OUTRIDERS

OUTRIDERS

• ——————— •

RODEO *at the* FRINGES *of the* AMERICAN WEST

REBECCA SCOFIELD

UNIVERSITY OF WASHINGTON PRESS
Seattle

Outriders was made possible in part by a grant from the Charles Redd Center for Western Studies at Brigham Young University.

23 22 21 20 19   5 4 3 2 1

UNIVERSITY OF WASHINGTON PRESS
uwapress.uw.edu

Chapter 2 is a revised version of Rebecca Scofield, "Violence and Social Salvation at the Texas Prison Rodeo," *Journal of American Studies*, September 27, 2018, doi.org /10.1017/S0021875818001305. Courtesy of Cambridge University Press. Copyright: Cambridge University Press and British Association for American Studies 2018.

LIBRARY OF CONGRESS CATALOGING-IN-PUBLICATION DATA
Names: Scofield, Rebecca, author.
Title: Outriders : rodeo at the fringes of the American West / Rebecca Scofield.
Description: Seattle : University of Washington Press, [2019] | Includes
    bibliographical references and index. |
Identifiers: LCCN 2019001684 (print) | LCCN 2019011459 (ebook) |
    ISBN 9780295746050 (ebook) | ISBN 9780295746067 (hardcover : alk. paper)
Subjects: LCSH: Rodeos—Social aspects—West (U.S.)—History—20th century. |
    Rodeo performers—West (U.S.)—History—20th century. | Cowboys—
    West (U.S.)—History—20th century. | Cowgirls—West (U.S.)—History—
    20th century. | Minorities—West (U.S.)—History—20th century. |
    West (U.S.)—Social conditions—20th century.
Classification: LCC GV1834.55.W47 (ebook) | LCC GV1834.55.W47 S36 2019 (print) |
    DDC 791.8—dc23
LC record available at https://lccn.loc.gov/2019001684

For my family

CONTENTS

ACKNOWLEDGMENTS

A community created this book. In order to finish this work, I needed succor from mentors, family, and friends. I express my deepest gratitude to Robin Bernstein, Andrew Jewett, Rachel St. John, and Susan Greenhalgh, each of whom provided unwavering support. Without each of you, I would have foundered before I had even begun. To my cohort and their partners, thank you for becoming my family. John Bell, Carla Cevasco, Chris Allison, and Dan Farbman, you are amazing colleagues and even better friends. Remember: "It's gonna alright." Andrew Pope, Amy Fish, Maggie Gates, Aaron Hatley, Mike King, Julie Miller, Charles Petersen, Theresa McCulla, Jennifer Ryan, Adam Sowards, Alyson Roy, and so many more, thank you for your editing abilities, particularly your unflinching grammar correction. Chris Hanson, thanks for always calling. My family, I would not have done any of this without you. To my parents, Clay and Margie, thank you for teaching me how to find adventure, both in books and in the world. And for giving me my own sense of roots to analyze. John, thank you for always listening—I hope I provide you even an ounce of the love, support, and laughter you give me. You are truly the reason I have the luxury of thinking and talking for a living. Here is to another five and a movie. My children, thanks for hurrying me along on this project.

This work has also depended on a great deal of institutional support. I would like to thank the Jacob K. Javits Foundation for four years of financial assistance during the development of this book. This project has also been sustained through grants from the Charles Warren Center for the Study of American History; Harvard's Graduate School of Arts and Sciences; the Autry Museum of the American West; Harvard's Gay and Lesbian Caucus (The Open Gate); the Center for American Political Studies; the University of Idaho; and others.

Likewise, I could not have conducted my research without the untiring aid of the dedicated archivists. The entire staff at the Autry Museum of the American West deserves my appreciation for their unfailing aid, particularly Marva Felchlin and Belinda Nakasato. In addition, this research would not have been possible without the work of Gregory Hinton, Frank Harrell, Patrick Terry, Roger Bergmann, Brian Helander, and all the people involved with the International Gay Rodeo Association. Thank you to all the archivists working at the National Cowgirl Museum and Hall of Fame, the African American Museum and Library at Oakland, the Okfuskee County Historical Society and Museum, and the town of Boley. I hope that this work stands as an ode to your dedication to history. Lastly, I would like to thank my UW Press reviewers for their insightful comments, my editor, Larin McLaughlin, who pushed me to continue improving and polishing, and my copyeditor, Sue Carter, who got me my edits before I delivered my second child, instead of after. Those days mattered.

OUTRIDERS

Introduction

Rodeo and the Outriders of History

RODEO IS VIOLENT, PAINFUL THEATER. IN THE ARENA, human beings undertake a series of competitions against and with animals. Speed, dexterity, and strength are all necessary to control another living creature. A tiny mistake—a finger misplaced between a saddle horn and a lasso or the over-rotation of a shoulder during a bull ride—can result in financial devastation, permanent injury, or even death. A rider who does not win will not be paid. Money, however, continues to be only part of the stakes. Combining sport and theater, rodeo is both athletic entertainment and the enactment of an imagined past. Often, especially for amateur or hobby riders, the stakes are and have been dignity, respect, and inclusion.

Outriders: Rodeo at the Fringes of the American West chronicles the efforts of several communities at the edges of rodeo to use popular performance to assert their definitions of western, masculine, and American. Examining female bronc riders in the 1910s and 1920s, convict cowboys in the mid-twentieth century, all-black western performance in the 1960s and 1970s, and gay rodeoers in the late century, *Outriders* illustrates that people who were cast out of popular western mythology and often marginalized from mainstream American life found belonging and meaning at the rodeo, demanding their right to grapple with the symbol of the cowboy in their own lives. As the cowboy has waxed and waned as an icon of national belonging, many communities have staked their claims to

3

Rodney Goings at the 1960 Cody Stampede in Wyoming demonstrated the danger of junior bull riding. Uninjured, the youth would lose that day's go-round to a female competitor, Kathy Harper, but his photograph captured national attention. *The Big Fall*, 1960. Photograph by G. C. "Kip" Hinton, courtesy of Gregory Hinton.

national inclusion through performance. These groups challenged the restrictive meaning of the cowboy while also furthering the idea of an authentic western identity.

Outriders poses several central questions about western performance and identity through an analysis of rodeo. First, as the image of the cowboy became increasingly white, straight, and masculine, how have the performances of women, incarcerated people, people of color, and LGBTQ+ people resisted this narrow definition? How have they strategically deployed complex notions like authenticity and heritage as a way to demand inclusion, but also, at times, exclude others? As a result, how have outriders used popular performance as a way to claim belonging in a larger national narrative?

While many may perceive rodeo to be marginal itself, with only a small percentage of the global population participating, rodeo's self-conscious performance and discrete communal boundaries address in explicit and overt ways the same questions about communal identity and belonging that all people strive to answer. Engaging with both cultural histories of performance and literature on the imagined American West, this study contributes to a long scholarly discussion of popular performance's role in shaping regional and national identity, especially as a strategic set of tools for marginalized peoples.[1] Performative spaces, whether the picket line, the basketball court, or the pow-wow, crystalize the racialized, classed, gendered, and sexualized dynamics of a given community and allow us to examine how people both enlarge and restrict group membership over time. Rodeo demonstrates how people utilize popular performance to claim authenticity and demand greater inclusion in national mythologies, while also at times reiterating the inherently exclusionary aspects of these myths. By looking at people at the fringes of communal identities, people I call the "outriders," we see the complex ways people police the boundaries of their identities, especially if that identity is threatened.

Claiming an identity as "real cowboys" has allowed marginalized people the ability to articulate other aspects of their lived experiences. An immigrant cowgirl could claim to be American because of her willingness to "go West." A convict cowboy could feel pride because his suffering in the arena paid for expanded educational opportunities for other inmates. A black rodeo rider could demand dignity because he performed an enactment of the range labor that his enslaved ancestors had been forced to endure. A gay cowboy could prove his masculinity through his willingness to walk into the arena. For many people, the love of stock, the thrill of competition, and the sacredness of camaraderie were foundational to their sense of self. As one Filipino American rodeoer told me, "I'm one person. I happen to be a gay man [. . .] I can't change that. It's like I can't change the color of my skin. I can't change the slant in my eyes. [Rodeo is] just where I fit."[2] Each of the communities discussed in this book argued that they belonged in the national imagination not because the West should be accessible to everyone, but because they fit.

Outriders analyzes rodeo performance as an epistemology of the West: a specific way of knowing, or making others know, that one is western.[3] Rodeo helps determine what characteristics, actions, and identities count as western. Scholars of gender, race, and sexuality have shown how epistemologies expand far beyond traditional knowledge production to incorporate embodied ways of knowing. Performance does not discover or uncover an essentialized identity, but rather allows individuals and communities to generate knowledge through bodily action.[4] The imagined West, meaning our collectively held notions of going west or being western, has often been produced through consumer-oriented industries like dime novels and film. In contrast, for over a century, rodeos have demanded the performance of these collective visions by real people and real animals, rendering ideals into flesh. Sitting at the crossroads of broad cultural categories like the imagined and real, urban and rural, traditional and modern, and liberal and conservative, rodeo shows that these dichotomies have rarely been as segregated as we assume in people's everyday lives.

• • •

The individual histories of varied rodeo communities took place alongside, and often in concert with, the longer development of the cowboy as a national figure. Rodeo, together with literature and film, drove the creation of the cowboy as the mascot of the imagined West in the twentieth century. The cowboy can be seen through media scholar Nicole Fleetwood's definition of iconicity: a single image that comes to stand for "a whole host of historical occurrences and processes."[5] North American rangeland labor in the mid- to late nineteenth century was influenced heavily by the *vaquero* mounted herding traditions of Mexico.[6] A racially diverse, homosocial, and nomadic ranching culture emerged that sat uneasily with Victorian notions of idealized manhood. Unlike landowning cattlemen, working-class cowboys were often portrayed in dime novels and travel texts during the 1870s and 1880s as riffraff who cavorted with prostitutes and cattle.[7] The supposed "closing of the frontier" in the 1890s, along with western cheerleaders like painter Frederick Remington, politician Theodore Roosevelt, historian Frederick Jackson Turner, showman Buffalo Bill Cody, and author Owen Wister, helped shift public perception of cowboys away from social deviants and toward knights of plains.[8] Astride a noble horse, the individual cowboy was no longer imagined as a working-class stiff who participated in collective bargaining and strikes, but as the very embodiment of America—democratic, brave, and stoic in the face of savagery.

Through the proliferation of popular representations of the West, the core of a national mythology cemented itself to the "frontier" and the characters who inhabited it. While scholar Frederick Jackson Turner articulated a specific "frontier thesis" grounded largely in agrarian advancement in his infamous 1893 speech, "The Significance of the Frontier in American History," other representations, such as Buffalo Bill Cody's, presented a far more violent depiction of this "civilizing" progression.[9] The cowboy at this time often appeared alongside other male-dominated occupational roles in the popular imaginary—mountain men, soldiers, scouts, and prospectors. Slowly, the "cowboy" began to appear in popular culture as an amalgamation of these once job-specific characters—a wanderer of the golden West, often with unclear connections to employment. Within the first several decades of the twentieth century, the cowboy had transcended his status as an occupational folk hero to represent a profound belief in American exceptionalism. Just as Theodore Roosevelt's Rough Riders used military conquest in the Spanish-American War to secure Anglo-America's dominance over populations in Puerto Rico, Guam, and the Philippines, so they used the image of the cowboy to communicate a global message about America's ability to "civilize" the world.

While the rangeland cowboy commanded newfound respect in the opening decades of the twentieth century, rodeo cowboys were not always considered "authentic" goods, at least by working range hands. As historian Michael Allen noted, "From the early ranch cowboy's point of view, a rodeo man was undependable—he drank too much, caroused with women, and had bad work habits. He was constantly quitting ranch work to follow the rodeo, leaving ranch cowboys to pick up the slack."[10] Derided by his occupational peers during these early years, rodeo riders carefully crafted ranch-raised backstories to support their stage personas and rodeo promoters relentlessly trumpeted performers' bona fides. In many ways, early rodeo actually reflected to a closer degree the diversity of rural working-class life in the West: women could bronc-ride, the rare African American performer could headline a show, and a Native American cowboy could be crowned champion.[11] Questions about who could and should be considered a "real cowboy" occupied a central place in rodeo culture from the very beginning.

Between 1900 and the 1930s, rodeos struggled to distinguish themselves from other forms of popular entertainment, like Wild West shows, sports exhibitions, circuses, and vaudeville. Rodeo cowgirls dove on their horses from platforms at Coney Island and participated in wrestling matches for dimes at county fairs. In the winter months, when the rodeo circuit ground to a halt, many rodeoers turned up in Hollywood, hoping to be cast as stunt doubles in western films. Local rodeos, such as Frontier Days in Cheyenne, Wyoming, often competed against touring rodeo shows, such as California Frank's rodeo company, to hire the best riders for an exciting performance. Early rodeos had the potential to draw in large crowds over their often monthlong stays in major cities. The 1936 Chicago Rodeo, for instance, provided both afternoon and evening shows, seating ten thousand people at each for several weeks.[12] In 1943, during World War II, over half a million people watched the Madison Square Garden Rodeo in New York City, with sixteen thousand people attending each of the thirty-six performances.[13] Due to the variety of rodeo venues, unregulated pay structures, and unpredictable travel conditions, early competitors traveled as far as Europe to participate in large rodeos with the possibility of being left behind broke and broken when the show moved on without them.

It was not until the 1940s that most people began to fully accept rodeo cowboys as "genuine" cowboys—around the same time that mainstream rodeo shifted to a professionalized sport and women and people of color were relegated to supporting roles. As rodeo grew in popularity and professional cowboys began to unionize in the 1930s and 1940s, the image of the rodeo cowboy became increasingly white, male, and heterosexual. With the advent of the Cowboys' Turtle Association in 1936 (which would later become the Rodeo Cowboys Association) and rodeo's growth into a multi-million-dollar entertainment industry, fewer women and people of color found a place in professional rodeo. Gene Autry not only cut women's rough stock riding from his popular Flying A Ranch Rodeo Company, he also helped establish the cowboy as an indisputably good guy with his "Cowboy Ten Commandments." These included patriotism, respect for women, and gentleness with children and animals.[14] Importantly, during the rise of global fascism, his cowboy code stated that cowboys should not hold racially or religiously intolerant ideas. Yet Jim Crow segregation ensured that men of color were prohibited from participating, even when associations did not explicitly ban their membership. Just when the imagined West lost much of its fluidity in order to be embodied by heterosexual white men, the rodeo cowboy ascended in American popular culture as the true inheritor of the cowboy legacy.

With the United States' newfound global power following World War II, cowboys once again enjoyed a massive surge in popularity. Television, Disney Land, and Louis L'Amour helped reinvigorate the fantasy of the "Old West," teaching millions of baby boomer children that the West was both a place of violence and, eventually, justice. Men like John Wayne established international stardom as they articulated the complex anxieties of American men who had returned from war to a national culture instructing them to embrace domesticity, global capitalism, and modernity.[15] The 1950s and 1960s produced the heydays of classic western film, television, and fiction. While the western genre experienced dips in popularity in the early years of the 1970s, films about rodeo and urban cowboys actually increased and, by the 1980s, *Urban Cowboy, 8 Seconds,* and *Dallas* had rewritten the setting of cowboys away from the range and into the bar and boardroom.[16]

By the late twentieth century, conflated with Cold War film gunslingers and memories of working range hands, rodeo cowboys were popularly portrayed as hard-living daredevils who, like their ancestors, valued the freedom of the range and refused to be domesticated. Rodeo cowboys have been both romanticized and sexualized: as one bullfighter told me, the point of rodeo is to "get on, get drunk, get laid." Buckle bunnies, or female rodeo groupies, provided much needed accommodations, meals, and even financial support for traveling rodeo athletes, as well as helping establish an explicitly sexualized culture at the rodeo.[17] Despite the growing number of arena-trained rodeo athletes, who had never worked with stock on ranches, these men were lauded as the booted foot that kept the gate from swinging shut on America's frontier past.[18] Framed as a potential venue for both physical pain and sexual pleasure, rodeo continues to enable the sexualized image of the white, masculine, anti-domestic cowboy to affect people's bodies, relationships, and livelihoods.

As mainstream rodeos and the cowboy icon became increasingly homogenized and more people were excluded from this vision of American identity, people fought back through the creation and expansion of niche rodeo circuits. The Girls Rodeo Association (organized in 1948), gay rodeos, and all-black rodeos continue today. *Outriders* traces this contraction and re-expansion of rodeo participation, noting how niche rodeos in the 1970s and 1980s provided the diversity that mainstream rodeos had once afforded, though to a limited degree. As the civil rights, feminist, and

gay rights movements wrought incalculable changes in the late twentieth century, many people personally protested their absence from the
imagined West by founding or joining new rodeo associations. While
many people, especially in nonpolitically engaged, non-eastern or -southern,
and non-urban communities, may have felt cut off from these large
social movements, rodeo demonstrates how people became intimate
with ideas about social equality and worked to access previously restricted
activities.

Simultaneously, other people rejected the cowboy as a figure of national
pride. The cowboy has always been and remains a contested icon. While
men like John Wayne may have enjoyed almost universal popularity in the
1950s, his real-life association with anti-communism, conservative politics, and pro-war policies allowed a critical public to associate Wayne, and
other play cowboys like Ronald Reagan, with America's rightward turn
toward patriarchy and racism in the 1970s and 1980s. Similarly, as country
music became nationally popular and artists like Merle Haggard self-
consciously associated themselves with nostalgia for a manlier, short-
haired America, the cowboy came to represent an inherently oppressive
force in American culture, making many people uneasy about the future.[19]

For over a century, people have invested their lives and identities in
being rodeo cowboys and cowgirls. As an activity increasingly mythologized within American culture and the imagined West, rodeo demonstrates the ways people understood and expressed new ideas about being
western and its connection to national, gendered, and racialized belonging
at specific moments throughout the twentieth century.

●　　●　　●

Outriders were historically the cowboys who rode at the edges of the
cattle drive. Pushed to the margins, these hands ensured that the cattle
kept moving forward in a straight line. While the lead, or point, cowboy
headed the drive and the tail, or drag, cowboy rode in the dust driving
reluctant stragglers, outriders maintained the boundaries of the herd.
White, heterosexual men may have taken over the position of the lead, but
the outriders of the rodeo have stood at edges of the imagined West, helping contain an ill-defined, malleable herd of ideas in order to claim their
place as cowboys.[20] As marginalized populations participated in the

construction of the imagined West, these communities demonstrated how western identity has always been performative, even as they endeavored to define themselves as authentic participants in that performance. The very process that allowed rodeo outriders to decenter and broaden western identity with their presence also ultimately strengthened the imagined West's normative center.

Historians of the US West have explained that the "real" West and the "fake" West have existed as inextricable entities, sharing their lifeblood.[21] The West was already being mythologized by authors, painters, and showmen when the US government began federal support for the systematic colonization of the trans-Mississippi West in the mid-nineteenth century. Today, people continue to perform the fantasy of the West—or the associated fantasies of the wilderness, the farm, and the range—on a daily basis, as can be seen across a wide variety of practices from hay-barn weddings and hobby ranches to whitewater rafting and survivalist training.[22] Unlike many of these self-ordained explorers, ranchers, and soldiers, rodeoers perform the life-and-death relationship between the real and the imagined in front of a paying audience and provide media packets that detail their right to belong as cowboys. As Louis Warren eloquently argued about Buffalo Bill Cody, studying the staged American West captures the "real embodiment of public fantasy" as well as the "personal cost of maintaining the illusion of a life lived in accordance with national myth" for those who choose to perform it.[23] From injuries to bankruptcy, the cost has always been steep.

The desire to live out the western myth has been driven in part by the place of the "frontier" in the American imagination. The growing need to associate the frontier with Americanness was solidified in Frederick Jackson Turner's influential "frontier thesis," through which Turner postulated that American conquest generated an exceptional American character. According to Turner, unlike Europeans, Americans had continuously wrestled their nation away from savage peoples and tamed it, becoming democratic and individualistic Americans in the process.[24] Wild West shows and later rodeos became the live performance of the link between westward conquest and national character in the twentieth century. Termed "as much a part of our red-blooded American civilization as the 'Star Spangled Banner,'" rodeo has not only defined western character, but has also been deployed to describe Americanness as a whole, encapsulating and eliding a longer regional history of conflict, colonization, and violence.[25]

As the *New York Times* noted about New Jersey's Cowtown in the early 1990s, "The rodeo is not only all action and thrills, but a colorful reminder of the mystique of the cowboy." Asked by a journalist why he still participated, a sixty-year-old cowboy simply stated, "I never done it for the money. [. . .] I love my horses and I love to ride 'em." He said that few men wanted money or glory; instead, "most of these riders want to buy into the romance and the legend of the American cowboy. And this is the very best way we know how."[26] Perpetually framed as the last of a dying breed, struggling to maintain an endangered way of life, the rodeo cowboy has come to enact a "tradition" that barely represented a ranching way of life even when it was popularized in the 1910s.[27] Yet, just as paintings, tourism advertisements, literature, and films helped establish rugged western landscapes like Monument Valley, the Grand Canyon, or Yosemite Valley as the visual representations of America as a nation, so rodeo cowboys in the late twentieth century have received praise as the inheritors of an idealized national character.

While heterosexual white men ultimately dominated this image of the cowboy, they have not been the only sculptors of the icon. Over the twentieth century, the cowboy's critics, as well as its supporters, helped shape the national debate over the meaning of the cowboy. For those who wished to embody the idealized "cowboy way of life," large communities emerged around particular rodeo circuits, such as the gay rodeo circuit, the collegiate rodeo circuit, or the professional bull-riding circuit. These communities, made up of bronc riders, prison wardens, and housewives, have staged multiple wests over time. Within these sprawling and fluid communities, people otherwise marginalized in American society have consistently linked their rodeo participation with a claim to western or pioneer authenticity, ranging from the Texas Prison Rodeo's claim to breed "real" cowboys through prison ranch labor to Black Power–era celebrations of black settlers' participation in western conquest. Rodeo has both demonstrated the intertwined natures of the real and imagined Wests and offered a tempting path to inclusion in that mythology for those previously excluded, grounded in the rhetoric of authenticity.

Authenticity is an ever-shifting cultural concept and has often influenced the popular performance of the American West.[28] In the early twentieth century, Colonel George Washington Miller called his Miller Brothers 101 Ranch Wild West Show the "Real Wild West" because it was important for him to communicate to his audience that the scenes his paid performers enacted were unaltered tableaux of Oklahoman life. Of course, he also hired women like Goldie Griffith and Tillie Baldwin, neither of whom had been raised on ranches, as trick riders and bronc busters.[29] Creators of the mythic West have always depended on people from other geographical regions to both perform and consume their visions. Yet, while the East often helped write the mythic West and vice versa, historians like Bonnie Christensen have demonstrated that "westerners have imbibed these images along with everyone else and have recognized the power that such identities might offer them."[30]

Westerners of all kinds have performed authenticity with self-conscious awareness. In 1934, an incarcerated cowboy in the Texas Prison System articulated the popular vision of the cowboy and the demand for real westerners to mirror these characteristics. He wrote in the prison newspaper that eastern "dudes," or those "unfamiliar with cattle ranches, cowboys, and horses," came West thinking cowboys spent their days "riding at a gallop, toward flaming sunsets, in pursuit of a black-browed villian [sic], (usually a cattle rustler with ambitions) for the purpose of rescuing some fair damsel from a horrible fate."[31] As a former hired hand on the Circle X dude ranch in Texas, this writer had dedicated himself to "conducting [myself] at all times so as to conform with the Dudes' ideas of a 'real cowboy, my deah!'" His duties included dressing in "gaudy, silk neckerchief, flaming-hued shirts, fancy chaps, ten-gallon hat, etc," doling out inaccurate information to painfully ignorant gentlemen, and posing as an "'isn't he romantic' cowboy" for the young women. While the author had never risked his job by openly challenging these tourists' vision of the West, he could later self-deprecatingly poke fun at the mythologized cowboy, the silly easterners who believed in him, and westerners' role in bolstering their dashing image.

Rodeo helps illustrate that western authenticity and heritage do not point to a universally understood set of characteristics, but instead represent tools that have been used to negotiate and define belonging and difference. People use rodeo, alongside many forms of popular performance ranging from hula, equestrian theater, and religious festivals, as a set of rhetorical and bodily strategies to imagine themselves into a culturally valued past. *Outriders* argues that the performance of belonging must be examined from the perspective of those supposedly excluded from mythic activities in order to reveal the elemental attraction of those mythologies.[32] As a generation of western historians has demonstrated, the cultural, linguistic, religious, and racial differences of the regional West were erased by Frederick Jackson Turner's "frontier thesis" and white Hollywood cowboys.[33] Yet, even as scholars work to recover the stories of those left out of the Turnerian vision of heroic settlers and voiceless Natives, we must also analyze, in the words of literary historian Daniel Moos, "those subjects who problematically endorsed western myths in their attempts at national inclusion."[34]

The robust scholarship on rodeo history has often focused on separating historical fact from fiction, distinguishing myth from reality, or simply celebrating the mythological West that rodeo itself has helped construct.[35] *Outriders* instead examines the ways communities have sought, rejected, and reconstructed the idea of authenticity through their performances. Using diverse narrative strategies, journalists, audience members, organizers, promoters, and participants have constructed discourses, or intertwined sets of ideas and practices, about the meaning of cowboy performance.[36]

Outriders in rodeo reappropriated a symbol of American national identity, struggling to imbue their communities with its cultural power. Outriders' continued participation in other culturally significant arenas from the National Football League to the US military illuminate the allure of those deadly settings and the potential costs for individuals and communities who assert their right to belong. Importantly, outriders flip the common practice of mainstream appropriation and resale of powerful minority symbols, from music to fashion.[37] For much of the twentieth century, "Indian" Halloween costumes and Hawaiian luaus were aspects of everyday American life, available for easy consumption and disposal. Yet the rage expressed toward gay people, women, incarcerated people, and people of color who dared to tread foot on the soil of the rodeo arena reveals the uneven flow of cultural symbols between the margins and the center. While mainstream appropriation of minority symbols often dilutes their radical meaning, outriders in many ways have reinforced the normative tenets of mainstream symbols. By providing those symbols with sustained, if rewritten, cultural significance, people at the margins have often aided in keeping dangerous practices with unsettling histories alive.

As foundational histories of diverse populations in the western borderlands have demonstrated, marginalized populations continued to thrive in the region despite being written out of this mythology.[38] Scholars like Susan Gray and Gayle Gullett continue to push against the remythologizing of the region by emphasizing "place" as a socially constructed site that individuals experience in different ways.[39] Building on nuanced understandings of how gender, race, ethnicity, sexuality, and religion have shaped people's understandings of their homelands, *Outriders* argues that the mythology of the region cannot be completely disregarded because it shaped the everyday decisions of diverse peoples. *Outriders* in particular explores the way these myriad groups have both contested the increasingly homogenized western myth and continued to invest in the cowboy as a symbol of personal devotion and the rodeo arena as a space of national belonging. Over the twentieth century, outriders in rodeo radically resisted hegemonic understandings of western identity and national belonging, but they did not openly reject the allure of the cowboy fantasy, creating their own versions instead.

These adaptations of the cowboy fantasy approach the notion of "disidentification." Theorized by José Esteban Muñoz in his foundational work on the performances of queer people of color, disidentification is a style of relating to dominant culture that stands between a full subscription to it and a complete rejection of it. This strategy of marginalized people "tries to transform a cultural logic from within, always laboring to enact permanent structural change while at the same time valuing the importance of local everyday struggles of resistance."[40] Although the numerous individuals who chose to rodeo did not always share radical or even progressive political aims, their refusal to submit to their own erasure from national mythology "crack[ed] open the code of the majority" and then proceeded to "empower minority identities and identifications."[41] *Outriders* demonstrates that the radical potential of rodeo can be found in repurposing dearly held notions like tradition and heritage to argue for an expansion of belonging, even as actors continue to be invested in other forms of exclusion.

Outriders reveals the processes by which some marginalized groups have persistently invested in an icon at times weaponized against them.

Previous interpretations of the imagined West, such as Anne Butler's "Selling the Popular Myth," deemphasize marginalized populations' participation in the imagined West, arguing that "although ethnic groups have adopted some aspects of the 'western' mode—clothing, jewelry, crafts, rodeos—they lack both internal capital and endorsement from big businesses and thus can point to only modest economic results."[42] *Outriders* does not analyze economic outcomes as a central factor in people's decisions to rodeo or their success in re-articulating markers of western identity. These communities' histories show that financial gain was not always the end goal. Instead, recognition as "real" Americans, westerners, or men tempted many down the rodeo road and helped nourish the cowboy as an image of national belonging even after it had become a well-recognized image of racism, sexism, and homophobia. That populations who were selectively erased from the public memory of the West fought to rewrite the cowboy illustrates both its power and its contingency as a national icon.

Using a particularly dangerous performance, the different outriders in this book helped resist restrictions on authentic knowledge and western belonging over the twentieth century. Yet they also helped police the boundaries of the West as a place connected to an "authentic" past rooted in the brutal experiences of settler colonialism. Their histories illustrate how real people have used popular performance as an epistemological tool, striving bodily to expand the ideals of the increasingly narrow mythic West—constructing and deconstructing multiple wests over a century. Rodeo served as a way for people to communicate that while others did not define them as cowboys, they "knew better."

· · ·

Outriders, along with all rodeoers, have experienced the evolution of rodeo as a professionalized and profitable industry into the twenty-first century, though few—and rarely those at the margins—ultimately share in those profits. While the conditions of the road have changed from wagons to airplanes, rodeo communities have shared crucial experiences that span time—namely the financial, familial, and physical demands of participation. Enthusiastically embraced by people from all walks of life, from wealthy Germans to poor Texans, and constituting a global activity in which people have constructed and consumed an image of the American West, rodeo uses violent performance to claim belonging in an imagined past and a national romance. From the youth rodeo organization Little Britches and the National Intercollegiate Rodeo Association to the professional circuit, a person can start his or her rodeo career in elementary school and ride until physically unable to climb over the fence and into the chutes.[43] The at times coercive brutality of rodeo has shaped both the allure and the costs of participating in the bodily performance of the cowboy.

Sports Business Daily reported that between 2000 and 2004, over ninety-five million people in North America attended professional rodeo events, outselling both golf and tennis. Roughly thirty million people watch the six hundred professional rodeo events held in thirty-seven states each year. Millions more attend the local, amateur, and single-event rodeos held worldwide. In 2013, the Houston Rodeo drew two million people over its monthlong run.[44] In 2016, the National Finals Rodeo officially sold out for the thirtieth straight year, a total of three hundred shows. Additionally, as rodeo has secured broadcast television contracts, American rodeo organizations have discovered their global appeal with international viewers in countries such as Australia, Brazil, and China. Non-US rodeo fans are especially vital to the international circuits, such as the Professional Bull Riders (PBR) association, which crowns world champion cowboys. Complete with corporate sponsorships and sports news coverage, rodeo has been transformed from local pastime to international sport.[45]

While international broadcasting of events may be new, rodeo, and the imagined West more broadly, has always held global appeal. In her memoir, bronc rider Vera McGinnis described visiting London and Japan in the 1920s as both wildly exciting and also, at times, deeply disappointing if weather, health, or crowds did not cooperate to make shows a success. McGinnis would make lifelong friends with an Englishwoman, exchanging letters for decades.[46] Traveling the world provided performers rare opportunities, particularly women and people of color, who otherwise faced sparse and unattractive employment opportunities in the early century. The ability to compete in international locales would not have been possible without global demand. As scholars like Renee Laegreid and Ruth Ellen Gruber have shown, Italy, Germany, France, England, Brazil, Japan, Israel, and many other countries have persistently adopted and adapted tropes from the romanticized American West. Global fascination with the American West was rapidly established with Wild West shows and early films, but also expanded into opera, literature, and horse associations.[47] Representing notions of wide open spaces, personal freedom, and economic opportunities, the West has offered a colorful setting for local populations to play out their own fantasies as well as providing American rodeoers the opportunity to compete abroad.

Investing their money, time, and emotions in rodeo, people have flourished and withered based on the travails of the rodeo road. Even amateur rodeos, including gay rodeo, take place on a year-round circuit, requiring extensive travel to dozens of events. An average participant on the gay rodeo circuit in 1990 spent six hundred dollars to travel to a single rodeo, where an average contestant might win nothing.[48] Many rural, and often impoverished, westerners have looked to rodeo with rags-to-riches dreams, though they often found disappointment. A single rodeoer could have a streak of luck and live large on the proceeds for a long time. Many rodeoers, however, have instead ended their lives with broken bodies in grinding poverty.

Due to the financial, physical, and emotional stresses of the rodeo circuit, rodeoers often construct a "rodeo family." These kinship networks include parents, spouses, friends, groupies, fans, other cowboys or cowgirls, and many others. Their invisible labor, such as shared rides, free beds, or home-cooked meals, allows rodeoers the ability to travel the country and the world. With no guarantee of a paycheck and high risk for expensive injuries, rodeo participants are dependent on these networks, even as the national imagination still sees rodeoers as rugged individualists.[49] Rodeo shapes not only the lives and identities of people who actually ride but also the considerable number of people who hold supporting roles for friends, loved ones, and community members who share their particular vision of the West.

As staged events, rodeos have evolved continually. An average rodeo in the early twentieth century would have taken place at an outdoor arena with wooden grandstands set far away from the action, no stock chutes to hold and release animals, and usually a large racing track. More informal events took place in ranch corrals or on baseball fields with cars parked close together to form a perimeter. The program might have included bronc riding for both women and men, a buffalo-riding exhibition, and a race with riders standing on horseback, called Roman racing. The local chamber of commerce organized some shows, individually inviting top competitors or hiring a touring company to perform. Occasionally, fly-by-night outfits raised local money to host the rodeo but then ran away with all the proceeds, leaving both participants and local contractors without their pay.[50] In contrast, professional rodeo today is a sport regulated by a variety of governing bodies, dominated by the Professional Rodeo Cowboys Association (PRCA), which emerged from the Cowboys' Turtle Association. These rodeos take place in both outdoor and indoor arenas, rarely include a racetrack, and maintain a tight rodeo program that includes numerous quick-release chutes to ensure a steady stream of action.

All mainstream PRCA rodeos must include standard events: bareback and saddle-bronc riding, bull riding, team roping, calf roping, steer wrestling, and barrel racing. Today, rough stock events (bronc and bull riding) require a rider to stay on the animal for a set amount time. Rides are then scored based on both the rider's and the animal's performance. Team roping includes a two-person team, one who catches the head and one who catches the heel of a calf, and, like calf roping, is a timed event. Today, most calf roping competitions involve breakaway roping, meaning the rope literally breaks away from the competitor's saddle once the calf is caught, instead of tie-down roping, in which a competitor would dismount and tie the calf's legs together. Steer wrestling, or bulldogging, features a rider chasing a steer, dismounting while still in motion, and wrestling the animal to the ground. This is also a timed event. Barrel racing, which in American mainstream rodeo is the only available event for women, requires a rider and horse to race around barrels in a clover pattern as quickly as possible without tipping the barrels. Each of these events has evolved over the past century and time standards vary between professional and amateur events. Local rodeos also tend to feature nonstandard events like chuck wagon races, goat flipping, and wild cow milking. While there remains a significant amount of uncertainty in professional rodeo, safety standards for both people and animals are rigorously enforced and winnings are reported as taxable income. The rodeo road, while still exciting and unpredictable, now delivers polished athletes rather than the sideshow performers of early rodeo.

Despite its professionalization, rodeo remains violent theater—raising the stakes of this particular form of cultural performance. As one rodeo cowboy explained, it is "about putting on a good show for the audience."[51] Frequently, "a good show" has meant making a spectacle of pain and blood.

In the early years of its existence, the Texas Prison Rodeo reportedly used fake packets of blood to keep spectators entertained.[52] Animal performers in particular achieve celebrity for their ability to brutalize contestants. As animal studies scholar Susan Nance notes, "From the beginning, the bucker—the 'outlaw' bronc—dominated the show and its iconography, effectively demonstrating to viewers and participants how a 'Western' animal behaved and reflected upon the character of Western people."[53] A cowboy's score was only as good as the star animal violently attempting to escape him. Animals have often bled, passed out, broken legs, or died in the arena.

Indeed, fake blood is not necessarily required in a sport that produces wince-inducing wrecks between human and animal. One study found that rodeo's injury rates are ten times greater than professional football and thirteen times greater than ice hockey.[54] Rodeo athletes have been reluctant

Bull rider Dusty Qualls competing with the National Rodeo Association during the 1980s. Photograph courtesy of Marilyn Qualls.

to wear protective gear, labeling it "not cowboy."[55] For men who work to fulfill an image of physically tough masculinity, protective gear threatens to demean the cultural ideals embedded in their performances.[56] During 1994 and 1995 in Louisiana alone, five cases of major spinal cord and brain injuries were reported at rodeos, with several stemming from competitions for the National High School Rodeo Association. In one case, a seventeen-year-old boy's head collided with the bull's head, shattering his nose and rendering him unconscious for five days. After forty days of acute care, the study found he still "had pronounced cognitive and behavioral impairment." Similarly, a twenty-eight-year-old man, with fifteen of years riding experience, fractured his fifth and sixth cervical vertebrae when he was thrown from his bull. Emergency medical services were not present and it took forty-five minutes for the ambulance to arrive. Discharged after a nine-day stay in the hospital, the man could not feed or dress himself.[57] Neither of these men was wearing a helmet.

Rodeoers not only sustain life-altering injuries from arena accidents every year, they also die. Because rodeo is a fluid world, with people participating in junior, local, and professional events, no centralized statistics exist for counting annual rodeo deaths. The PRCA maintains that their association averages less than one death per year, but that is still far higher than other professional sports. At times, these tragedies have had a high public profile, such as when PRCA bull rider Lane Frost died after a broken rib punctured his heart during the 1989 Cheyenne Frontier Days. But usually these deaths do not receive much national attention. For instance, in 2009, a twelve-year-old boy was killed in a junior-level Little Britches rodeo when the steer he was riding stepped on his chest and ruptured his heart.[58] While the use of helmets is now mandated for new riders in most professional associations, the decision to wear helmets or reinforced vests may not always be enough to save rodeo riders.

Like other professional sports, including boxing, football, and hockey, rodeo is now facing the consequences of repeated brain injuries. The majority of reported injuries in the PRCA between 1981 and 2005 were head and face injuries, representing roughly fifty percent of major injuries, especially in the rough stock events.[59] These statistics did not take into account the injuries sustained by bullfighters, also called rodeo clowns, who are at significant risk of head injury. By 2015, rodeo doctors were concerned that they had not seen a decrease in concussion rates despite the increasingly widespread use of helmets.[60] While a helmet may protect one's skull from being crushed, a kick in the head from a bull weighing twelve hundred to two thousand pounds or the force at which a rider can hit the ground will still produce a concussion. Indeed, even the force of a bull spinning can cause the brain to forcibly slosh into the skull. Some rodeo athletes experience four or five concussions a year on the circuit, often riding while concussed.

In 2017, Ty Pozzobon, a top Canadian bull rider with the PBR and PRCA, was the first rodeo athlete to be diagnosed with chronic traumatic encephalopathy (CTE). CTE is a degenerative brain disease that causes anxiety, aggression, depression, memory problems, and eventually dementia. Pozzobon had reportedly suffered at least twelve concussions during his career, the worst of which was a sickening blow to the head that cracked open his helmet. He most likely also sustained a number of blows below concussion level that still contributed to long-term brain damage. Ty Pozzobon was only twenty-five when he took his own life. While the PBR has instituted some limited concussion protocols for their top riders, PRCA and other associations have not. Because rodeo athletes can be members of a variety of associations or take part in local, nonsanctioned events, they do not always self-report any injuries sustained outside the PBR, making concussion protocols difficult to implement.[61]

Bull riders are not just competing in a sport: they are performing their vision of the cowboy with their lives—and possible deaths. Unlike mass-produced fiction and film, rodeo mandates the live enactment of the cowboy ideal by real people, from the chewing tobacco rings permanently imprinted on the back pockets of their jeans to the staggering yearly hospital bills that can bankrupt a family. Despite the unrelenting deaths, people continue to participate in this distinctive cultural performance— in part because people enjoy dangerous and thrilling activities, but also because it connects them to an imagined past and a national mythology. The gore of the arena reflects a commitment to reenacting the violence of western conquest, venerating a narrative of bodily sacrifice by bold men willing to confront savagery.[62] The danger of the arena has been central to the ways that various communities have performed their belonging in the West over the twentieth century.

• • •

Outriders focuses on how rodeoers, their promoters, and audiences have challenged strict definitions of cowboy identity through narrative and performance, while also at times policing the boundaries of acceptability and authenticity. While these case studies cannot represent all the outriders of rodeo, they do address core aspects of the evolving cowboy mythology. If the cowboy by the late twentieth century was defined by being male, white, heterosexual, and free, how do people who existed beyond these definitions fracture the narrative of the cowboy over time? Each chapter analyzes a crucial rupture as communities fought to define the cowboy on their own terms.

Chapter 1 examines gender and nationality in the imagined West through the mediated story of Norwegian immigrant-turned-champion-cowgirl Tillie Baldwin. Born Anna Mathilda Winger in 1888, Baldwin immigrated to Brooklyn as a teenager and worked as a hairdresser. After discovering trick riding while visiting Staten Island one weekend, she went on to win bronc-riding championships across the United States and Canada. Interweaving an analysis of her tactics of self-promotion with that of other female bronc riders and rodeo performers, I explore the various forms of western authenticity a woman could claim in the early twentieth century amidst national debates on women's suffrage and immigration restriction. While most cowgirls emphasized their ranch upbringings, Baldwin strategically deployed her immigrant story to craft a new definition of authentic western womanhood as someone who successfully performed being western in the arena. After two decades on the rodeo and Wild West circuits, Baldwin settled in New England in the 1920s as a ranch manager and riding instructor, becoming a western mascot for the area. Her journey from immigrant hairdresser to working cowgirl to local celebrity affirmed that by performing an idealized image of the American West, she could claim to be a genuine pioneer and a true American.

Chapter 2 scrutinizes the Texas Prison Rodeo's evolving discourse of violence, race, and social salvation. Prison officials, convict cowboys, and audience members used this rodeo, which ran from 1931 to 1986 and often bordered on blood sport, as a needle that could stitch together prison violence and prisoner redemption at midcentury. The brutal action of the rodeo provided imprisoned men a unique form of social salvation for both themselves and other inmates. This deliverance was bestowed in the form of ticket receipts, which were donated to the Educational and Recreational

Fund to pay for all educational, religious, and recreational activities for Texas prisoners. Used to promote the prison system's postwar reform efforts, the rodeo operated as a marketing campaign for the penitentiary's ability to reshape failed men into productive citizens. The penal system in this former slave state claimed that by exposing their own bodies in the arena, outlaw cowboys could redeem themselves and other prisoners and thereby lay claim to both true American masculinity and grit.

Chapter 3 chronicles the importance of heritage in all-black cowboy performances, particularly in post-1960s America. In the context of an increasingly "colorblind" mind-set among white Americans in the Black Power era, black rodeoers called for greater inclusion on mainstream circuits but also leveraged their long history of ranching and rodeo experience to illustrate their place in the cowboy legacy. Focusing on the communities that supported black western performance in the 1960s and 1970s, particularly Boley, Oklahoma, and Oakland, California, this chapter explores the ways in which rodeo organizers and riding associations explicitly linked their own performance of the cowboy to the range labor conducted by people of color, both free and enslaved, during the nineteenth century. Protesting their erasure from national memory, African American cowboys and cowgirls enacted western pageantry and competition as a way to encourage civic engagement, promote community education, and demand national recognition of their unique role in the history of the American cowboy.

Chapter 4 turns to gay rodeo performance in Reagan's America, exploring the meaning of masculinity and camp in an era that embraced playing cowboy. In the 1980s, as gay rodeo shifted from a novelty event held in a single city to a full-blown rodeo circuit under the International Gay Rodeo Association (IGRA), tense debates about the meaning of gay rodeo erupted among participants. While some members argued the rodeo should be a space for fun and inclusion, others perceived the rodeo as an avenue to prove their dedication to tradition, masculinity, and western heritage. These internal disputes articulated Americans' growing sense of unease about authentic manhood in the late twentieth century. As Ronald Reagan and Ralph Lauren repopularized the cowboy as the birthright of white American men, gay, often white, men demanded access to this birthright. Ultimately, IGRA members pushed cowboy masculinity to the edge of drag, threatening to unmask all cowboy masculinities as performance.

Each of the four communities came to rodeo for different reasons and with different results, but they all invested, in specific ways, in claims to cowboy authenticity. From 1920s rodeo cowgirls' dedication to the healthy white American family to 1970s black cowboys' invocation of settler heritage, however, a staunch commitment to authenticity also potentially allowed for new exclusionary definitions. These ideas of western heritage and, more broadly, authenticity have not carried stagnant meanings across time and space; instead, these notions have fluidly adapted to bolster specific stories people desire to tell. Told together, these disparate rodeo histories render visible the changing debates about western inclusion over the past century.

While outrider cowboys and cowgirls often saddled up from the fringes of a whitewashed and masculinized West, their performances often underscored the desire to maintain the borders of both a regional and a national identity. Even as participants, organizers, and audiences have contested the meaning of the cowboy through every new form of rodeo, however, they have failed to entirely rewrite the history of the cowboy in the national consciousness. Indeed, today more than ever the cowboy continues to be connected with a conservative political agenda and white masculinity. This very failure illustrates the imagined West's capacity to simultaneously offer a much needed haven to a variety of people and still represent an inflexibly white, masculine, and heterosexual image within the culture at large. The dual elasticity and intractability of the imagined West exposes how outriders of all kinds, reaching far beyond rodeo's grandstands, participate in bodily performances in order to earn communal belonging while also ultimately protecting specific cultural icons from complete subversion.

CHAPTER 1

Coiffeuse to Cowgirl

Pioneering and Performance of Western Womanhood

ANNA MATHILDA WINGER DID NOT LIKE STYLING HAIR,
or at least we can assume as much. She dropped the profession as soon as
she learned how to hang off a galloping horse and snatch a handkerchief
from the dirt. Around the turn of the twentieth century, having emigrated
from Norway as a teenager, Winger lived and worked with an aunt in New
York City. On a fateful weekend excursion with some friends to then rural
Staten Island, Winger saw "a troupe of show people" performing equestrian tricks for a film. Winger later described being amazed by the "won-
derful costumes and apparently colorful lives" of the entertainers. She
desperately wanted to learn to ride a horse so that she could join the
troupe. "Back to New York I would go and dream."[1] Unlike so many other
young women, however, she did more than just dream. She reportedly
returned to Staten Island and paid one of the performers to teach her
to ride.

Within a couple of years, New York hairstylist Anna Mathilda Winger
had become Tillie Baldwin, "Champion Lady Bronco Buster." By the mid-
1910s, she had performed with the Miller Brothers 101 Ranch Wild West
Show and competed at the largest rodeos in America and Canada, winning titles in racing and riding against some of the toughest ranch women
and men in the business. Despite this illustrious career, in 1916, she
exclaimed to the *World* magazine: "Cowgirl? I'm no cowgirl . . . I've never
been on a ranch in my life."[2] In this mediated moment, Baldwin exposed

deep debates about women's performance and western authenticity. Her air-of-innocence response articulated the performance of nonperformance cowgirls worked to achieve. At times appropriating larger tropes of "authentic" western womanhood, Baldwin also often cheekily resisted these narrow definitions, especially after her retirement from rodeo. Competing in an era defined by anxiety about the closing of the frontier, the growing number of immigrants, and the increasingly loud political demands of women, Baldwin negotiated her nationality, inexperience on stock ranches, and gender in order to assert her place as a true American pioneer.

The term "cowgirl" did not come into popular usage until the end of the nineteenth century.[3] White women who went west throughout the nineteenth century did not celebrate the moniker cowgirl or its predecessor "cowboy girl." As historian Joyce Gibson Roach has explained, most white women who lived on stock ranches in the mid- to late-nineteenth century carried Victorian gender ideals, including eastern fashions and a

Tillie Baldwin in her classic bloomers costume exhibiting her trick-riding abilities. *Fancy Riding by Tillie Baldwin Champion Lady Buckaroo*, Pendleton Round Up. Photograph by W. S. Bowman, courtesy of National Cowgirl Museum and Hall of Fame, Fort Worth, Texas.

strict division of labor.[4] For instance, despite the rough terrain, the use of a sidesaddle was still encouraged for women in order to protect their sexual productivity. Oregon resident Elizabeth Ludley took exception to the notion that riding astride was more comfortable, challenging women in 1872: "I fancy that twenty miles' experience on a man's saddle, over rough road, will convince almost any of our ladies that she can't do everything 'as well as a man.'"[5] Outside work was men's work. Only desperate need would drive a cattleman to let his wife or daughters consistently participate in herding practices.[6]

As the nineteenth century waned, however, alongside the cultural emergence of the cowboy hero, writers and theater directors increasingly promoted daring dime novel heroines and Wild West gals, crafting a new image of the western "cowgirl."[7] While Theodore Roosevelt has often been credited with coining the term in reference to Wild West performer Lucille Mulhall, historians have noted its usage in Wild West programs and news articles in the 1890s.[8] Based on these historical realities and the diversity of cowgirl experiences, twentieth- and twentieth-first-century historians have made a careful delineation between cattle women and rodeo entertainers. The National Cowgirl Hall of Fame, for instance, has separate categories for "women who had kinship with the land" and "women who went into the arena."[9] Yet, from the 1900s through the 1920s, rodeo producers and performers made no such distinction. Performers often sold audiences on the notion that rodeo cowgirls were the daughters of true pioneer mothers with ranching in their blood.

Women working and living on the early professional rodeo circuit performed a specific form of what gender theorist Jack Halberstam has called "female masculinity."[10] Female masculinity refers to the performance of a masculine identity by women who were otherwise blocked from masculine privilege. Lacerated skin, shattered bones, and excruciating deaths often resulted from riding broncs, wrestling steers, and racing horses. The media continually reiterated the "heroic" and "brave" natures of rodeo women. As one show program proclaimed, "And then the cowgirls! [. . .] the kind of girls who never hesitate to join the cowpunchers in the great cattle drives and who brave the lonely prairie rides with all the attendant dangers of outlaws and renegades, with never a thought of danger."[11] As women's suffrage debates raged during the 1910s, with many western women already enfranchised, the paying public embraced this form of female masculinity under the exceptionalist premise that these women were bred in the unforgiving environs of the West. Unlike other women in show business during the early twentieth century, their authenticity protected them, at least partially, from undue moral scrutiny.

Historians like Renee Laegreid and Mary Lou LeCompte have shown the complex realities of balancing femininity and masculinity in both cowgirl and rodeo queen performances in the early twentieth century. As local queens vied with glamorous, if rowdy, touring cowgirls, debates about who was an authentic participant in western culture emerged.[12] Tillie Baldwin's ability to navigate the American public's growing obsession with the West and her own impulses to claim a western identity, her immigrant story, or both illuminates the crucial intersection between nation and gender in western performance during the early decades of the twentieth century.

Indeed, the American public desired western women, imagined as strong mothers, forged on the frontier, as dual panics about white womanhood and immigration created anxiety about modern society. As waves of immigrants from southern and eastern Europe poured into the country and the United States spread its imperialist influence around the globe, white elites began to craft a discourse of "over-civilization." Many people were concerned about preserving the hardiness of native-stock, white Americans, seeing a lack of vigor in urban life. Adherents to the theory of race suicide, which postulated that falling birthrates were a harbinger of inevitable racial extinction, urged women to remember their primary duty to the nation in bearing healthy children who would become fit citizens.[13] Popular cultural movements like antimodernism and primitivism, which celebrated "the frontier" as cultivating more genuine forms of existence, provided tropes that cowgirls could invoke. Within the performative arena of rodeo, cowgirls could also reject a growing concern about rural degeneracy. As people fled farms for cities, social scientists worried that the country's vital stock was dwindling, making rural places as deviant as the city.[14] Cowgirl performers actively drew attention to both their fit bodies and their homemaking skills in order to protect their respectability and to craft themselves into antimodern heroines, often reinforcing traditional gender norms and anti-immigrant sentiments.

Tillie Baldwin both broke with and bolstered this longer narrative about the place of easterners, European immigrants, and women in the imagined American West as she strategically emphasized particular physical and behavioral attributes that allowed her to be marked as genuinely western. Importantly, Baldwin's image was crafted in large part by the media stories published over her lifetime. An immigrant who at times openly scorned notions about a woman's place throughout the 1910s, Baldwin's story had the potential to counter the idea that authentic western womanhood was rooted in blood and upbringing, but she often strategically decided to uphold that definition. She was able to do so in part because, as a blonde Norwegian, she faced far less anti-immigrant sentiment than southern and eastern European, Mexican, or Chinese immigrants experienced. While during her early career she often shared or withheld the particularities of her birth at different events, meaning some people knew she was an immigrant while others did not, during her retirement in Connecticut, she actively combined her immigrant and cowgirl stories, defining herself as a true pioneer.

This is not a biography of Anna Mathilda Winger, or of her alter ego Tillie Baldwin. She published no memoir to tell her own story, no diary to reveal her inner thoughts. Instead, this is an examination of how women like Baldwin crafted their own identities in the media. Many women like Baldwin earned a living by selling a standard definition of the cowgirl that emphasized ranch-born narratives of hardy domesticity while also actively resisting that definition by participating in masculine wage-earning performance, supporting the expansion of women's political and social rights, and embracing their own east-to-west stories. Placing Baldwin alongside her competitors and compatriots from the 1910s and 1920s, including Lucille Mulhall, Mabel Strickland, the Greenough sisters, and Vera McGinnis, we can analyze how white women in these decades used the tools available to them, specifically ideas about their birth and upbringing on the rugged frontier, to ensure the acceptance of their rodeo performances. When Baldwin left the circuit, she continued to rework the meaning of the cowgirl, asserting her right to be a western performer without being ranch born. In her retirement, as national concerns about immigration and women's rights waned, Baldwin claimed to be western and ultimately American on her own terms. Instead of lamenting her lack of pioneer pedigree, she was recast as the "good immigrant," a true pioneer who, through a trial by fire on the old frontier, overcame her Norwegian heritage and became fully American. Walking dangerous tightropes between public adoration and public scorn, outrider cowgirls played with concepts of western authenticity to gain acceptance as full citizens in the United States.

• • •

In 1912, the *San Francisco Chronicle* announced, "Tillie Baldwin, the young Oklahoma girl who recently created a sensation at the recent rodeo at Los Angeles by winning all the prizes for bucking bronchos [*sic*], defeating some of the best-known cowboys in the exhibition, will be a feature of the 101 Ranch Wild West."[15] Riding as an "unknown" in the 1911 Los Angeles Rodeo, Baldwin swept the riding trophies and the media gleefully reported on the homegrown cowgirl, "recruited from the Miller Brothers' famous 100,000-acre ranch." The 101 Ranch Wild West Show, dubbed the "Real Wild West," advertised its authenticity, inviting only "bona fide cattle men of the ranges" and "genuine, blanket-wearing" Native peoples, alongside "Clever Ranch Girls."

The woman from whom Baldwin stole the crown in Los Angeles was Bertha Blancett. Born Bertha Kapernick to German immigrants in Ohio, she moved with her family to a Colorado ranch when she was very young. Historian Mary Lou LeCompte dubbed her a "typical cowgirl, [who] spent most of her time riding."[16] In 1906 she joined Pawnee Bill's show and then married a successful rodeo cowboy, Dell Blancett, after meeting him at the first Pendleton Round-Up in 1910. In 1911, she almost won that rodeo's All-Around Champion title, placing ahead of almost all her male competitors in points. Her successful performances spurred rodeo producers to create separate "ladies' events."[17] The expansion of these events, with different rules and smaller cash winnings, ensured that cowgirl performers could participate in rodeos, but with carefully established limits.

Throughout the 1910s and 1920s, cowgirls readily participated in the construction of a narrative that linked their masculine abilities to their supposed upbringing on the rugged frontier. Many women explained their own transgressive behavior in terms of a celebrated notion of pioneer motherhood and hardy domesticity. Baldwin's story demonstrates the tenacity of the equation of cowgirl performer with ranch-born daughter. The narrative of cowgirls as fiercely dedicated to serving the home, strong through necessity, and healthier than their eastern sisters, however, meant a single, childless, and immigrant performer like Tillie Baldwin should not have existed; yet she did. As she attempted to establish her career, Baldwin successfully played on particular physical and behavioral traits in order to portray herself as a "genuine" American cowgirl.[18]

At the turn of the twentieth century, Baldwin was one of the hundreds of thousands of young Norwegian immigrants fleeing a time of rapid economic and political change in their homeland. As self-sufficient farms gave way to market production, factories provided ready-made fabrics, and railroads carried goods from the interior to the coast, the number of available jobs decreased. In more rural areas, a patriarchal structure of land inheritance meant the small farms could only be passed down to eldest sons. Most young people needed to engage in domestic service or farm labor in order to support themselves. Baldwin was born in 1888 in the coastal town of Arendal, which had for centuries depended on the timber trade and shipbuilding. As steam replaced sails, the town's merchant fleet required a large economic investment to modernize. Timber purchases from Europe decreased unexpectedly, however, and the investment did not pay. Just before Baldwin's birth, in 1886, Arendal suffered a significant economic crash, with three of four local banks going bankrupt.[19] The catastrophic economic downturn that marred her childhood may have made it necessary for Baldwin to leave her home at a young age for the perceived economic stability of America. Having an aunt already residing in New York would have offered her a safe destination. In the late nineteenth century, Norwegian communities expanded in Brooklyn and points further west, like North Dakota. During this time, only Ireland saw a larger ratio of its people immigrate to the United States. With a population of two million in 1900, Norway lost three-quarters of a million people between 1865 and 1915.[20]

As the United States experienced mass immigration and undertook imperialist wars to win new territories stretching from Puerto Rico to the Philippines in the early twentieth century, decades-old debates about the place of women in American social, economic, and political life continued to rage. After the passage of the Reconstruction amendments, granting freedom, citizenship, and voting rights to African American men following the Civil War, many white women activists, including Elizabeth Cady Stanton and Susan B. Anthony, explicitly invoked racial hierarchies to urge for their political inclusion. As Ida Weaver of Boise, Idaho, stated during the 1896 suffrage debate in the state: "Is it unfeminine to cry out for justice when an ignorant foreigner, or debased wreck of a man can vote to tax an intelligent woman's property to sustain an almshouse which he helps to fill? Is it right to class a large number of our wage earners and property holders with the Indians, Idiots and lunatics?"[21] White women, many argued, could bring the benefits of Christian morality to bear on America and the world, offering a safeguard to white American democracy through the measured expansion of political participation.

Bridging political parties, many Americans viewed white womanhood as particularly crucial against the onslaught of over-civilization and the supposed failing of the "white," or Anglo-Saxon, race. The rapid urbanization and industrialization that accompanied global and regional migration were thought to have corrupted white masculinity with vapid weakness. Rural communities, too, left with a dwindling gene pool bereft of natural talent, were thought to be weakening as well. Immigration restrictions, Jim Crow laws, and eugenic legislation increasingly limited anyone who was deemed "unfit," either mentally or physically, from entering the country, gaining employment, or reproducing.[22]

As a tall, blonde Norwegian woman, Baldwin would still have faced some nativist attitudes during this era of anti-immigration sentiment, but Scandinavian women met the Anglo-Saxon ideals of racial health. As Madison Grant wrote in his work on race suicide, "Only in Scandinavia and northwestern Germany does the Nordic race seem to maintain its full vigor."[23] Most importantly, Baldwin's immigrant background, like her anti-domestic sentiments, could either selectively be ignored or deployed by the press for the first half of her career as she contributed to an idealized notion of western femininity.

Increasingly, the cowgirl moniker was understood to be white, despite the roles many women of color played in western performance. Mexican American, Native American, and African American women often participated in riding and shooting exhibitions, yet they were also often singled out by their race. In Buffalo Bill's Wild West Show, "Prairie girls" were pitted against "Indian and Spanish girls" in horse races.[24] In 1911, *Billboard* noted that those who witnessed Tillie Baldwin and Señorita Valdez's bronc-riding act with the 101 Ranch "had never seen such an exhibition of bucking horse riders by ladies in any arena." Whereas Señorita Valdez was introduced as "the Spanish girl," Baldwin's whiteness required no modifiers;

the article simply assumed she belonged in the Wild West as a cowgirl.[25] While white cowgirls received widespread news coverage, women like Mrs. Sherry, an African American trick rider in the early 1920s, received very little media attention. Likewise, Native women were either lumped together as "squaws" or celebrated as "princesses," but never understood as cowgirls.[26]

The assumed whiteness of cowgirls contrasted with a slightly more flexible definition of cowboy at the time. As the cowboy hero emerged in novels, paintings, theater, and film at the end of the nineteenth century, the cowboy image no longer fully incorporated the racial diversity and working-class labor politics of the ranching industry. Yet this whitewashing did not completely extend to western performance, and men of color found a limited amount of acceptance in early rodeo. The famous African American cowboy Bill Pickett, for instance, toured with the 101 Ranch Wild West Show in order to perform his bulldogging technique. Bulldogging, an event Baldwin would later attempt, featured a participant on horseback dropping from a speeding horse onto a steer and wrestling it to the ground. Pickett would bite the lip of the steer, just like a bulldog, in his exhibitions. Native American cowboys like Tom Threepersons also made names for themselves on western circuits. These positions were precarious, however, often facing racialized commentary, for example, the persistent media association of Pickett with animalism. In keeping with the complexity of this racial landscape, Pickett was often forced to identify as Native American or Mexican American to skirt Jim Crow prohibitions.[27]

Indeed, Will Rogers, one of the most prominent American celebrities of the era, negotiated his race and cultural affiliation daily. As scholar Amy Ware demonstrates, if we understand "the Cherokee Kid" within his tribal-nation context, we see the ways "the hokey meanderings of a homespun cowboy-philosopher" were actually specific enactments of "Cherokee artistry" that operated as modes of survival for Rogers and other Native people.[28] Born in 1879 into a family of prominent Cherokee politicians and landholders in Indian Territory, Rogers was a trick roper, vaudevillian, journalist, comedian, and a beloved figure on the early Wild West circuit, with Tillie Baldwin considering him a close friend.[29] The conundrum of an Indian being a cowboy, however, at times mitigated his audience's ability to recognize him as Native or specifically as Cherokee. As an outrider of western performance, both resisting the emergence of a specific cowboy icon while also being foundational to its creation, Rogers shifted his own representation over time. Also, as the son of Cherokee Confederates who had owned slaves prior to the Civil War and were participating in the hotly debated Freedmen issue at the time he left Indian Territory, Rogers, like Baldwin, often left the racial hierarchies of the day unchallenged.

In many ways, the window of racial inclusion was closing even as it opened, as rodeos and cowboy performances by the 1910s became exhibitions of white Americans' growing concerns over racial supremacy and America's place in the world order. The antimodernism movement emerged in response to these concerns. Anxious that the modern age would create racial and gender weakness, a growing group of politicians, psychologists, and capitalists encouraged a return to "antimodern" authenticity, through manly interactions with nature and sport, as pathways to recapture the supremacy of white American males.[30] Through physical fitness, outdoor excursions, and traditional crafts, otherwise urbanized and unfit men and women could regain their mental and physical well-being, allowing them to be more productive citizens.

As Teddy Roosevelt famously stated in his 1899 speech on the necessity to expand America's colonial territories, "I wish to preach, not the doctrine of ignoble ease, but the doctrine of the strenuous life, the life of toil and effort, of labor and strife." In particular, Roosevelt derided men who "fear the strenuous life." "The timid man, the lazy man, the man who distrusts his country, the over-civilized man" would "shrink from seeing the nation undertake its new duties, shrink from seeing us build a navy and an army," which were necessary to bring "order out of chaos in the great, fair tropic islands." As scholar Gail Bederman has argued, in linking strenuous masculine activity with imperialistic foreign policy, Roosevelt merged the need to reassert white supremacy worldwide with the need to reassert masculinity at home.[31]

Wild West shows and rodeos aided this rhetoric of a strong, white America rooted in a frontier past. At the 1904 St. Louis World's Fair, one Wild West outfit staged the widely publicized "Contest for World Supremacy," which was designed to show white supremacy through a roping competition between "American Cowboys, Indian riders, Patagonian plainsmen of South America, and Mexican vaqueros."[32] Buffalo Bill's famous Congress of Rough Riders of the World similarly staged the victories of American cowboys over other horse-centric cultures.[33] Roosevelt and many of his contemporaries promoted the West, or the imagined frontier, as one place to journey in order to find this new strength and vitality.[34]

These cultural producers and politicians increasingly praised the frontier mothers of hardy western children. Theodore Roosevelt drew on the success of the idealized western woman to argue for women's right to vote. Roosevelt, writing for *Outlook* magazine in 1912, explained: "The service of the good mother to society is the most valuable economic asset that the entire commonwealth can show." That unremunerated labor, he continued, needed to be protected at all costs. Anything that threatened the home threatened the nation and civilization as a whole. Roosevelt argued that women deserved the vote because their superior moral fiber would help pass stricter labor laws and enforce harsher penalties on absent fathers. Using western women as evidence, Roosevelt asserted that women would not forget their places once given the vote. He explained, "In those Western States it is a real pleasure to meet women, thoroughly womanly women, who do every duty that any woman can do, and who also are not only in fact but in theory on a level of full equality with men. I fail to see that these women are any less efficient in their households, or show any falling off in the sense of duty; I think the contrary is the case."[35] Women, particularly pioneer women who were both strong and feminine, were central to the moral uplift and racial survival of the nation.

In their own promotion of their careers, cowgirls often connected their performances to the production of healthy citizens. In the early twentieth century, medical professionals were concerned that over-civilization had created a gambit of maladies running rampant through the upper classes. Many men and women were diagnosed with "neurasthenia," a disorder defined by lethargy, irritability, and decentralized aches. In 1881, physician George M. Beard, who first discovered this illness, described it as "nervelessness—a lack of nerve force" in his work *American Nervousness*.[36] These complaints, which mostly plagued the middle and upper classes, who had ample leisure time, were perceived to be the costs of civilization. Urban living, domesticity, and white-collar jobs were sapping the strength of America's citizens.

Cowgirls particularly stressed the healthful aspects of a necessity-drive lifestyle, emphasizing that over-civilization was as harmful to women as it was to men. Rider Mamie Francis Hafley assured her audience:

> In the west where I was raised, women are by no means the weaker vessel. Inured by lives of hardship, inconvenience, and sometimes privation, the western girl has learned to take her place in the saddle and often behind the trenches with her brothers. She has learned the art of marksmanship, not merely as a pastime, but as a means of protection and defense. When necessary, she has shouldered a gun and, side by side with her brother and father, fought the Indians or the desperados. She has ridden wild horses and enjoyed the excitement of the round-up. She knows nothing of broken down nerves and neurasthenia.[37]

Purportedly hardened and made fit by the harsh climate, the racialized enemies, and the loneliness of the West, cowgirls were fit citizens prepared to defend their homes, even against social diseases. This healthfulness produced female happiness. As bronc rider Alice Greenough explained, "Western women are happier, I believe, because they have to be tough—and that means strict rules of physical and mental health. [...] A cow-woman takes no coddling and gets no martyr complex just because she is going to have a baby." Indeed, western women had hard bodies from physical toil; they did not wear "binding clothing" because they had no excess flesh to wrangle into submission.[38] A perfect balance between healthy and feminine, the cowgirl epitomized the ideal "American girl."[39]

For Tillie Baldwin, this narrative of physical, and therefore mental, strength served to bolster her racial place in America. Standing "five feet ten, 180 big-boned pounds, with a crop of blond curls and a paradoxical pink and white complexion," this solidly built Scandinavian woman showed herself to be a "buxom girl . . . rounded out into young womanhood of unusual strength and proportions."[40] Baldwin's image communicated her racial fitness to her audience. She also demonstrated her moral fitness by refusing to participate in late-night carousing, telling reporters that she needed to sleep in order to stay strong and physically fit. As women across the nation looked to outdoor pursuits like hiking, swimming, and tennis to strengthen their bodies, cowgirls situated themselves as role models.[41] Mildred Mulhall, Lucille's sister and fellow member of the

In full cowgirl regalia, Baldwin fulfilled idealized notions of health and western womanhood. Photograph courtesy of National Cowgirl Museum and Hall of Fame, Fort Worth, Texas.

101 Ranch Wild West Show, asserted, "It is the most healthful form of exercise for women, more vigorous and wholesome than golfing or yachting. [. . .] I'm glad I've never have had to call upon the services of a doctor since I began to throw the lariat and I hope to be able to ride a horse as long as I live."[42] Women like Baldwin promoted the physical benefits of their lifestyle in order to communicate their fitness as athletes, women, and Americans.

These traits of frontier-tested physical and mental fitness could then be instilled in the nation's youth. In 1914, the Girl Pioneers of America's official manual exhorted, "The pioneer women were strong. You can be strong. The pioneer women were upright. You can be upright. The pioneer women were unselfish and self-sacrificing. You can be unselfish too."[43] Similarly, the Camp Fire Girls program urged young women to use camping, exercise, and dieting to "become sturdy and rugged" like their pioneer foremothers. Young women needed to resist modern entertainments and distractions, which were thought to debase young women into a life of childless immorality. Girls were taught instead to celebrate "old-fashioned womanhood."[44] The periodical the *Continent* noted that the Camp Fire Girls "bear in their faces the rich color that is evidence of sodas and candy foregone, and of nights spent in healthful sleep out of doors. Their hands are scarred with wounds where the darning needle slipped, or a hot kettle slid off the holder."[45] In rejecting empty consumerism and performing their domestic duties with fearless sacrifice, young women of the modern age could overcome their era's failings and live up to their foremothers.[46]

Cowgirls capitalized on and contributed to these larger cultural ideas about western femininity while also enduring the harsh realities of a competitive entertainment industry. Making a living on the rodeo road could be backbreaking, heartbreaking, or both. In the early twentieth century, rodeos were not yet standardized competitions. Staged in both small western towns and booming eastern cities, they were often presented in large arenas with no stock chutes and a distant grandstand. In order to make a rodeo worth watching, organizers tried to pack in as much excitement as possible, including trick riding, wagon racing, bronc riding, fancy roping, sharpshooting, and a variety of other events often based around local preference, with women performers in many of these competitions.

Women were no strangers to western performance. By the time Tillie Baldwin was just beginning to train on horseback, women like Annie Oakley and Lillian Smith had already been performing in Wild West shows for fifteen years. Acting out her sharpshooting routine as a robust country girl during the show, Oakley was well known for staging her Victorian virtue outside the arena, including dressing modestly, insisting on social decorum during her travels, championing temperance, and voicing opposition to women's suffrage. As historian Glenda Riley has explained, Oakley often stated that her greatest wish was "to be considered a lady."[47] She and other Buffalo gals helped establish white women as part of the western tableau in the popular imagination and contributed to a standard narrative of proper western femininity.[48]

These rehearsed performances began to give way to riding competitions at large western rodeos. In 1896, Annie Schaffer became one of the first woman bronc riders to be recorded competing at a local rodeo in Fort Smith, Arkansas.[49] In 1904, Bertha Blancett, then Bertha Kapernick, rode broncs as an exhibition at the Cheyenne Frontier Days.[50] By 1912, roughly forty women were actively participating on the growing circuit of big rodeos. Tillie Baldwin made sure she was consistently part of the pack and often the champion in bronc riding and relay racing.[51] In 1914, the

Oregonian exclaimed, "Tillie Baldwin has won her spurs in the bucking-horse riding; won them again and again as a trick and fancy rider [. . .] She is one of the most popular little cowgirls ever appearing at the Round-Up."[52]

While many women started down the rodeo road with an idea of glamorous costumes and audience adoration, the reality often fell short, being marred with all manner of physical and emotional agonies. Eleanor McClintock Williams, a decorated cowgirl, left her daughter with her wealthy parents to be brought up in a more proper manner, commenting, "We're out on the road so much, it would be hard for us to look after her . . . And I wouldn't want her trailing around with the circus—not my little girl."[53] Despite having run away with a cowboy to join the rodeo herself, she imagined a more socially appropriate, and perhaps easier, life for her daughter.

The rodeo season was a grueling nine-month trek from one rodeo to the next, traveling first by wagons and trains and later cars and trucks. During this period, female performers at times signed up as contract riders for a particular show, traveling with the entire cast and crew, and at other times were simply contestants, responsible for their own transportation, food, and accommodation. On the road, rodeoers lived out of tents, trucks, and even horse stalls for months, and women were expected to keep up with the cooking and cleaning for their male family members in addition to practicing tricks, exercising their animals, and finding paying jobs.[54] As early trick rider Juanita Hackett Howell explained, "It was a hard life. We went the hard way. We had to earn our money to keep afloat. We managed to save enough to buy our 40 acre farm. The rest of our money was spent on the road with flat tires and gas and traveling was expensive. It was a hard life."[55]

Wrecks, both in the arena and on the road, could lay women up for weeks as they tried to catch back up with the circuit, nursing broken bones, black eyes, collapsed lungs, and concussions. At the Winnipeg Stampede in 1913, Baldwin collapsed but ignored the advice of physicians in order to continue to ride in the Roman Races. Roman riding (standing astride two horses at once) was extremely dangerous even for a healthy person.[56] Baldwin and other women did not want to lose paying contracts or forfeit their entry fees in competitions, so they often rode injured.

Surviving, let alone thriving, on the road necessitated the construction of a "rodeo family." These networks of friendships and dependencies were

Roman racing was extremely dangerous. At the 1913 Winnipeg Stampede, Baldwin finished ahead of her male competitors. *Tillie Baldwin, Roman Race*, Winnipeg Stampede, Manitoba, August 1913. Photograph courtesy of Glenbow Archives, NA-1029-18.

created through both blood and affective ties. Marriage, of course, was the most prominent way in which women hitched themselves to a rodeo circuit. Marriage offered cowgirls both literal protection from the dangers of the road and the protection of their reputations. As rodeo historian Mary Lou LeCompte has noted, young, single women were not always welcomed into the rodeo family and "most cowgirls married rodeo cowboys within a year or two of joining the circuit."[57] After divorcing her first husband, trick rider Vera McGinnis related the trepidation she felt: "Rodeoing isn't a lark for a lone woman, yet I had a career to keep alive."[58] As McGinnis reminisced, "Even though Earl had not been on the road with me all the time, I had still been a married woman—married to a cowboy in the profession. As such I rated help and protection from the other cowboys, even if they didn't like me personally—or if they liked me too much. To rodeo alone was a challenge I had to prime myself to meet."[59]

Cowgirls also had to protect themselves from sexual attacks, at times from audience members who perceived them to be sexually available. A drunken crowd once attempted to pull Vera McGinnis from her horse.

One man "put his big hand up the leg of my leather skirt, and said: 'Little cowgirl let daddy feel.' My reaction came before my thought; I grabbed my bottle of beer by its neck and walloped him across the head."[60] As their travels took them all over the world, cowgirl performers faced sexualized forms of exploitation and danger.[61] Marriage offered women protection from sexualized and gendered violence within their own community.

Not only did marriage help protect women against the unwanted advances of rodeo cowboys or audience members, it also constructed a public image of white western womanhood as virtuous. Marriage and motherhood allowed cowgirls to publicly promote their connection to domesticity and allowed them to distance themselves from the associations of other women performers like theater actresses, vaudevillians, and burlesque dancers. Sensationalized horseback marriages at rodeos offered the audience a spectacle of heterosexual romance, reassuring audiences that, like any respectable woman, cowgirls desired marriage.

In reality, women could be coerced into these public displays of respectability. In 1913, Buffalo Bill Cody gave Goldie Griffith away in marriage in front of eight thousand spectators at Madison Square Garden.[62] Dressed in a red leather riding outfit made by Sioux women, with beads and fringe covering her gauntlets, hat, and scarf, Griffith stayed mounted on horseback next to her groom. Griffith's fiancé had not even proposed to her himself, leaving that task to the business-minded Cody. The wedding was meant to sell tickets, to be a public ode to the traditional western family. Indeed, after Griffith had been injured badly in a horse crash during the previous night's show, she had been given the mind-altering drug laudanum by a doctor for her pain. Her fiancé, however, insisted the wedding move forward. Through the haze of pain and drugs she remembered little about her wedding day. She told a reporter years later that the injury and anxiety over potentially missing the well-advertised wedding was a "nightmare." Within three years, Griffith was reportedly pressured into having an abortion, learned her husband was already married, and attempted to shoot him.

Yet, in the press, cowgirls often maintained their respectability by performing heterosexual domesticity. Indeed, cowgirls often contended that the family unit was their sole concern. As performer Alice Greenough asserted, "Asking city women what they want from life is not generally the opening to a pleasant conversation because in their anxiety to rope in their desires they have become hysterical and frustrated. (Words cowgirls seldom ever hear). They are too eager to *get* and too ignorant of *giving*."[63] Western women, by contrast, lived healthful lives because they worked hard to provide for others, with little time to work themselves into hysterics. Defense of the home and the need to toil for prosperity made cowgirls antimodern heroines and allowed them access to a masculinity otherwise still prohibited for many modern women. Even the staunchest defender of femininity among cowgirls admitted that she was a tough businesswoman, but in the name of her daughter. Mabel Strickland, well known for her distaste of unladylike behavior, including "vulgarity and chewing gum," explained that when signing any contract, there better not be "anything cute above the signatures that will keep the money from our little April."[64]

Women who exhibited their skill with stock performed a particular type of female masculinity—one that could have been threatening to the white, middle-class American public. Marriage provided a way for cowgirls and their promoters to distinguish between the arena and the home: "To the Rodeo Crowd she is Fox Hastings, cowgirl extraordinary. To neighbors, she is Mrs. Mike Hastings, a good cook and tidy housekeeper."[65] Indeed, famous cowgirls who failed to marry or married outside of the rodeo often left the business, as Tillie Baldwin eventually would do. Not only did they lack the formal protection of a legal bond, but they were also often perceived as threats to marriages, placing them at odds with other performers. While on the rodeo road, Baldwin herself had to negotiate questions about both her immigrant background and her familial belonging.

Unlike other cowgirls who married, often multiple times, or had a baby to show the cameras, Baldwin simply changed her name. Prior to becoming a recognized champion in 1911, Baldwin first joined a local show in New York for six dollars a week.[66] Eventually, she joined up with Captain Jack Baldwin's Wild West show. While her stated reason for changing her name was that she simply liked it better, the change helped her manage public perception. Just as the media often assumed that she was an "Oklahoman girl," they frequently named Jack as Tillie's brother or husband.[67] Billed as husband and wife duo Johnnie and Tillie Baldwin at times and as the Baldwin Twins at others, the pair performed joint riding acts at fairs and in larger Wild West shows. They also traveled to rodeos and competed individually. In 1913, at the Winnipeg Stampede, *Billboard* magazine reported that John Baldwin and W. B. Steele bragged loudly, and even made a bet, about whose "wife" could ride a bronc better. While there is no evidence that she married during her fifteen years as a rodeo rider, Tillie Baldwin thus did have a male riding partner, allowing her to pass as part of a well-established Wild West family. As Baldwin, and women like her, struck out on the rodeo road, they were often utterly devoid of connections to western communities or the western life they were supposed to represent—making carefully mediated maneuvering a necessity for survival.

Many early rodeo profiles actually used her supposed marriage to explain away her immigrant past. In 1912, an Oregon paper explained that "contrary to natural opinion," Baldwin "is no girl of the west, neither is she a girl of the east. In fact she is not native American at all but claims Sweden as her fatherland."[68] Before her "marriage" to Jack, she knew as much as any "effete eastern girl," but when she married a Texan, "she did not lose much time in adapting herself to be a true helpmate." Despite her whiteness, and people's therefore "natural" assumption about her place in the West, in this instance, Baldwin becomes both authentically American and western because of her domestic dedication to serving as her husband's "helpmate."

While marriage may have offered her strategic protection, Baldwin, or her chroniclers, were also not always so upfront about her immigrant story. During the months of the year in which she performed with the 101 Ranch Wild West Show, Baldwin was most often subsumed under the "Oklahoman cowgirl" description. Only a few months prior to being dubbed "no girl of the west," Baldwin was heralded as one of the "Clever Ranch Girls" alongside the "Real Cowboys and Bedecked Indians" in the show.[69] She often passed as a homegrown cowgirl by emphasizing her ability with stock. In 1913, the year she competed at both the Pendleton Round-Up and the Winnipeg Stampede, the *Idaho Statesman* asked Baldwin how she learned to ride. She responded: "I just rode, that's all. Got on the horse and got dumped, got up and got on him again and got dumped again." The article calls her a "girl 'cowboy'" and hypes her promise to bulldog a steer at the next Pendleton Round-Up. This brash woman, who openly rejected a "woman's sphere" and bragged that "there is nothing [at Pendleton] I can't ride," claimed to be devoted to horses because "she was raised that way."[70] Interestingly, later in life, she would say she learned to ride broncs from Will Rogers, a fellow performer and friend.[71] Yet, this particular narrative, of learning show business rather than ranch business, did not serve her well at the time. As she promoted her abilities as a rider, Baldwin did not always contest the assumption that she was ranch-raised or at least experienced with stock.

Instead of highlighting her own east-to-west trajectory, Baldwin often played into a popular idea of cowgirls' west-to-east journeys. Promotions for cowgirls' performances heralded their arrivals: "Beautiful but Brave These Cowgirls Here from the West," and "Cowgirls Arrive from Prairies."[72] For many eastern Americans, the West was a place to visit, explore, and test one's mettle. By the 1920s, rodeo producers like Tex Austin were staging shows in large eastern cities like Chicago and New York. Taking advantage of the exoticization of the West, Austin often noted how "his country has little in common with the East and the East seems so very far away." The West was "something separate and apart from the rest of the United States."[73] In this separation from the everyday lives of eastern cities, cowgirls could be advertised as "novelties."[74]

As exotic exceptions, existing slightly outside the realm of everyday eastern life, cowgirls could offer the language of necessity as an excuse for their masculine performances. They were celebrated as strapping lasses of pioneer stock, both deeply American and gaze-worthy. A 1917 Buffalo Bill program said of its female performers, "A fine healthy, sun-browned, robust lot they are."[75] The press hailed Tillie Baldwin with descriptions of her ability to ride "the most untamable ponies with out [sic] the slightest evidence of fear."[76] Yet demonstrations of this type of novel bravery also potentially tainted cowgirls.

In the early decades of the twentieth century, medical journals, child-rearing books, and psychological studies all suggested that a masculine mother, a monstrosity in herself, could only produce weak and effeminate children. As the New York Medical Journal stated in 1900, "The female with masculine ambition is always amusing and often pitiable; but the attenuated, weak-voiced neuter, the effeminate male: pity him, but blame his mother for the false training, and give scorn to the father for his indifference."[77] Cowgirls had to walk a tightrope between entertaining their audiences with daring acts and justifying these acts as both confined to the arena and necessitated by their upbringing.

Most importantly, the ideal cowgirl never felt the need to seek independence for its own sake. Buffalo Bill's program explained: "She is a development of the stock-raising West comparing with the bachelor girl and the independent woman of the East. She is not of the new woman class—not of the sort that discards her feminine attributes and tries to ape the man, simply a lively, athletic young woman with a superfluity of nerve and animal spirits, with a realization that in affairs where skill is the chief qualification she has an equal chance with her brothers."[78] Embodied in the figure of the "New Woman," the "bachelor girl" and the "independent woman" were self-centered creatures of the modern age who fussed with fashions or, worse, attempted to usurp masculine professions.[79] Cowgirls, unlike the political New Woman, desired to retain their femininity, even if forced into masculine pursuits by the caprices of birth. Cowgirls like Mabel Strickland reassured audiences that they were not "gender inverts," or women who desired to be men.[80] Strickland explained, "I can't tolerate the mannish woman any more than I can stand the womanish man."[81] Of course, many of these women had already gained the vote in their own states, allowing them to distance themselves from questions of a Constitutional amendment. Many cowgirls did not want to be associated with political calls for greater political equality; they were simply performing their duties as the sturdy daughters and wives of the frontier.

The image of the western woman as being morally and physically strong pervaded American culture. In 1903, the *New York Times* ran an article praising the capable women of the frontier. While women in the East were making progress in the professions, women "in every part of the raw, new West" were "not only adapting themselves to a crude and strange environment but are winning fortune and fame." Miss Amelia Dunn, for instance, took over her family's ranch when her father died, tending to four thousand head of cattle over "200 miles from home across sandy wastes and among foothills and mountains." In this celebration of both the enduring pioneer spirit and living women making a living on the range, the *New York Times* argued that women like Amelia simply did what was necessary while also remaining dedicated to femininity. "While on the range Miss Dunn dresses in true cowboy fashion—wide-brimmed white felt hat, long gauntlet gloves, a lariat coiled about the saddle horn, and a revolver at her belt—and rides the wildest bronco with thorough ease. When off duty she is a quiet, unassuming young lady, the last one that would be suspected of such masculine accomplishments." Indeed, the *Times* reported that her only regret was "that I have never had an opportunity to gain any of the womanly accomplishments." The harshness of life in the West did not dampen women's supposed desire for genteel femininity in the midst of necessary masculinity.

While Amelia Dunn did not enter the arena, her image and that of the professional cowgirls were often conflated because of the belief that cowgirls were real western gals. As one article noted, "It's one thing to preserve a complexion of peaches and cream, along with a daintiness that would make any flapper envious, and it's another to master a plunging, fighting 'outlaw' broncho [*sic*], rope and throw a running calf, or ride a wild horse bareback. But to achieve both of these extremes is a problem that probably only some of the champion cowgirls of the far west have solved." Beauty and health could be achieved through taking "fresh air and exercise" and "shunning too many sweets." Mabel Strickland "never touched rouge to cheek or lip," yet lacked "nothing in the softness of femininity."[82] In an age of rapid industrialization and urbanization, cowgirls cast themselves as living artifacts of a dying age. They could balance their essential feminine natures with the necessary tasks of masculine labor pursuits, and balance their commitment to traditional gender roles with modern beauty and glamour.

Just like Dunn, cowgirls worked and used their skills in service to family survival, defining themselves as active participants in the expansion and protection of American civilization. Trick rider Tad Lucas stated in the *Boston Evening Post*: "[We are] normal girls who fell victim of their environment—rugged daughters of a rugged frontier. In fact . . . any eastern 'perty' lass of the lipstick and fluffy female type might have taken to bronc busting if born in the leathery surroundings of a daddy-owned stock ranch, cradled in the saddle, teethed on a cinch buckle, and nourished on cooked cow."[83] Even popular postcards of cowgirls often showed them in action, throwing a lasso or jumping their horses over cars, separating them from other stage women, particularly theater actresses, whose postcards tended to be beauty shots of them draped over luxurious furniture or statically posed in costume.[84] By framing themselves as undertaking necessary action, cowgirls carefully framed their theatrical professions as the live performances of their rugged upbringings.

This commitment to courage could be transmitted through performance, as cowgirls urged city dwellers to toughen themselves up. Mamie Hafley, described as a "lithe, familiar figure in rodeo, vaudeville and carnival acts since 1908," dove horses from fifty-foot platforms into pools of water to the delight of children at Coney Island, even as she won riding and roping competitions in the trans-Mississippi West. She defined her feats as socially significant because acts of bravery executed in front of an audience emboldened viewers to be daring in their own lives: "It is foolish for people to feel that a man or woman who is doing an act of daring in a Hippodrome or circus, is jeopardizing his or her life with no end in view—with no permanent good to humanity. I maintain that every act of daring performed in public contributes something to the sum of human courage. The force of example is all-powerful." While Hafley did not expect men and women to rush to dive on horseback, she had the "self-satisfaction" of knowing that "every time I make my perilous descent someone has been impressed and imbued with a greater bravery and more courageous spirit." Exhibitions taught people "better nerve" and "more self-reliance," especially eastern women who did not have the experience of riding "wild horses" or participating in a "round-up." By performing the West, Baldwin, Hafley, and other cowgirls encouraged all Americans to find their nerve. Hafley lamented the "rank injustice to performers of my class to give us no credit beyond mere temporary glory of having amused and thrilled."[85]

From the early 1900s until the 1930s, women in professional rodeo created public personas that espoused robust health over vapid over-civilization. Their connection to the West and its harsh environmental demands allowed this otherwise overly masculine performance to be converted into a defense of the white, heterosexual home. Using this language of authenticity, professional cowgirls and their promoters created an acceptable form of female masculinity that placed cowgirls firmly in a domestic vision of the white American polity.

• • •

While this narrative, constructed by the performers, their promoters, and the press, rooted women's western authenticity in birth and upbringing, the allure of the rodeo drew women from all walks of life. As Vera McGinnis, no ranch-born girl herself, explained: "Secretly the pageantry and excitement of the arena throbbed with a deep bass rhythm against our very souls."[86] Indeed, historian Mary Lou LeCompte has noted that most of the prominent cowgirls in this era were working-class women born into first- or second-generation immigrant families, many from outside the geographical West.[87] While learning to ride on Staten Island, Tillie Baldwin, like so many before and after her, did not so much learn to love ranch labor, but instead learned to love the idea of western glamour.

As Mitzi Lucas Riley, daughter of famous trick rider Tad Lucas, explained, "If you wanted to run away from home and join the rodeo, just like people did the circus, you just did it."[88] Her own mother had run away from her parents and twenty-one siblings on a Nebraska farm to join the rodeo. At the dawn of the modern era, women gravitated toward opportunities to travel and earn a living in popular theater, dance, and cultural exhibitions.[89] This desire to buck the system was true of socialites as well as poor immigrant women and farm girls. Eleanor McClintock Williams, daughter of wealthy Pittsburgh artists, attended the Madison Square Garden Rodeo in 1928, meeting and marrying a rodeo cowboy.[90] Even after two divorces, she stuck to the saddle and earned a living as a champion bronc rider. For the performers, artifice was a natural part of their careers and they deftly navigated the concerns of the public as they subtly resisted definitions of authenticity that would have barred them from rodeo performance.

Despite the perception that women's childhood connection to horses or their experiences rounding up cattle brought them to the rodeo, many women found the arena through theatrical careers. Juanita Hackett Howell saw her actress mother sewing costumes for a Wild West show and asked to be brought along on the road. For the next twenty years, Juanita worked rodeos, circuses, fairs, and horse shows performing trick riding.[91] Other female masculinities, like female athletics, were a popular attraction in the early twentieth century. Goldie Griffith, for instance, worked as a wrestler with Blanche Whitney's Lady Athletes. At carnivals and amusement parks, customers could pay ten cents to watch Griffith wrestle other women and occasionally men. Like Baldwin, Griffith eventually became a member of the 101 Ranch Wild West Show and performed with Lucille Mulhall on her "Girl Scout" vaudeville tour. Many rodeoers, not just Baldwin, found their way to the arena by way of occupations having little to do with stock ranches.

While other women in the public eye were subject to suspicion, cowgirls sidestepped infamy by associating themselves with genuine range work. One newspaper described famed cowgirl Lucille Mulhall as the "best practical quickest handiest cowpuncher her daddy had. That's where she learned the business. She's not a vaudeville performer, just struck onto a novelty. She didn't go to a riding professor and get taught. She learned to rope steers and lasso wild horses like a bird learns to fly, she just tried."[92] Indeed, the distasteful business of show business wasn't quite befitting a person with such real-life experience. "Some vaudevillians are born to grease paint—they have no personality outside of it; others attain grease paint and like most ready-made things, it never exactly fits; but Lucille Mulhall, the Oklahoma girl at the Temple this week is a shining example of those who have grease paint thrust upon them—and in her particular case it is safe to prophesy—it isn't going to stick."[93] In 1912, while riding with 101 Ranch alongside Mulhall, Tillie Baldwin and Lulu Bell Parr received praise as "daredevil girls." Parr was a top hand because she had spent her life on ranches and "the ranch life appeals to her as the only one that is really worth while [sic]."[94] This performance of non-performance epitomized cowgirls' ability to use ideas about "authenticity" to embrace theatricality and earn an independent living without being labeled New Women or actresses.

All western performance was ultimately a show produced for a paying audience. Lucille Mulhall, the handy cowpuncher, was part of a show-business family. Her father designed his 101 Ranch Wild West Show around her performances of riding and roping, illustrating the inextricability of the real and the imagined wests. Despite her intentions of staying home in Oklahoma, "I always return to the road after a short interval at home. I suppose I always will, too. At least as long as I am able to do it and public enjoys my 'stunts.'"[95] The most "real" of cowgirls understood the gap between what she did in the arena for applause and life on a stock ranch. To Mulhall, her performances were exciting stunts, meant to thrill the audience, not to authentically reflect the drudgery of ranch life.

Cowgirls even understood their clothing as costume. Over the 1910s and 1920s, cowgirls increasingly embraced bright colors, large bows in their hair, and even pants. This western style was itself a contrivance of early rodeos and Hollywood.[96] Vera McGinnis liked to refer to dressing in her costumes as being "Westerned up" in her "loud rags." While staging a rodeo in London, hosts would ask cowgirls to dress in their supposedly authentic garb at parties: "boots, hats, spurs, and all. We were not individuals, but the colorful west."[97] One 1930s rodeo queen from Pendleton laughed at her cowgirl getup, calling it a "novelty."[98] Indeed, Will Rogers connected Mulhall's authenticity to her ladylike dress: "Lucille never dressed like the Cowgirl you know today, no loud colors, no short leather skirts, and great big hat, no sir, her skirt was divided, but long."[99] Rogers marks a divide between generations of cowgirl costuming, but split skirts were by no means standard wear for western women when Mulhall was performing. For most women performers, being a cowgirl always included a costume, no matter their background.

Early cowgirls did not confine themselves to a predetermined notion of what rodeo or western equestrianism encompassed. Unlike today's fairly limited offerings of rodeo queening and barrel racing for women in rodeo, women of this golden era created and performed all manner of exciting stunts and shows for their audiences. Just as Mamie Hafley created her horse-diving act, so Lucille Mulhall ran her own vaudevillian production. Starring as a scout, she rode a horse on stage, threw lariats, and handled guns. Many women displayed their trick-riding expertise in rodeos during the summer months and then performed similar routines for a film camera or a circus audience during the slow winter months. The rodeo was not a hermetically sealed arena where ranch-raised daughters demonstrated their practical stock skills but rather a permeable space filled with women performing a number of impressive feats.

The variety of entertainment also meant a variety of spaces. Western producers took advantage of large, spectacle-focused structures like urban hippodromes and rural fairgrounds. At a Connecticut fair in 1918, the Baldwin riding act appeared alongside theatrical recitals by dogs, acrobats, high-wire walkers, and an anteater.[100] A diverse array of people also participated in the staging of western performances, including "frontier contestants, Wild West performers, contest managers, and Wild West show owners."[101] Native American performers and encampments continued to be central to fairs, rodeos, and Wild West shows, especially in places like Pendleton, Oregon, which was located near a reservation. Pendleton even crowned Native queens from the local Umatilla reservation during the 1940s and 1950s.[102] In the early decades of the twentieth century, professional cowgirls displayed their talents on film, in circuses, at county fairs, and in rodeos.

World War I and Buffalo Bill Cody's death in 1917 generally mark the moment when rodeos replaced the Wild West show as the predominant form of western performance, but rodeo cowgirls continued to work as Wild West entertainers, vaudevillians, and circus performers through the 1930s.[103] Mamie Hafley's daughter, Reine, or Reno, as she was called, started her show business career as a three-year-old in her mother's vaudeville shooting act. By twenty, she had done almost every task necessary to make a Wild West show successful: "stock care, setting tents, costume making, cleaning and packing tack, bally-hooing, performing in several acts, working the arena, leading broncs to the next town when trains were not available, working guns for Mamie's shooting act, grooming and exercising the specialty horses in off-season."[104] She also rode elephants and performed as a flamenco dancer. Riding in rodeos made up only a small percentage of these performers' tasks.

The fluidity between rodeos and other forms of performance meant these women were both athletes in an emerging competitive sport and actresses in a broad range of turn-of-the-century entertainments. As vagabond career women who risked injury and death, cowgirl performers like Baldwin straddled a gendered, racialized, and sexualized line between beloved pioneer heroines and scandalous oddities of the American West. In an era of liberalizing ideas concerning sex and marriage, their performances were also scrutinized for potential improprieties, whether sexual or professional.

Despite their best efforts, cowgirls could not entirely distance themselves from the rough-and-tumble world of theater. As Michael Allen has noted, rodeo cowboys were not always considered real western cowboys, but instead a rowdy crowd of ne'er-do-wells shirking ranch business for show business.[105] This reputation held true for rodeo women as well. In an oral history about her experiences as a rodeo queen for the Pendleton Round-Up in its early years, Ella Granger suggested that the cowgirls who came to town weren't quite "proper women"; they "would play cards and maybe drink and associated with men all the way around more so than we did . . . We didn't know that kind of life."[106] As part of a second generation of cowgirls during the 1920s and 1930s, Margie Greenough described Baldwin's era: "I'd heard of quite a few fights before I came around. That was a pretty tough bunch there to start with. I don't think they hesitated to use a knife, or anything, from what I hear. I think there was probably a lot of jealousy."[107] Indeed, cowgirls slung accusations of sexual impropriety at each other, impugning the respectability of their competitors. Vera

McGinnis punched another woman for calling her a "chippie."[108] The term "chippie" denoted women accused of rodeoing for the main purpose of socializing with the cowboys and granting sexual favors to the judges in order to win titles.[109] Cowgirl Pearl Mason stated during an oral history interview in the 1980s, "Some of the girls only rodeoed so they could be around the men. [. . .] I was nice to the judges . . . but I never slept with them."[110] Cowgirls needed to keep these accusations of moral laxity out of the press, but they could not entirely keep them out of the public consciousness.

Some cowgirls, like Baldwin, also openly embraced suffragist stances, though their views were rarely presented as radical. While Mulhall was "not much interested" in debates about the vote, Lulu Bell Parr was described as "a suffragette in every sense of the word." The newspaper, however, immediately distanced her from British "militant suffragettes," who found "no symposthizer [sic] in her."[111] As agitation for women's voting rights grew, and the image of western women was actively used to promote these demands, Baldwin made a show of rejecting the home as the only sphere for a woman. A 1913 article exclaimed: "Tillie Baldwin says she would rather ride a relay race any day than attend a sewing circle, make the backdrop pickup from any horse than cook the three family meals per day, and ride the worst bucking horses that can be found than do the family wash." Once again pointing to the notion that she was "raised" to ride, the article takes her opinion on a woman's place in stride. She is quoted as saying that she would rather "give an exhibition ride on a milch cow before the Society of the Prevention of Cruelty to Animals" than be "roped and hog-tied by what's advertised as society."[112] Buttressing her identity as an authentic westerner by playing up her disgust of both effeminate housewifery and effeminate animal-rights activists, Baldwin also playfully asserted her abilities as a rider and her desires as a public woman.

Baldwin's performances became renowned for their blatant refusal to bow to feminine norms. She introduced wearing a gymnast's costume, complete with bloomers, while riding. Denounced by early cowgirls like Mulhall who found bloomers unladylike, Baldwin helped reshape cowgirl costume. Long skirts presented the danger of tangling and also became increasingly outdated in national fashion trends; bloomers, and later pants, were far safer attire.[113] She also may have been the first female performer to bulldog, or wrestle steers, as an exhibition at a major rodeo.

Introduced by Bill Pickett, a fellow member of the 101 Ranch Wild West Show, bulldogging was seen as the ultimate display of brute force because of the agility and strength it took to bodily throw a steer to the ground. Wide publicity preceded her attempts at bulldogging at the 1913 Pendleton Round-Up, and later articles recalled how people "gasp[ed] in delight" as she threw a "wild bull."[114] Baldwin adjusted her persona throughout her career, sometimes downplaying her immigrant past and allowing audiences to believe she was married, and other times rewriting gendered norms on the rodeo circuit and explicitly acknowledging the political significance of her performances.

In 1916, Baldwin asserted that she lacked the upbringing required to be called a cowgirl. Trick rider, bulldogger, or racer—but not a cowgirl. While much of the public may not have previously known about her immigrant background, people within the industry knew from the beginning of her career. In 1915, Whistling Annie, author of the cleverly named *Wimmin's Writes* column for *Billboard* magazine, wrote, "Tillie Baldwin—Is the report true that you will again open a manicuring parlor in New York? We were under the impression that you were a Wild West exponent for good."[115] An "exponent," a person who believes in or promotes a particular cause, was precisely the position imagined for Baldwin. She could be in the West, but not entirely of it. She could be a promoter for the West, but not entirely an example of it. Just as Baldwin refused to remain a hairstylist, to marry early, to celebrate domesticity, or to wear long skirts, so she refused to hide stories of her migration, her city life, or her hairstyling. Yet, with her rejection of the cowgirl title, she also upheld the popular narrative that linked western women's authenticity to birth and upbringing. Baldwin's story not only demonstrated the complexity in staging "real" western femininity during the early twentieth century, but also how definitions of the authentic change over time. By the time Baldwin retired from the arena, her story had transcended the very boundaries it helped construct.

•   •   •

While Tillie Baldwin ultimately did not refute the prevailing notion of the "authentic" cowgirl, she also did not perceive herself as disqualified from performing westernness or claiming a western identity. Like other performers, she strategically crafted herself in the media as racially, physically, and mentally fit to be an American. Alongside other non-ranch-born women, she helped rodeo thrive in a polyglot environment that staged the West as a part of a larger national spectacle. She even donned bloomers and at times publicly rejected domesticity as the dominant meaning of her performances. Most importantly, in the second half of her life, she retold her story as a triumph in American pioneering. As an immigrant she lacked a pioneer mother and father, yet she was a "pioneer" herself. As she moved back toward the East, marrying, retiring from the circuit, and reassuming her life as Anna Mathilda Winger, the legend of Tillie Baldwin and her unparalleled achievements only solidified. Instead of being authentically western through upbringing, she had gone westering herself.

In Baldwin's mid-thirties, her life began to shift back toward the East Coast. In 1916, just months after saying she was no cowgirl, Johnnie and Tillie bought a farm in New Lyme, Connecticut, reportedly as brother and sister.[116] She told a Montanan newspaper that far from defining her identity, rodeo was her "season profession." She used performance as a way to make a living: "When the shows are on and there's money to be made, I'll stick to it for all it's worth. I'm very anxious to make money." The article, which dubbed her the "Little New York Hairdresser," both celebrated her abilities as a rider and reiterated that with her "pink and white complexion" and beautiful curls, she was still as much "coiffeuse" as cowgirl.[117] From 1919 until 1923, Baldwin performed mostly in New England at "society circuses and benefit rodeos," most likely small community shows that included trick riding and other exhibitions.[118] In 1924, she married William Slate and together they moved to Four Mile River Road in South Lyme, Connecticut.

As with many women before her, marrying outside the profession meant the end of her rodeo career, but not the end of Tillie Baldwin as a piece of local color. The neighborhood was quite interested in the woman who had once had her name in lights, her face on cigar wrappers, and an adoring audience roaring its approval of her shows. The *Hartford Courant* wrote in 1925 that there was "nothing unusual" about Mrs. Slate living in South Lyme, "unless one happens to know that Mrs. Slate was formerly Miss Tillie Baldwin, world's champion lady broncho [sic] buster, buckaroo, bulldogger, trick rider and relay racer."[119] Over the next thirty years, the *Courant* ran articles every decade or so reminding people of Tillie

Baldwin's accomplishments. Her life story was periodically honored, often with the same article with minor revisions, as being both exotically fascinating and quintessentially American.

During the 1920s and early 1930s, after Baldwin retired from the rodeo circuit, many white Americans were reinvesting in their own personal westering narratives. Increasingly commemorated in beloved children's literature like Laura Ingalls Wilder's *Little House on the Prairie* series, the days of dusty cattle drives and log cabins were gone. But one could also still experience the untouched West through dude ranches, national parks, and automobile tours.[120] The growing tourism industry ensured that many Americans saw the West as a place to experience "authenticity," even if it was grounded in fantasy.[121] Dude ranches exploded in popularity around the country, allowing average Americans the ability to play cowboy and cowgirl for a weekend, a month, or a summer.[122] Aching to see the West before the "calamity" of settlement, wealthy white girls like Loraine Hornaday Fielding wrote about their trips, emphasizing the authenticity of their experiences. Fielding described her summer in Montana in her memoir, *French Heels to Spurs*: "Here was a real ranch—not a summer resort, but an honest-to-goodness cattle-ranch—equipped with the finest ranch buildings possible, situated in a truly ideal place."[123] It was not necessarily the pioneer woman's experiences Fielding yearned to perform, but rather those of the daring cowgirls she had seen in films, rodeos, and novels. Having purchased for herself all the trappings of a western costume, she found out that "most of the girls . . . wore overalls, but where was the romance of the West if you couldn't wear chaps and everything that goes with them?"[124] In order to embody the popular image of the West, one had to be extraordinary and not mundane.

The desire for the performative West allowed readers of a local Connecticut newspaper to define Anna Mathilda Winger Slate as an exemplary cowgirl. Unlike her compatriot cowgirls, she was not a cowgirl because she had grown up in the West; instead, she was authentic because she herself was a pioneer. "And when one learns that Mrs. Slate, formerly Tillie Baldwin, is no native to the American West, but was christened Anna Mathilda Winger in Norway and was, but a brief span of years back, a New York coiffeuse, one's interest in her becomes extremely keen."[125] An immigrant and an oddity, Winger proved herself willing and able to Americanize, a fact that pleased the decades of activists who had claimed that white ethnic immigrants would adapt to American culture if given the opportunity.

Baldwin earned her authenticity as a "real" American through her association with the West. The *Hartford Courant* explained, "The West claims Tillie Baldwin as its own. And the West has a good claim for it was there that Tillie became a cowgirl and it was in the land of cattle and trails that she won her spurs. The West is the land she loves and there is no disputing that she is a real rider of the West." Even though she actually learned to be a cowgirl in the East, her performances were retroactively read as being part of the true westering tradition. Indeed, the author continued, she surpassed many of the homegrown cowgirls. She performed "stunts too much for many girls, natives of the golden west."[126] Baldwin, with her proven abilities as a racer, trick rider, and bulldogger, earned her spurs not through birthright but through her dexterous performance of the idealized cowgirl.

Her immigrant story only added to the honor of her achievements, making her an even more genuine product of the West. "Her early life is mentioned that honor may be given her for a victory over all manner of obstacles." In this telling, her ethnicity, once elided in her public persona, was reinterpreted as a handicap that she had conquered. Even the manner of her arrival changed with each telling. At times she "sneaked in," while at others she simply arrived. Sometimes she was a young girl of twelve, while others she was almost a full-grown adult. Yet, no matter her means of entry or age, within the narrative she always moved "up the ladder of fame." Slowly and surely she overcame all impediments, pulling herself up by the proverbial bootstraps. She was "Tillie Baldwin, working, resting, and leaving no stone unturned in improving her art and strengthening the muscles of her robust body."[127] Just as significant immigration restriction was stemming the tide of southern and eastern European immigrants with the 1924 Johnson-Reed Act, Baldwin and her chroniclers recrafted a story of the immigrant who overcame her birth and outcowgirled the cowgirls. Upending earlier concerns about needing a pioneer bloodline to be a cowgirl, Baldwin became a true western woman by westering herself. Her physical characteristics, her willingness to go West, and her preservation of that character in her new life illustrated the ways in which Baldwin leveraged her stage persona in order to be accepted as a "real" American.

Indeed, her exotic association with the West allowed for her legend to grow for decades, especially as women disappeared from rougher forms of western performance. After Baldwin's retirement, the heyday of cowgirl rodeoers' participation in rough stock events drew to a close. Around the mid-1920s, young white women began to shift their involvement in rodeos away from rodeo competition and toward serving as community queens and sponsor girls. These queens, often elected through fund-raising or ticket-selling competitions, were expected to personify the respectable values of their small western towns. Eventually, this neo-Victorian version of the western woman came to replace the rodeo cowgirl as the main form of rodeo participation for women.[128] By the late 1920s, fears of over-civilization were lessening, and Americans were losing their fervor for a domestically centered female masculinity. Amid this cultural shift, in 1929, a famous Idaho bronc rider, Bonnie McCarroll, died from injuries she received during the saddle bronc contest at the Pendleton Round-Up. She was trampled severely by her mount when her leg got tangled in her stirrups, which were tied together, or hobbled, under the horse's belly. Hobbling was thought to make the mount easier for women to ride because their legs would not flail about in all directions. This safety measure, tied to propriety, actually resulted in many injuries because women could not untangle their legs from the tied stirrups when they were thrown.[129] McCarroll's tragic death marked the moment when mainstream western rodeos began eliminating women's rough stock events. Indeed, this incident demonstrated the tenuous position of women riders in the eyes of not just an "outsider" eastern public, but for western audiences as well.

While western rodeo committees slowly phased out competitions for women, eastern rodeos continued to hold ladies' events throughout the 1930s. The financial instability of the era, however, restricted the amount of time and stock women could secure from rodeo producers. Ladies' events were expensive to maintain at big city rodeos, particularly because of the need to have separate strings of stock for both men and women to be able to ride fresh mounts, which would buck more enthusiastically. As historians have shown, World War II permanently changed women's place in mainstream rodeos. As Americans once again became interested in rodeo after the war, rodeo organizers like Gene Autry refused to reintroduce ladies' rough stock events in part because of the cost and the desire to streamline shows for eastern, indoor rodeos.[130] Additionally, the Rodeo

Association of America, organized in 1929 by rodeo managers and producers, and the Cowboys' Turtle Association, started in 1936 by cowboys and later renamed the Professional Rodeo Cowboys Association, refused to list ladies' bronc riding as an event that sanctioned rodeos were required to hold. Unlike many rodeos in the West, the associations did not outright ban women's rough stock events, but simply refused to support them.

The end of the war consolidated the new world order for rodeo, with women's place often being decorative and supportive. Cowgirls were increasingly absent from events like bronc riding or horse racing, providing them space in the arena only as potential brides to cowboys. In 1940, the *New Yorker* wrote, "The cowgirls, though they do not compete in the more strenuous events, are on terms of affectionate equality with the cowboys, and there is almost no prosperous bachelor cowboy who does not dream of marrying a cowgirl someday and raising kids and a herd of white-faced steers."[131] Indeed, even as women-only rodeo grew in the aftermath of World War II, rodeo organizers desired to enforce proper behavior. The Girls Rodeo Association, which formed in 1948, listed "rowdyism" in 1949 as one of the reasons a woman could be barred from participating.[132] By midcentury, the mainstream rodeo cowgirl had become appropriately feminine and programs were more likely to list her bust and hip measurements than her skills on a bronc or exploits with a gun.

Yet, even as the door closed for the next generation of cowgirls, Tillie Baldwin managed to hold her place. As her story continued to be told, Baldwin's masculine feats only served to prove her authenticity as an Old West roughrider and pioneer. These tricks were "almost unbelievable," yet "authentic reports" tell "of the many mad bulls she has wrestled with, finally throwing the powerful animals to the earth." A strapping Norwegian woman with a "panther-like" body and a no-nonsense attitude, Tillie Baldwin continued to be a "fearless, intrepid, rough riding horse-woman."[133] In 1936, an article noted that she "[blew] into New London in a ten-gallon hat, breeches and bead-studded, high-heeled boots, with old faithful lariat in the back of her touring car. She wears these things because she has worn them nearly all her approximate forty years, and isn't comfortable in anything else. Conservative New England, which should be shocked, protests it's not a pose."[134] Baldwin's femininity was no longer called into question because she was the authentic product of the American West. Over the years, local papers chronicled her exploits as she managed a local ranch for actor Fred Stone, ran her own riding school, bodily removed rowdy cowboys from her bunkhouse, and reportedly applied to be the first policewoman in town.[135] While small western towns were attempting to assert proper femininity for their female rodeo riders, Baldwin's verve proved to her new eastern audience that she was the original article.

Anna Matilda Winger Slate became an American by going west, and by becoming Tillie Baldwin. The fragments of her story allow us to understand the ways in which authentic western womanhood was deeply connected to the perception of respectability, hardy domesticity, and upbringing, even while many women did not fulfill those standards. Her own unwillingness to call herself a cowgirl bolstered these definitions, even as her rejection of domestic respectability defied them. Baldwin's story demonstrates the multiplicity of paths that first-generation immigrants took to claim Americanness during times of anti-immigrant sentiment. By deploying her whiteness and her physical fitness, and by performing culturally valued acts, even ones that demanded a careful balancing act between femininity and masculinity, Baldwin could claim belonging.

As national concerns shifted away from women's suffrage and anti-immigration sentiment, so too did the parameters of authenticity. While the lack of pioneer parents had once excluded her from being a "real" cowgirl, this lack was later leveraged to define her authenticity as an American. Baldwin and other outrider cowgirls used their performances to foreclose on the multicultural West in favor of Anglo-Americanization and the tale of the good immigrant. Rodeo became a tool with which Baldwin could achieve her own belonging in the United States, reiterating the need for white ethnic immigrants in the early- and mid-century to go west, or to the imagined West, to learn to be "real" Americans.

Tillie Baldwin, an outrider in American society when she arrived in New York, embodied early twentieth-century anxiety about immigration, financially independent women, and racial strength. She both self-editorialized her life story and strategically capitalized on her racial and physical characteristics in order to outmaneuver public concern about her place in the performative West. Ultimately, Baldwin's story exposes the ways in which professional cowgirls, particularly those at the edges of this industry, understood, appropriated, and changed preexisting discourses about American identity and western performance.

CHAPTER 2

Restorative Brutality

Violence and Social Salvation at the Texas Prison Rodeo

THE MAD SCRAMBLE WAS INDEED MAD. ANGRY ANIMALS, eager inmates, and wild crowds all waited in anticipation on an October Sunday afternoon in Huntsville, Texas, in 1941. Speeches had been delivered, picnics had been eaten, officials had been introduced, and the rodeo was finally about to begin. Convict cowboys had been waiting months for this moment. Rodeo and prison officials had been planning for a year. Despite some rain, eighteen thousand audience members had driven hundreds of miles early in the morning to get seats in the sold-out stadium.[1] For the past decade, during October, "All roads led to Huntsville."[2] With a loud clang, ten chutes swung wide, releasing ten Brahma bulls with outlaw riders on their backs. "Cheering crowds [rose] to their feet" as each bull battled to unseat an incarcerated cowboy, each of whom was known to be "a pretty tough hombre himself." The bulls, products of the correctional system's vast agricultural holdings, demonstrated the "lust to kill" in their "fiendish gyrations." These animals used "every ounce of brutal energy within their mountainous hulks to unseat their riders."[3] The 1941 Texas Prison Rodeo had begun and the madness was exhilarating. For more than fifty years, the Texas Prison Rodeo sold the spectacle of outlaw beast against outlaw man. The violence of this clash, prison officials reassured the crowd, was not without purpose.

The Huntsville *Item* praised the Texas State Prison Rodeo as an uplifting, life-altering event for incarcerated men. One "rough and tough inmate" had even left the rodeo arena with "tears in his eyes," saying, "Until today I thought no one cared if I lived or died." The applause, however, made him feel as though "things are going to get better for me in the days ahead." Sure enough, the article assured readers, after a conditional pardon, this man was "making good" in the free world. Convict rodeoers not only found a path to rehabilitation for themselves, the newspaper rejoiced, but through their selfless cowboy performances ultimately delivered the "salvation of humanity."[4]

This deliverance was found in the form of ticket receipts, which were donated to the Educational and Recreational (E&R) Fund, the sole source of funding for all religious, leisure, and educational activities for the incarcerated population of Texas. Convict cowboys may have found personal validation through the roars of the crowd, but for rodeo officials, the real meaning of the rodeo was the profits. State appropriations allotted no financial support for inmates' recreation or education, so the rodeo was promoted as the saving grace of the system. Men, advertised as hardened criminals, risked their lives and laughed at death, but they were also paying for "an ever expanding library, good movies, baseball, volleyball, horse-shoes, dominoes, special holiday meals, vocational training program, and a lot of other things." All could "see how great things can be by a bunch of Convict Cowboys."[5]

Prison officials and the public used the rodeo to illustrate the supposedly redemptive possibilities of an abusive labor regime. In the official narrative crafted through media stories, rodeo programs, and the inmate-written, prison-censored newspaper, the *Echo*, prison officials defined the "salvation of humanity" as economic rehabilitation, self-sustenance, and profitability. At the rodeo, "making good" described a man's ability to earn money and then to feed that money back into the prison system so as to free prisoners from taxpayer charity. Goodness did not mean a moral shift in character, but instead the reclaiming of men's labor for society. From the late 1930s until the late 1960s, the Texas Prison Rodeo staged the state's exploitative and violent labor system as the path to social redemption.

Created in 1931, the rodeo was a Texas tradition until 1986. The first and almost all subsequent rodeos took place within the system's main unit at Huntsville, referred to as "the Walls." Within a decade, the rodeo drew upward of fifty thousand spectators over the month of October with sold-out and ever-expanding grandstands. In order to participate, inmates usually auditioned for the rodeo in September. Prison officials encouraged participation through prize money and other less tangible enticements, like interaction with the outside world. Riders were not excluded based on race but, as the rodeo capitalized on and created specific forms of racialized violence, white men tended to dominate the image of the convict cowboy during the first decades of the rodeo's existence. At its peak only about two hundred people rode in the rodeo, but hundreds more participated in entertainment and service roles. In the 1950s, one hundred thousand people annually trekked to the penitentiary over the month of

Incarcerated men and women were separated from free-world crowds, though concession sellers, cowboys, musicians, and other selected inmate participants moved more freely. *Inmate Seating Section*, Prison Rodeo Photographs, 1973, Texas Prison Rodeo records, Texas Department of Criminal Justice. Photograph courtesy of Texas State Library and Archives Commission.

October to sit in the inmate-built stadium, be served by inmate concession sellers, and watch convict cowboys in close proximity to an incarcerated audience.[6]

Previous interpretations, such as Mitchel P. Roth's *Convict Cowboys* and Ethan Blue's *Doing Time in the Depression*, have read this rodeo as both a straightforward fund-raising mechanism for an otherwise deprived system and an instrument for regulating the prison population.[7] Blue labels the rodeo, alongside other forms of prison recreation, a "technology of control," teaching inmates discipline through gendered and racialized codes of sport. Beyond this fundamental dynamic, however, the public came to see the rodeo precisely because it was not entirely controllable. The spectacle of the rodeo catered to the desire to celebrate and ridicule incarcerated men, to racialize and sexualize inmates in specific ways, to potentially see their bodies broken, and to hear a specific story about the successes of the prison's labor regime and its ability to save men from criminality and nonproductivity.

Other states in the South and the West, from Oklahoma to Louisiana, drew inspiration from Texas and expanded their institutional tourism through rodeos, capitalizing, in anthropologist Melissa Schrift's words, "on the public's fascination with criminality through the spectacle of animalistic inmate others subdued by a progressive penal system."[8] Over the twentieth century, film, literature, and prison tourism allowed the American public to construct particular narratives about the experience of prison and its potential for reforming social outcasts.[9] In her examination of the still-operating Angola prison rodeo in Louisiana, Mary Rachel Gould argues that prison rodeo creates a "spectacle of discipline." This latter-day prison rodeo emphasizes inmate inexperience with stock, portraying the punitive pain of a just prison system with only superficial nods to "rehabilitation." Whereas Angola continues to promote its inexperienced riders as the stars of the "Wildest Show in the South," earlier days at the Texas Prison Rodeo promoted its supposedly experienced cowboys as the authentic products of rangeland prison farms, linking the rodeo directly to prison farm labor and the potential for inmates to produce food, goods, and funds for the prison system as a whole.

These stories were grounded in Texas's place in both the South and the West. In Texas, the prison system enforced ten-hour workdays for inmates on its remote assemblage of cotton plantations and cattle ranches. In this adaptation of the plantation labor regime, man and animal alike felt the burn of the Texas sun, the weight of the cotton crop, and the crack of the whip.[10] Disproportionally, these were men of color as they were incarcerated at far higher rates throughout the twentieth century and were routinely relegated to farm labor instead of learning trades at the Walls.[11] The rodeo exhibited this southern system to the public by framing it as the taming of the "Old West."[12] Unlike the prison and plantation, sites of carefully maintained control, the "frontier" was imagined as a place of freedom, even lawlessness. Exemplifying Richard Slotkin's foundational notion of "regeneration through violence," prison rodeos embodied Americans' belief in the civilizing abilities of wildness: by touching savagery, and defeating it, men could choose to return to productive citizenship.[13] The 1939 rodeo program declared, "It is a love of clean, manly sport together with a benevolent interest in errant mankind that brings you here to witness the only show of its kind in the world."[14] By attending a wild rodeo, audience members could assure themselves they were actually investing in civilization, as their admission fares paid for vocational classes, eyeglasses, and baseball bats. Beginning with their creation in the nineteenth century, American penitentiaries attempted to inspire behavioral changes through bodily penitence, especially labor, increasingly hiding the violence of correction behind penitentiary walls.[15] Yet the rodeo, far from hiding the violent labor of incarceration, provided a thrilling spectacle of brutality that claimed to redeem men previously lost to society by allowing them to make "crime pay."[16]

The Texas Department of Corrections documented the rodeo well, at least from the perspective of the institution. Within this record, only censored inmate voices appear, universally supporting the rodeo. Dissenting opinions from incarcerated people were not allowed to be published or promoted. The idea that imprisoned men and women enjoyed the opportunities for recognition and financial gain that the rodeo provided cannot be discounted. These outriders often reworked a show grounded in exploitation into a positive reaffirmation of their identities as outlaw heroes. Yet even the prisoner-run newspaper, the *Echo*, must be viewed as part of the prison official narrative because of prison control over the content. In this narrative of the rodeo, prison officials, audience members, and imprisoned people used the Texas Prison Rodeo to transform the violence of prison life into a story of social uplift.

Rodeo mimicked the "breaking" of a wild horse into a productive working animal by ranch hands, allegedly saving the animal from uselessness and making it into an instrument of labor. The prison rodeo purported to use a socially sanctioned form of violence to help break bad men of bad habits, providing funding for them to learn how to be economically productive citizens. Yet neither rodeo animals nor competitors could actually be broken without being rendered useless as objects of entertainment, allowing the rodeo to both publicly punish and celebrate the untamed outlaw. This brutal spectacle was highly racialized as people of color were overrepresented in the Texas Prison System, yet routinely erased or caricatured in a rodeo that glorified plantation labor.

Founded during the Great Depression, when administrators were seeking to find new ways to sustain an impoverished prison system, the rodeo provided a new source of economic support. Organizers emphasized the spectacle of prison labor, actively assuring audiences that these were "real" cowboys. Their supposed authenticity derived not only from the ranch labor they performed before and after being imprisoned, but also from their outlaw lives, which personified the rough-and-tumble ethos of the rapidly disappearing mythic "Old West." As the rodeo matured during the early Cold War, prison officials sutured their own plans for system modernization, meaning self-sustenance, to this celebration of violence. Prison officials effectively used racialized cultural performances to depict an exploitative labor system as self-salvation.

By the mid-1960s, however, the tone of the rodeo began to change. Introducing new forms of racialized and sexualized spectacle and increasingly emphasizing the individual, the rodeo at first enjoyed several years of sustained popularity, only to see a slow decline of interest. Through the 1970s and early 1980s, prisoners' rights movement began exposing prison labor as a system of horrific abuse and not a transformative process that produced ideal citizens. The Texas Prison Rodeo consistently displayed incarcerated men, and at times women, as dehumanized objects of violence. Bolstering a national narrative of restorative brutality, the rodeo stitched the performance of prison violence to an espoused belief in prisoner rehabilitation. As the rodeo shifted its narrative toward individualistic gain in its final decades, the rodeo ended amid its own inability to tell a tale of social salvation.

• • •

Lee Simmons, general manager of the Texas Prison System from 1930 to 1935, saw himself as a hardworking man, a fair-minded patriarch, and a true Texas cowboy. Raised on an East Texas farm, Simmons had had an obsession with rodeo since the day he sold his first pig to buy a saddle.[17] This fascination with breaking stock was lifelong. At age seventy, Simmons boasted in his memoir, he broke a horse his farmhands had "spoiled."[18] Pitching and bucking, the horse threw him twice. "I just naturally had to bust him to show him who was who." He "crawled back on the critter" and "I busted him. I rode him. I rode him good and proper." Bruised and sore, Simmons reveled in the knowledge that through his "one-man, one-armed rodeo," he had redeemed an animal and rendered it profitable again. As the general manager of the Texas Prison System in the 1930s, an era defined by both financial desperation and local resistance to a burgeoning national welfare state, Simmons applied this same logic to the incarcerated population, seeking to save them through the violence of the rodeo arena with the creation of "Texas's Fastest and Wildest Rodeo."

Texas built its first penitentiary around 1848, complete with an attached cotton mill. The cloth produced by the mill went into a ready market, often for enslaved people's clothing. After the Civil War, the prison population grew steadily as people freed from slavery were increasingly imprisoned. In the 1870s, the state began leasing incarcerated men out to companies in order to save taxpayers from assuming the cost of their upkeep.[19] Women were often sent to work as domestic servants in wealthy Texans' homes. State leadership thus took full advantage of the stipulation within the Thirteenth Amendment to the Constitution to the effect that citizens could still be enslaved in punishment for a crime. Described by historian Robert Perkinson as "the most corrupt and murderous penal regime in American history," convict leasing allowed predominantly African American groups of low-level offenders to be leased for railroad construction, mining, and iron smelting.[20] They experienced dangerous and squalid conditions as companies cut costs by depriving men of adequate food, clothing, and medical attention. Inmates were sexually and physically abused by their keepers, with little oversight by the state.[21]

In the early twentieth century, labor unions complained that convict leasing threatened fair compensation, and Progressive reformers urged the state to end the practice and its inhumane treatment of prisoners; yet in Texas and elsewhere, the practice of prison labor continued to grow.

Having already purchased land in the late nineteenth century, the Texas Prison System began undertaking land acquisition in earnest. In 1908, the state purchased the Ramsey estate, a sprawling eight-thousand-acre farm on which to set its inmates to work. Within a decade, the state owned almost a dozen prison farms, and inmates, on average young, nonwhite, and uneducated, were impressed by the state to grow crops like cotton, sugarcane, and corn.[22]

The idea for the rodeo emerged in the context of a state reform movement in the 1920s. After decades of scandal about prison living conditions, the public began expressing concern for the well-being of inmates, especially as environmental factors overtook biological explanations for crime.[23] In the late 1920s, the prison management system was restructured, with the introduction of a nine-person prison board, of which Simmons was a member. When he became general manager in 1930, he had the care of 4,868 incarcerated people, more than seventy thousand acres of land, and thirteen separate prison farms.[24] Describing the state of the system upon his arrival, Simmons commented that "the conditions which confronted me were appalling," lamenting that "the slave camps of olden times could not have been more unsanitary."[25] The economic insecurity that millions of Texans encountered during the Great Depression simultaneously increased the inmate population and decreased the money available to the prison system. Simmons worked to address living conditions at the Walls by installing additional toilets and showers, expanding the gardens to foster better nutrition, and encouraging a range of recreational activities. The farms, which housed predominately men of color, however, were not updated in similar ways, and the men incarcerated there rarely benefited from these changes, continuing to live and work in terrible conditions.

Under Simmons, aided by his eventual athletic and recreational director, Albert Moore, the prison added a baseball league and hosted theater productions. Moore, son-in-law of Huntsville's warden (Walter Waid), was hired in 1931 to direct the new inmate welfare fund. As historian Ethan Blue explained, Texas's incorporation of recreation and entertainment into its prison system promoted "key features of labor discipline, sublimated aggression, gendered notions of sportsmanship, racial hierarchy and national belonging."[26] These activities provided incentives for good behavior alongside brutal punishments like whippings, starvation, and humiliation. Masculinity scholars like Don Sabo have demonstrated how sports can help men "sustain sanity in an insane place" and provide inmates with important tools for crafting self-identity.[27] While Moore worked to create diverse recreational opportunities for inmates, from boxing matches to minstrel shows, Simmons focused on the idea of a rodeo: "That was 'our' rodeo, his and mine."[28] Like other planned activities, the rodeo was originally aimed at providing enjoyment for the employees, not a paying audience. Yet unlike other forms of prison sport and theater, prison rodeo had the ability to risk lives while purporting to save them.

The first rodeo, held in 1931, boasted about a dozen inmate riders for the viewing pleasure of employees, their families, and an unexpected crowd of two hundred townspeople. For many years afterward, employees attended the rodeo for free with their families, framing the spectacle as a bonus for employee loyalty as much as "a reward to the inmates for meritorious behavior and a strict attention to the tasks to be performed."[29] The audience was therefore instructed to feel grateful for the opportunity to step into the prison stadium and watch a rodeo not designed for their benefit, but supposedly for the benefit of prisoners and employees.

For Simmons, reforming erring men did not differ much from reforming an errant horse: violence was key. Simmons portrayed himself as a man who did not tolerate guff from anyone, whether his children or the inmates. In his memoir, he acknowledged the growing anti-violence sentiment in penology, saying, "I do not belittle the methods of correction advocated by the modern sciences, and I have made use of them, but I am a firm believer nonetheless in corporal punishment—in the home, in the schoolroom, in the reformatory, in the penitentiary." While "sympathy and tender care" were praiseworthy traits for a patriarch, "the rod is needed."[30] Faced with five thousand people imprisoned in a dysfunctional system, Simmons rationalized, "I had to make it perfectly clear to everybody that I could and would discipline them."[31] For Simmons, good horses and good men earned their own keep.

As Paul Lucko has argued, despite his well-crafted public persona as a benevolent and even reform-minded leader, much of Simmons's efforts worked against the reforms he was supposed to represent.[32] When legislators sought to ban the use of the "bat," a leather strap four inches wide and two feet long, Simmons compared this whip to spurs: "You don't have to use the spurs, because all [the horse] needs is to know that the spurs are there."[33] To quell strikes and escapes, Simmons urged for the spurs, supporting the use of devices like "The Horse." Consisting of a beveled piece of wood affixed horizontally to vertical supports, inmates would be forced to straddle "the horse" in excruciating pain for hours with their feet dangling.[34] Simmons's logic in leading the prison system provided the guiding narrative of the rodeo: violence forged social good.

Just as the prison rodeo was forming, mainstream rodeos, or "free-world" rodeos as they were referred to by inmates, were becoming safer and more standardized. Mainstream rodeos between the 1910s and early 1930s still incorporated traveling troupes and independent community contests. The confusion and uncertainty of mainstream rodeo was amplified by the fact that every major rodeo, from Madison Square Garden to the Pendleton Round-Up, crowned their own "world champion," leading to a fair number of world champions walking around. As paid positions with Wild West shows disappeared, and performers were increasingly responsible for paying their own way to competitions, professional rodeoers began issuing demands that production companies pay them a fair purse if they won.

As cowboys and cowgirls nationwide sought standardization in management, events, and officiating, they began to collectively organize. In 1929, the Rodeo Association of America brought together various planning committees, but it still did not represent cowboys. In 1936, protesting the unfair division of prize money between contestants and management, cowboys went on strike at the Boston Garden Rodeo and voted to unionize, forming the Cowboys' Turtle Association to represent their interests. These early organizations would eventually produce the Rodeo Cowboys Association, later renamed the Professional Rodeo Cowboys Association. While convict cowboys celebrated the opportunity to compete, no matter the danger, both rodeo committees and professional rodeo cowboys were working to eradicate low pay, unfair rulings, and dangerous events.[35] The Texas Prison Rodeo thus faced plenty of competition for its paying attendees. Audience members could see rodeos much closer to home and for far less trouble. From the beginning, despite the homage paid to the idea that the rodeo was not for the audience, organizers and participants sought to create a rodeo that would surpass all others in terms of sheer spectacle. As other rodeos got safer and more standardized, the Texas Prison Rodeo advertised itself as the opposite.

Under Simmons, who oversaw the system until 1935, the rodeo mainly featured events similar to mainstream rodeos, including roping, racing, and riding, yet the intensity of the events set them apart. The Mad Scramble, which often kicked off the rodeo action, was described as a contest "designed to make the blood turn to ice." This event amplified the bucking competitions at free-world rodeos by featuring ten bucking bulls or broncs at once, instead of only one. This spectacle of danger was used to "awaken the fans to the fact that this is a real rodeo, styled and performed as the 'Wildest and Fastest Rodeo in the World.'"[36] "No quarter is asked or given [. . .] each contest is a purely personal struggle between man and beast."[37] While the *Echo* praised this contest as "purely personal," the event was not strictly between man and animal because riders had to avoid being trampled by ten animals instead of one, fostering mayhem that was simply unthinkable at mainstream rodeos. While mainstream rodeos had at

The Mad Scramble, featured from the early years of the rodeo, kicked off the action every Sunday in October in Huntsville, Texas, with ten bucking animals being released at once. *Mad Scramble*, Prison Rodeo Photographs, c. 1980, Texas Prison Rodeo records, Texas Department of Criminal Justice. Photograph courtesy of Texas State Library and Archives Commission.

times featured these types of events, they were increasingly banned as "too neck-breaking," eliciting a media cheer as "Huntsville's bad men eat it up."[38]

As the crowds grew over the first decade of the rodeo's existence, rodeo officials replaced standard rodeo competitions with rougher contests. Incarcerated clowns raced chariots harnessed to brahma bulls and cowboys rode in washtubs strapped to horses' backs. The prison board, inmates, and organizers wanted people to see a show "worth the money," which led to a ratcheting up of expectations for the rodeo.[39] Inmate writers boasted, "Without the least bit of faltering over superlatives that the show put on by 'The Men in White' is the roughest, toughest, wildest, high falutinest, and most stupendous coliseum of animation that could be wrapped up in three hours of entertainment."[40] The Texas Prison Rodeo distinguished itself as entertainment by proving that the riders were much more willing to endanger themselves than free-world cowboys.

As public ticket sales soared, profits took center stage. Prior to the creation of the prison board in 1927, no systemwide recreational committee or funding apparatus existed, which had undermined earlier attempts at reform.[41] The Prisoner Welfare Fund, later the E&R Fund, became the destination for the large amount of money flowing into the prison system from the rodeo.[42] Audience members' admission fares provided the money necessary for a discourse of "rehabilitation by rodeo."[43]

The rodeo also perpetuated deeply racialized visions of Texas's southern and western past. Through the 1930s and 1940s, both formal and informal prison policies increasingly focused on retraining white inmates for industrial jobs while relegating men of color to the farms.[44] The majority of cowboys were white in this era, but a growing number of African American riders dominated the top-hand prizes and also participated as singers, clowns, and riders. They performed in front of segregated audience stands who cheered for "their" cowboys. In the 1930s and 1940s, African American inmates were often featured in the rodeo as entertainers to help stage the Lost Cause spectacle. The Cotton Pickers Glee Club—Simmons's other personal initiative—was an all-black, all-male singing group. Often pulled in the rodeo parade on an oxen-drawn wagon, they were to serve as happy "reminders of yesteryear."[45] Sitting at the nexus of the South and the West, the rodeo evoked the slave plantation as much as the cattle ranch and illustrated the inextricable relationship between slavery and the cattle industry in Texas.

Despite this pastoralized enactment of slavery, the prison rodeo provided the opportunity for black prisoners to cross, or at least weaken, certain lines of racial order. In this Jim Crow state, prison rodeo was the only place a black cowboy could compete against white men. Other sporting events, like mainstream rodeo and prison baseball, remained segregated by rule or by practice until well into the postwar period. As 1978 prison rodeo champion Willie Craig explained, "I was riding before I got here. But it was always hard for a colored man to break into rodeo in those days. The white boys didn't want me."[46] *Ebony* magazine explained in 1953 that "because of the great number of Negro participants in the annual rodeo, Negro spectators come from all over Texas."[47] African American inmates and audience members used the rodeo as a singular place to compete directly against white men.

Even as men of color proved their skill and worked closely with stock, however, most cowboys were still imagined as white, an image supported by promotional materials. For instance, the 1939 program included two photographs portraying white men and black men conducting rodeo labor. One featured several white men in cowboy hats, leaning on a fence, and was captioned "outlaw wranglers watching an outlaw horse." Immediately below this photograph, a group of black men held several horses still for the cameras. The caption merely read, "The system owns some fine brood mares." The program failed to caption these black men, who actually wrangled stock, effectually erasing the black labor that produced the system's prize animals.[48] Like the labor system they portrayed, black men served as romanticized memorials to Texas's slave past. For instance, O'Neal Browning would be the all-time winningest cowboy at the Texas Prison rodeo, with seven titles in three different decades. In a 1955 rodeo program featuring cartoons of top-hand cowboys, Browning's photo appeared snuggled up to a minstrel-style racial caricature of an African American woman.[49] White outlaws functioned as cowboys without racial justification; black prison rodeoers faced both a small measure of acceptance and persistent racism.

The image of black men as convict cowboys, moreover, always referred back to the ready acceptance of black men as criminals.[50] Having less access to legal protection and being barred from serving on juries, men of color had faced higher rates of incarceration since the end of slavery. By 1940, African Americans made up roughly fifteen percent of Texas's population, but represented forty percent of the prison population.[51] White men were heavily underrepresented in the prison system and overrepresented in the first decades of the rodeo. As media scholar Peter Caster has noted, "The history of racial incarceration in the nation tacitly criminalizes black masculinity in the cultural imagination."[52] While the rodeo offered both black and white men the opportunity to construct themselves as heroic cowboys in these early years, the setting of the southern prison rodeo maintained boundaries of race through the performance of an encaged black masculinity, the erasure of unpaid labor, and the nostalgic yearning for the slave plantation.

Like the rodeo's invocation of Texas's southern past, the achievements of the criminal cowboy were also leveraged to celebrate the state's role in the conquest of the continent. In 1938, the prison newspaper, the *Echo*, characterized "American Rodeo" as "a three-ring circus, and Indian massacre, a Lindy Hop and a Mexican bull fight all rolled up into one. Few are those men who have not sighed with regret at not having lived in the 'days of 49,' when you not only tamed wild animals but the wilderness as well, to say nothing of the numerous 'Bad Hombres.'"[53] The rodeo offered even incarcerated Texans, outriders thrust to the margins of the imagined West, a tool with which to narrate their contribution to the construction of America as a "mighty nation" and their role in bringing civilization to a wild place once dominated by Native and Hispanic peoples.[54] While many incarcerated men, especially men of color, may have held negative or complex feelings about the rodeo, and the association of it with conquest, these voices were stifled in the official record. Inmates, invited to celebrate the rodeo as the embodiment of a glorious regional past, were never allowed to openly question the classed, racialized, and sexualized violence of the rodeo.

The rodeo, as an enactment of the "frontier," ensured that men had a gender-appropriate space to purge their supposed criminal impulse for violence. As the Depression years created a surge in the prison population, overcrowding tested an already strained prison system. In the early 1940s, proponents commonly cited the concept of "venting," or a release of passion in a socially appropriate manner, as a service the rodeo provided for the inmates. Performers could purge "any pent up feelings" and use the "rodeos to let off steam and show the others how a man with 'guts' goes about doing difficult tricks."[55] Rodeo also served as a metaphor for self-control. One incarcerated man described the process of self-rehabilitation as an internal rodeo, wrestling the beast of "the criminal tendencies which crop up inside of us."[56] To successfully redeem himself, a convict had to embrace a form of heroic, violent masculinity by fighting his own internal beasts. These stories assured the public that the answer to prison violence was not reduced workloads or systemic overhauls but rather a space for men to purge their masculine frustration in order to regain control over their unruly desires.

The promotion of racialized cowboy masculinities in the early rodeo also necessitated the construction of particular forms of incarcerated femininity. In 1938 and again in 1952, two women imprisoned at the only women's facility, the Goree State Farm, petitioned to be allowed to ride in the rodeo because of free-world experience as cowgirl performers.[57] Both of these requests were denied. Female prisoners were allowed to watch the rodeo from race- and gender-segregated stands, and they spent many hours sewing the uniforms worn by male rodeoers. From the mid-1930s, the Goree Girls, an all-white string band, performed at the rodeo and became a well-loved feature.[58] The band portrayed a whitened vision of female decorum and happiness at the Goree prison farm, standing in stark contrast to the horrific conditions of the farm, which housed a population of primarily African American women. Beginning in the early twentieth century, a string of sexual scandals emerged from Goree, revealing that white male guards had routinely raped the incarcerated women and held them in appalling living conditions.[59] The black women who experienced some of the most isolating and intolerable injustices of the Texas Prison System were the people most unlikely to benefit from the rodeo in any way.

Rodeo was believed to offer social redemption in part because it staged inmates' experience with rangeland labor. As the prison newspaper noted: "In our humble opinion the most important step in rehabilitating a convict is to engage him in creative or productive labor."[60] A brutal labor regime produced "expert cow-hands, rope-twirlers, trick-riders, cow-punchers, hired-hands and bronc-busters."[61] Promoting performer authenticity was standard operating procedure for the prison rodeo in its early stages. Cowboys like Milt Good, a ranch hand, roper, and cattle rustler, held a prominent place in early rodeo promotion, and each year the *Echo* would trot out names of new likely contenders.[62] In 1938, for instance,

Roy White was a major hopeful. He "was born and reared on a West Texas ranch" and had participated in rodeos all over the country. Harkening back to "the great ranches of the Old West," which used riding and roping competitions to celebrate the end of the round-up, rodeo both staged "the cowboy's work-a-day world" and provided "recreation" "after the principal work of our vast farmlands" was complete.[63] Audience entrance fees thus paid to see this combination of recreation and labor.

Despite the insistence that many men had experience with free-world rodeos or were former wranglers from Texas's rangeland, very few identified themselves as professional cowboys. As historian Mitchel Roth has noted, in 1931, only eleven of five thousand inmates actually claimed to be cowboys prior to their incarceration, while seventeen described themselves as ballplayers. More characterized themselves as dairymen or farmers, but these still did not make up the majority of the prison population.[64] As these numbers continued to drop over the decades, promoters of the rodeo began arguing that these men were forged into convict cowboys by their time in prison. In 1941, the "convict press agent" told reporters that many of these men had learned to rope and ride on the prison farms. Yet, rooted in the long-established public obsession with western outlaws like Billy the Kid or Jesse James, even those without cowboy experience could claim to be bona fide criminals: they were "stiff-walking outlaws on high heels, hard-eyed from peering over their shoulders while pounding down the trail with gun-slinging sheriffs in ten-gallon hats behind them."[65]

Framed as hardened outlaws willing to risk life and limb to bust a bronc, incarcerated men were spectacularly staged as social outcasts. In the early 1940s, the *Echo* described convict cowboys as a "crossbreed of civilization," including, "professionals, western rangehands, dudes, and outcasts from all over the United States." These men—dudes and experienced hands—had cut "the fences of society" and would be demonstrating "little things picked up in all parts of the cattle raising world."[66] The media gleefully reported on "murderers, highwaymen, kidnappers, and cattle rustlers," listing their crimes and their sentences in their news reports like cowboy credentials.[67] Objectifying inmate pain beyond broken bones, rodeo announcers joked about the length of sentences: "He'll be riding in a lot more rodeos here at the Walls. [. . .] His sentence is 307 years."[68] The crowds, too, displayed their enthusiasm to "help" the prisoners by tossing cigarettes, money, and other small objects into the encaged bleachers. The gifts were appreciated, though much of the largesse was lost in the dirt under the bleachers.[69]

Audience members especially enjoyed the thrill of mingling with incarcerated men. Prison officials selected a small group of inmates to show distinguished guests to their seats and sell concessions and programs. Journalists remarked on the experience of being served by a deferential man who was capable of great violence: "The grinning, toothless Negro selling snow-white pillows is serving life for killing his wife."[70] Proximity to criminals, as well as the opportunity to save them with their ticket purchase, produced audience enjoyment. Unlike many rodeo communities, who rodeoed for themselves, the prison rodeo was a production by social outcasts for the socially accepted, casting incarcerated outriders as dehumanized objects of spectacle even as they fought to cast themselves as heroes.

The portrayal of convict cowboys as real outlaws solidified with the use of prison stripes as standard dress for rodeo riders. Striped uniforms were introduced in the Texas Prison System in the nineteenth century but were discarded in favor of an all-white uniform in the early twentieth century, resulting in Texas prisoners often being referred to as the "men in white."[71] Stripes, however, were kept around to mark particular inmates as troublemakers. While many incarcerated cowboys used the rodeo as an opportunity to wear fancy dress shirts, often sent from home, many began wearing stripes at the rodeo in the late 1930s. In 1943, when the prison board voted to reserve the striped uniform as punishment for prisoners who had committed mutiny in their labor unit or attempted escape, this usage only increased.[72] Prison officials used stripes to humiliate the man who fought for his personhood within the dehumanizing system. They were also used to remind the audience they were not there to just see cowboys at a rodeo, but convict cowboys at a prison rodeo. By the 1960s, nearly all the rodeo cowboys wore stripes "proudly."[73] At the rodeo, bucking the system—in prescribed ways—became a marker of accomplishment instead of shame.

While mainstream rodeos increasingly policed their participants, such as through the blacklisting of cowboys of low character, the Texas Prison Rodeo selected its performers based on their "crowd-pleasing abilities." Inmates submitted written applications, and Albert Moore selected men with clean records to audition. Race, class, and crime did not matter: "You get the job if you can ride the stock." Being a real convict cowboy did not even mean you needed to be southern or western: "Damnyankees, who did their teething on model 'T' steering wheels and learned about hawses while reading pulp westerns" could even participate.[74] Damn Yankees did fairly well in the early years. Sim and Will Hodge, two African American brothers who had owned a juke joint and who reportedly had never rodeoed before, won most of the roping competitions in the late 1930s.[75] When they were given unexpected clemency in 1941, the prison newspaper called the event a "godsend" for other ropers.[76]

Alongside real criminal cowboys, promoters of the rodeo also pointed to the genuine wildness of their stock. Until 1965, the prison rodeo used prison-raised stock. "Corralled in bottomland pastures, where they're getting meaner and wilder by the hour, the toughest, roughest herd of Brahmas" awaited the rodeo.[77] An "outlaw" horse was one that could not be broken—by design, of course. Animal studies scholar Susan Nance notes that the "outlaw bronc" was selected for its violent tendencies, and riders never attempted to actually break the animal during the rodeo, which would render it valueless in terms of entertainment.[78] Lee Simmons's successor, O. J. S. Ellingson, gave a speech describing the clash between outlaw rider and outlaw beast, with "inmate buckaroos, many of them real cowhands from the plains and hills of Texas, matching their skill and daring against the animal's brute strength and cunning." He continued, "From the vast grazing lands of the prison system we have endeavored to bring you the wildest hardest bucking horses and meanest Brahma steers ever to exhibit." This "mean stock" could only be contested by the "toughest and hardest riding bronc-busters and bareback riders in the prison."[79] The prison's stock had such a reputation that other rodeos rented the animals from the prison system.[80] Just like the inmates, animals also faced significant injury rates. In 1942, the *Echo* assured people that "there will be plenty of stock on hand to replace any hurt or tired by previous contests."[81] By using prison stock, rodeo officials not only saved money but also claimed the superiority of animals, as well as men, that were products of the prison labor system. Like inmate riders, prison animals were supposed to perform being broken while maintaining their wild personas.

Faced with the physically and socially violent reality of the arena, imprisoned men had a variety of reasons for participating. During the financial instability of the 1930s, imprisoned people looked to the cowboy as a symbol of both freedom and bravery. Describing the allure of the rodeo, historian Ethan Blue observes: "In the thick of the Depression, the image of the independent cowboy roving the range embodied the freedom that so many white men (all men, really) desired, while in truth, they were financially dependent on wage-labor jobs."[82] The popular image of the cowboy distracted men from the realities of financial precarity and transformed outlaws into cultural heroes. One inmate crowed, "I have always heard that a criminal is a coward, but it would take a magnanimous prevaricator to say that those fellows who risk their lives out in the arena with that writhing, plummeting, murderous mass of flesh are cowards!"[83] In a short story, one inmate described the joy of a successful ride on a particularly fierce bronc given the racialized name Apache: "He felt the freedom he had not experienced since his youth. Walking around the arena on shaky legs, he was a winning cowboy, not a robber, a thief, a murderer, or a convict. He was a man, a cowboy who had taken all Apache could give!"[84] By breaking "Apache" the horse, inmates could narrate their participation in the settlement of the nation, using the rodeo to taste a bit of the love, freedom, and white masculine heroism they were denied as prisoners.

Prison officials and rodeo organizers advertised that the rodeo allowed men to break down the boundary between free and imprisoned, providing them with much-needed recognition. In the arena, Simmons and other officials often insisted, any man could win recognition. He recalled one incident in which "one of my boys came out of the chute on an outlaw [bronc] . . . with hat and hand high in the air all the way until the whistle blew."[85] As the crowd went wild, Simmons rode into the arena, offered the convict rider a hand up, and together they waved to the crowds from his horse. This moment was the "spontaneous recognition of as good a bronc rider and of as fine a ride as ever I saw." Simmons, sitting with the bronc rider on the same horse, stated that he and the inmate were "just two of the hands with the outfit."[86] Through a dexterous display of domination, the convict cowboy earned his right to be redeemed and hailed as a hero instead of a criminal. Yet Simmons did not provide a name for the remarkable cowboy, referring to him only as "my boy." This term, which Simmons used to refer to both employees and inmates, asserted ownership as well as a stratification of station, exemplifying the promise of recognition alongside the erasure of personhood that the rodeo perpetuated.

The emotional and financial realities of prison life also encouraged men to participate in the rodeo, dubbed the "best morale builder" for the prison.[87] Travis Brumbeau, a prison shoe shop worker who spent countless hours hand stitching the leather equipment used in the rodeo, explained that "in the absence of old friends and dear ones," imprisoned men's emotions were "keyed up so strongly with the urge to give their very best."[88] Within the controlled space of the *Echo*, inmates promoted the rodeo as a focal point for the loneliness and despair of the system, encouraging the tireless effort that men and women dedicated to its success. Each September, the *Echo* would relate the sense of joy that preceded the rodeo: "The yard is taking on more color daily. Loud neckerchiefs, ten-gallon hats with gaudy bands, hand-tooled boots, flaming shirts and an assortment of other odds and ends are causing this usually prosaic stamping grounds to resemble a vast dude ranch when the Eastern visitors are assembled en masse."[89] This colorful and festive October would inevitably slide into a gray November. "The air has lost its spiceness [*sic*] and the laughter on the yard is a bit more subdued . . . Gone the gay colored shirts and the high-heeled boots . . . Gone the cowboys back to the farms . . . The rodeo is over." Yet, the *Echo* reminded readers, the rodeo had provided them with a sense of pride. They would never forget the "vision of intrepid cow-waddies that valued courage more than skill . . . a vision of hideout outlaw riders that broke an arm one week and came back to contest that outlaw stock the next week."[90] The rodeo, as a communal effort committed to portraying the system in a positive light, allowed incarcerated men and women to feel genuine excitement even as it coerced them into risking their lives.

Many incarcerated people expressed a desire to see and be seen. The rodeo provided people the opportunity to come watch their loved ones perform, often year after year. For seven years Leroy Rideaux, 1970 top-hand champion, was able to see his mother sitting in the stands. The rodeo program congratulated his mother: "You have a real champion there, Mrs. Rideaux."[91] People were afforded rare opportunities to feel pride in their wayward children, husbands, friends, and parents. In another kind of visibility, although women were sidelined in many ways from the rodeo performance, they were at the heart of many heterosexual men's rodeo experiences. As the rodeo began to add non-incarcerated performers, including trick riders and singers, in the 1940s and 1950s, rodeo officials invited non-incarcerated female performers to participate. Imprisoned men enthusiastically cheered as Anita Bryant kissed an inmate on the cheek after her performance in 1962.[92] The excitement felt about the presence of women, and often free-world women, was palpable. When asked why they wanted to rodeo, men throughout the rodeo's history stated that they enjoyed seeing women so they "wouldn't be so shocked" when they went out.[93] Convict cowboys were not alone in their pleasure of the visual consumption of female bodies, as one inmate poet wrote from the grandstands: "You boys may itch / to toss and pitch / on the back of a buckaroo / but give me a seat / out of the heat / with the Goree gals in view."[94] While the inmate crowd surely enjoyed the entertainment of the rodeo, the *Echo* reported in 1941 that the imprisoned men cheered the loudest when attractive blonds and brunettes walked by, imbuing the rodeo with sexual spectacle.[95]

Prison officials also crafted a system of inducements to promote participation. In 1939, O. J. S. Ellingson assured audiences that prisoners had "entered the contest of their own accord."[96] Two years later, officials even provided an image of the waiver that inmates were required to sign prior to participating. Yet monetary gain was a significant incentive for incarcerated men. While inmates were not paid for their labor in the fields, if selected to perform in the rodeo, they were guaranteed a small paycheck called "day money." This increased from roughly two dollars in the 1930s to ten dollars in the 1980s. By midcentury, a cowboy finishing in the top ten could take home several hundred dollars in prize money. The money was deposited into the inmate's commissary account, to be used for "luxuries" like snacks, coffee, stamps, and cigarettes—items they were otherwise unable to afford.[97]

Anyone who did not participate in the rodeo faced distinct disadvantages. By the 1950s, programs like visiting hours and vocational training shut down during the month of October because the paid employees were occupied with the organization of the rodeo, preventing them from seeing to their regular duties.[98] The programs the rodeo was supposed to fund were put on pause due to its demands. Inmates not allowed to attend the rodeo could face a month of little outside contact, while their peers interacted with, or at least could catch a glimpse of, the outside world. The cotton harvest also coincided with the rodeo and demanded additional labor.[99] Men not needed for the rodeo were often shipped out to the farms to endure the backbreaking labor of cotton-picking. As one official explained,

"If he can't stick to the saddle [in tryouts] then he is tossed back to the cotton patch."[100] In the 1930s, the mortality rate for inmates in Texas was double that of the general population, with many of these deaths resulting from heat exhaustion, beatings, and lack of medical care on the farms.[101] Many prisoners deemed potential broken bones or ruptured organs in the rodeo worth the respite from potentially deadly farm labor. The rodeo demanded everyone's involvement, in the name of prison uplift, and those who failed to participate had to deal with the consequences.

The early years of the rodeo established the narrative of social uplift through violence, culturally staging the prison system's own commitment to corporal punishment and labor. Induced to participate, individual inmates could gain redemption by pitting themselves against animals for the entertainment of the crowd. By the late 1940s, fewer and fewer American men identified themselves as cowboys, and yet the notion that the prison rodeo was a real rodeo continued to be grounded in the sheer madness of the spectacle. One inmate who was also a rodeo aficionado had seen shows "from Madison Square Garden to Pendleton, and all the little shows in between," but "never in his life has he seen a rodeo as fast and dangerous."[102] As the rodeo emerged from the dark years of economic depression and world war, prison officials shifted the emphasis from merely individual redemption to include the system as a whole.

• • •

By 1948, prison reform had stagnated, even as the rodeo continued to evolve. Oscar Byron Ellis, recently appointed prison director, had a plan to change that. After the Texas Prison System was criticized for "the worst" in the nation, Governor Beauford Jester and the Texas Prison Board selected Ellis because of his experience running an ostensibly self-sustaining and scandal-free penal farm near Memphis, Tennessee. Immediately, Ellis called for the comprehensive "rehabilitation of the Texas Prison System," which could, he argued, pay dividends in "reclaimed human lives."[103] Rehabilitation to Ellis meant modernizing the labor system, updating hiring procedures, and investing in infrastructure. Mechanized farm equipment, a more qualified staff, and new dormitories would cut down on escapes, murders, and "abnormal sex practices," Ellis argued.[104] While taxpayers would initially need to invest four million dollars in this plan, it would pay for itself in the long run by creating a self-sustaining, modern, and just prison system that would return productive citizens to the national fold. At the height of the early Cold War, the rodeo served as a major marketing apparatus for this plan, as prison officials appropriated the already existing narrative of violent self-transformation.[105] The postwar rodeo stitched together prison reform and violence.

While Simmons had maintained that only violent punishments, like whippings, could maintain order, the Ellis plan reworked well-established systems of control, drawing on an expanded guard force and building tenders, or inmate guards, to implement his modern vision of coerced labor.[106] In order to "modernize" Texas's agrarian plantations, Ellis created a new form of prisoner segregation that assigned jobs based on race, number of offenses, and sexual crimes, formalizing previously informal systems of discrimination. White first offenders were offered more opportunities to learn industrial work at Huntsville, while black and Mexican men continued to be sent to the farms, albeit with tractors instead of mules.[107] As the prison population grew in postwar Texas, a growing set of liberal welfare programs invited policing of minority communities through the language of rehabilitation and recouping of lost productivity.[108] In Ellis's vision, a modernized version of violence, whether through coerced labor in the fields or the arena, would forge both industrious citizens and a new prison system that operated on internal profits.

The rodeo served as a primary marketing apparatus for Ellis's plans. While the rehabilitative aspects of the rodeo had previously been attached directly to inmates, now the audience was invited to save the system as a whole. The 1948 rodeo program featured detailed reform plans, explaining Ellis's desire to "protect society from the criminal and the criminals from each other." In order for a man to be truly rehabilitated, the state must "punish" him for his crime and also provide training so that he could "earn a living and live in peace" after release. Glossy photos of modernized equipment and new buildings worked to persuade readers that the system truly was experiencing a total reformation and producing healthy, happy inmates eager to earn their own keep. The prison board invited audience members to "see for yourself how your money is being spent to save human lives—besides making your Prison System self-supporting in its vast operations."[109] As Ellis attempted to rehabilitate the system's national image, one newspaper exclaimed, "With sufficient money in the E&R

Fund, the Texas Prison System may someday take its place among the more enlightened penal institutions of the country."[110] The rodeo narrated for the public the experience of imprisonment and the improvements officials were supposedly creating in the late 1940s and 1950s. Focused on inmate productivity, the rodeo and the inmates were expected to create profits for the benefit of all society.

As Ellis promoted his vision of a self-sustaining prison system, rodeo promoters emphasized the need to make "crime pay" for prisoners as they relied on their own labor and not "charity" from the taxpayers or their families. In 1953, Huntsville warden H. E. Moore explained to *Ebony* magazine that "the rodeo proves there's a lot of good in prisoners that can be salvaged. The event helps to rehabilitate these men by putting them to work for their own benefit."[111] The well-organized and high-earning rodeo pumped resources into the prison system at no direct cost to taxpayers, rendering it necessary to the salvation of the entire system and the goal of self-sustenance. As the 1946 rodeo publicity director exclaimed, "Ever since they unveiled their first rodeo to the public, Texas convicts have been lifting themselves by their cowboy bootstraps."[112] The 1950 rodeo reportedly netted the E&R Fund $100,403 through ticket and program sales.[113]

As reform efforts progressed and the E&R Fund grew, so too did the marketing of rodeo violence. Texas's Fastest and Wildest Rodeo shifted to become the World's Fastest and Wildest Rodeo.[114] The 1950 chair of the Rodeo Committee greeted guests by saying, "Do not be surprised or shocked at the viciousness of the untamed stock or the amazing light-heartedness of the untamed performers as they laugh at death in utter abandon."[115] Vicious and untamed, the rodeo provided audiences with "the fastest, rowdiest, ruggedest rodeo," which was "unmatched anywhere for the rough recklessness of the convict riders, and the wild, savage, unbroken, untamed temper of the stock."[116] The rodeo drew hundreds of thousands of viewers in the postwar period because of "its unrehearsed ruggedness and the complete disregard of inmate contestants for personal safety in opposing the brute strength and savagery of the wildest rodeo stock in the world."[117] The need for prisoners to prove that they were untamed and strong enough to contest savage cattle and horses translated to a fast-paced rodeo, strictly timed at three hours. This could result in stock being released from chutes before the previous rider had cleared the arena. The "show of shows" only continued to expand its reputation for violent entertainment.[118]

The rodeo produced scenes of violence beyond the boundaries of the prison stadium. C. C. Springfield, head of rodeo advertising in the 1940s, leapt at the chance to explain to free-world readers the "unexpected spice" the rodeo added to life at the Walls. After a disappointing day at the rodeo, a white cowboy "tried to rob a couple Negro prize-winners in the prison yard. Armed with a knife, he shook one down, then started to the other. But he made a grave error in failing to note that a two-by-four lay nearby. His first victim grabbed it as soon as he was free, and proved that it was more effective than a knife."[119] Through the raising and shattering of hopes, the rodeo created new tensions and potential for violence in the everyday lives of imprisoned men. This violence was often racialized, as white men were galled at competing side by side with black men.[120] The prison board expressed concern about transporting and housing the rodeo performers because of their penchant for "trouble" while they lived together in cowboy-only quarters. There were complaints about same-sex practices between the cowboys, their stealing of narcotics and barbiturates from the prison hospital, and their gambling and drinking.[121]

While the rodeo celebrated convict violence, prison officials also had to show their ability to control these passions. Domination of the inmates became a standard form of entertainment at the rodeo, as guards patrolled and oversaw the massive crowds with loaded weapons.[122] As one rodeo official joked, at the Texas Prison Rodeo, "No holds are barred, but all bars must hold."[123] Under Ellis, prison staff ruthlessly enforced order, producing the highly efficient production quotas and low official reports of violence in the reformed system.[124] While escapes had occurred at the rodeo in earlier decades, Ellis did not allow one on his watch.[125] In the 1960s, as rates of incarceration began to accelerate in black communities, an increasing number of black cowboys won the champion title.[126] Discipline continued to be exercised through racialized images, however. One photograph portrayed an inmate treed by baying hounds, recalling the hunting of enslaved people for the amusement of the audience.[127] These types of controlled pantomimes represented the desire for the system to exert racialized control over inmates even as it congratulated itself on its modernization and progressivism.

Just as postwar westerns enshrined the gunslinger as the protector of American progress, so convict cowboys symbolized bold outlaws fighting social inequalities. Richard Slotkin defines the Cold War gunfighter as using his "professionalism in the arts of violence" to battle "powerful institutions" that were both socially corrupt and producers of change, like railroads.[128] In the rodeo, outlaw riders became all the more celebrated in the 1950s as "rough and reckless" and "a breed apart."[129] The very flaws that made men outlaws in society made them excellent cowboys, enabling them to save their fellow man and themselves: "The indefinable 'something' that makes some men react, as to a challenge, to the laws and the rules of society, is the same thing that makes them unable to resist the challenge of a snorting horse or bellowing bull that refuses to be ridden."[130] The rebellion that marginalized them outside the Walls supposedly rendered them star outlaw cowboys, an association that solidified the connection between the outlaw and the cowboy. While the annual event took an immense amount of unremunerated and arduous labor, including program printing in the print shop, tack repair in the leather shop, and stadium expansion by the construction crews, the cowboys represented the central characters in the culmination of the redemption narrative.[131] Their performances could make or break the profitability of the rodeo, which could make or break the programs offered by the prison in any given year. According to the fiction of the rodeo, inmates who were able to live unmolested and violence free during the rest of the year were invited into the arena to mimic heroically criminal gunfighters in saving others through violence against themselves and animals.

Maintaining this narrative required the few to suffer for the many. Injuries, including broken bones, concussions, and ruptured organs, occurred frequently at the rodeo and at least one man was killed.[132] Promotions of the rodeo continued to extoll the "rip-roaring spectacle" of "bronc-busting, cow-wrestling, bone-smashing buffoonery that is wild to the eye and wilder beneath the surface."[133] Bordering on blood sport, the rodeo provided a specific form of entertainment: "the cowboys in stripes risk their criminal necks in a hilarious show of unshirted violence."[134] Audiences both laughed at and praised convicts' efforts to earn money and redeem themselves and others through bodily injury.

By the early 1950s, prison officials were arguing that the rodeo was not only saving criminals, it was saving society. The "Social Gospel" of the

New Deal era, which proclaimed a social need to care for the collective community, began to erode after World War II under pressure from corporate leaders, who instead supported the "salvation of the individual" through economic independence.[135] Rehabilitation, in Texas, meant "returning to good citizenship hundreds of men who are now a total loss to the state and to society."[136] Both the arena itself and the programs it funded purportedly offered inmates a sense of masculine productivity, providing skills that society had failed to offer. The *Echo* explained: "Many whose inability to get by in society could be traced to improper education and downright illiteracy are now returning to society, literate, and often with a special trade or skill."[137] A group of concerned citizens even thanked Ellis for his reforms in the 1949 programs, lauding his efforts to provide men "who deserve an opportunity of remolding their lives to become useful citizens."[138] The value of prison reform lay in training deserving white men in particular trades and thereby reclaiming their labor, and the dehumanized labor of prisoners of color, for society.

Like the need to break horses for labor, the rodeo performed the prison's need to break men to be useful to society. In line with Simmons's commitment to corporal punishment, Ellis remained dedicated to promoting the idea that coerced labor saved lives. Prior to Ellis's arrival, imprisoned men often resorted to self-harm, such as "heel-stringing," or cutting one's own heel tendon with a smuggled razor, in order to protest the harsh working conditions on the farms.[139] As Texas prison historian Robert Perkinson explains, Ellis met resistance with force. Heel-stringers were bandaged and sent back to their farms and able-bodied men refusing to work were denied food rations. Under Ellis's tightly controlled system, inmates continued to pick cotton under the scrutiny of horse-riding masters who beat, sexually assaulted, and routinely humiliated them.[140] Ellis declared that "idle men cannot be rehabilitated," and neither could an idle prison system.[141] The 1959 rodeo edition of the *Echo* assured readers that reform had been achieved: "I have ample food, adequate shelter [. . .] And work, of course . . . productive, organized, and regulated work."[142] Ellis's regime indeed produced an economical system: in 1951, it could cost up to $3.59 per day in other states to maintain one federal prisoner, while in Texas, it only cost forty-nine cents.[143] In this vision of reform, sweat and toil could transform both men and the system into productive self-earners. Yet, like the rodeo stock, which could not actually be broken or they would be rendered useless for the show, inmate outriders had to perform wildness without becoming seriously injured or killed in order to keep earning money.

Even as Ellis focused on the rehabilitative prospects the rodeo provided for prisoners, he and his staff used the growing funds to pad employee salaries. In the late 1950s, media and political scrutiny revealed that as much as forty percent of the fund was used to give top rodeo officials, like Ellis and Moore, bonuses and pay full salaries for part-time employees like the band director and craft shop supervisor. Over five years, Ellis had received $20,000 from the E&R Fund. The *Houston Post* reported that of the $314,236 available in 1959, at least $100,085 was used on payroll. Ellis defended the bonuses by saying the state would have lost key employees if he had not be able to pay them more money.[144] For Ellis, the proceeds of rodeo were not solely meant to benefit inmates, who at best might earn a couple hundred dollars, but to reinforce the system as a whole.

During the late 1940s and 1950s, prison officials harnessed the rodeo to solidify a prison reform discourse that used violence to offer social salvation defined by productivity. In 1959, O. B. Ellis died just as the New Frontier and the Great Society were beginning to pump federal money into state programs aimed at lifting people out of poverty. This federal money came with strings, however. As scholars like Elizabeth Hinton and Naomi Murakawa have demonstrated, 1960s liberal programs launched under the simultaneous War on Poverty and War on Crime actually helped increase local forms of surveillance and fuel the growth of incarceration rates even before the 1970s drug laws.[145] Ellis's successor, George Beto, continued to ruthlessly enforce the labor regime, using the rodeo to assure the public that prisoners no longer suffered at the hands of an antiquated prison system.[146] Beto maintained that prisons were worthy of small investments that would enable prisoners to achieve their own social rehabilitation through programs like the rodeo. Texas's prison rodeo exemplified the paradox central to notions of uplift promoted by the federal government during the Cold War: social redemption was possible, but you had to do it yourself with the smallest possible amount of help from the federal government.

Lyndon B. Johnson, himself a Texas rancher and New Deal Democrat, used the nostalgic image of the cowboy to symbolize the need to balance community commitment with a dedication to individualism. In his presidential foreword to a classic history of the Texas Rangers, Johnson urged an urbanized America to "preserve the equality of opportunity, the dignity of the individual, the commitment to justice for all that derive from the spirit of the Frontier era. Our affluence, our abundance, our strength and power have not dulled the values experience taught us through the challenge of opening the Frontier."[147] As civil rights activists staged mass demonstrations and Congress passed major pieces of legislation meant to create a more equal society, Johnson's Great Society initiatives also helped ensure the rapid expansion of the incarceration state as he sought to stamp out social disorder. Likewise, as historian Robert Chase argues, just as Texas earned high national praise "as a harbinger of modernity, the internal prison society bristled under the authoritarian grasp of a brutal and violent labor regime."[148] In the 1960s, the rodeo began to change its programming. Over the next twenty-five years, as mass incarceration blossomed and imprisoned peoples demanded new rights, the narrative of the convict cowboy's ability to save his fellow inmates rapidly dissipated.

• • •

In 1963, a new prison rodeo event dubbed "Hard Money" debuted. A Bull Durham loose-leaf tobacco sack was filled with fifty dollars and tied between "the horns of the meanest, mangiest, orneriest Brahma bull in the System." Cowboys were then invited to flood the arena and "walk up to the bull, friendly-like, say a few kind words, and remove the sack from the bull's horns." The attempts to snatch the bag of money from the bull induced hilarity. In its inaugural year, "when time was called on this event, the big, 2,000-pound monster was still trotting around the arena, observing the fallen heroes, with the sack still dangling securely between those horns!"[149] As Hard Money became a beloved feature of the rodeo over the next two decades, the narrative path of the rodeo shifted away from a fairy-tale of community uplift toward a story of individualistic gain, in many ways accurately capturing the reality of the rodeo. The rodeo increasingly invested in different forms of racialized and sexualized violence, grounded in the humorous spectacle of the economically desperate inmate.

First appearing in a moment of civil rights protest, the shift away from the prison's "rehabilitation through rodeo" narrative accelerated in the

1970s as the prisoners' rights movement publicly contested the notion of rehabilitative labor. Indeed, even as the individual took center stage in the rodeo narrative, collective protest by incarcerated people demonstrated to the larger public that Texas's system of unpaid prison labor harmed instead of helped.[150] Changes like Hard Money, the subsequent creation of the Redshirts, and the short-lived introduction of female contestants defined the rodeo's final stages of development. While these changes continued to draw large crowds initially, by the 1980s, the rodeo foundered amid financial scandal, public scrutiny, and its own inability to frame itself as improving life for incarcerated Texans.

As the rodeo changed form, rodeo officials and the media also focused greater attention on the performance of the individual instead of the outcome for the larger imprisoned community. Previously, the rodeo had been the means to build a "model prison system" that could "rehabilitate its inmates so that they become law-abiding, honest citizens after they are released from prison."[151] In 1978, however, the rodeo program announced: "Individualism seems to be the name of the game—an age old western frontier ethic still prevails. It's as if the prison rodeo cowboy is saying to himself and the world, 'I'm an individual; I am what I can show people I can do.'"[152] Hard Money was described by one rodeo press release as "every man for himself."[153] By the end of the 1970s, prison officials no longer celebrated the commodification of inmate labor as serving the greater community.

Events like Hard Money especially began capitalizing on the display of individual ineptitude. By the mid-1970s, the inexperience that would come to define prison rodeos like the one held at Angola replaced the insistence on authenticity in Texas. While audiences had always found enjoyment in inmates' lack of abilities, rodeo officials encouraged inexperienced riders to "stick to the grandstands." In 1973, the *New York Times* expounded: "The seriousness of most spectators at regular rodeos is replaced here by laughter" as men "cling desperately to their mounts before they are usually sent sprawling to the ground."[154] In 1975, the *Wall Street Journal* noted that one did not attend prison rodeo to "see riding" but instead to "see the convicts get kicked, and thrown and everything else."[155] The population of Texas rapidly urbanized in the postwar period, with the rural state population dropping to twenty percent by 1980. The vast majority of inmates in the 1970s were therefore inexperienced with ranch animals. Rodeo programs explained: "Unlike the freeworld cowboys, prison cowboys are not always men with a great deal of experience." These "rookies" ride through "sheer determination."[156] Given that the Texas Department of Corrections itself touted its move away from agrarian labor, labeling their inmates as experienced stockmen no longer seemed reasonable or even desirable.[157]

Inmates and audiences increasingly expressed anxiety about the meaning of the cowboy and role of the outlaw in this mythology. A central joke of the prison rodeo centered on the equating of the color white with good and the color black with bad in western popular culture. Cowboys were supposed to be inherently good, yet here were apparently bad men acting as the heroes. In the 1960s, several cartoons expressed both the audience's and the participants' frustrations with the good and the bad. One rodeo cartoon read, "I can't help it if I'm one of the *bad guys* . . . I'm still gonna wear m' *white hat*."[158] This black/white dichotomy of good and evil was further confounded by the fact that Texas prisoners wore white uniforms. Another cartoon featured in the 1969 program showed a woman asking a guard, "But if you're the good guys, how come they're wearing white."[159] Like the midcentury cowboy, the color white was supposed to denote virtue and morality, but that notion was turned inside out by the prison system's all-white cotton attire and criminal cowboys. The notion of criminal good guys was increasingly reduced to a caricature.

The rodeo also continued to stage the violence of prison life for the humor of the audience. For instance, in 1966, two inmates paraded a sign through the arena reading: "Would you believe we like girls?"[160] This banner, presumably created by the inmates themselves, exposed the raw reality of prison rape as a public joke. In 1945, based upon the growing public and prison concern for situational homosexuality in prison, the Texas Board of Criminal Justice listed prison rape as the third greatest concern created by crowded housing, with stabbings a close second.[161] Yet the prison system also ignored the extensive internal sex trade inmate "trustee" guards used to assert power over their peers.[162] By the late 1960s, these inmates used the arena to explicitly address prison rape but also render it as humorous, eliciting public mockery instead of compassion.

Money often sat at the center of these forms of malicious humor. In 1939, the rodeo program assured readers that "the prizes are not held before the prisoners as an inducement to join the rodeo; rather they are given as reward for courageous and cooperative service."[163] Despite the reality that most men had always participated for financial reasons, to the public, the convict cowboy was a daredevil inspired by the challenge of unbeatable odds, not a desperate man lured into the arena by the prospect of a small amount of money to make life more bearable. Hard Money erased this particular narrative. Glen Gustafson, a man who would become one of the greatest proponents of the rodeo, was asked why someone would risk his life for fifty dollars. A self-proclaimed "poor misdirected city boy," Gustafson responded, "I'm not a hero. [. . .] But, right now, I'm broke, so I guess I'll be out there again trying my luck for the money."[164] Violence out of economic desperation was portrayed as "all part of the fun at the prison rodeo." In 1985, the *Wall Street Journal* recounted the triumphs and woes of a man who "grabbed the cash and won [the] $400 prize" the week before, but failed the following week when "his feet [weren't] quite fast enough." Instead, "he end[ed] up flat on his back with a broken jaw."[165] Hard Money exposed imprisoned men's reasons for risking their lives in much starker terms than the thrill of the challenge.

The purely monetary nature of this event also solidified the racist image of the bumbling, greedy inmate in contrast to the talented convict cowboy. Between 1963 and 1972 the Texas inmate population swelled from 12,850 to almost 16,000. Over the 1970s it ballooned to 36,000.[166] While African Americans and Mexican Americans comprised only thirty-two percent of the state population in 1975, they made up sixty-two percent of the prison population.[167] While racialized violence and laughter had always been part of the rodeo, men of color had previously participated in the same events as white men. As the rodeo continued to evolve in the 1960s, Redshirts, a group of roughly forty men who only participated in nonstandard and highly dangerous events, took a greater role in the action. Unlike the convict cowboys, who were still predominately white men, Redshirts were almost exclusively African American or Mexican American men. Their inexperience with stock was lauded, profiling many of them as "Yankees, who have never been to a rodeo before."[168] Unlike the cowboys who had "earned" their cowboy stripes through individual efforts, Redshirts were portrayed by news reports as an indistinguishable mass who gave pleasure through their antics of chasing and being chased by enraged animals for the sake of money. This spectacle of the desperate inmate was amplified in 1979, when the rules changed to allow the audience to donate

Being a Redshirt was extremely dangerous as steers clashed with contestants. Prison Rodeo Photographs, 1972, Texas Prison Rodeo records, Texas Department of Criminal Justice. Photograph courtesy of Texas State Library and Archives Commission.

money to the tobacco sack.[169] When first introduced in the 1960s, a certain amount of work would guarantee a certain amount of money, but by the 1980s, it was the luck of the draw. One might strike it rich with over a thousand dollars, or one might have risked life and limb only to be left holding ten dollars.[170] The spectacle of desperation, and often disappointment, became key aspects of the entertainment.

As interest in western popular culture sagged in the 1970s and the rodeo's bottom line began to suffer, rodeo officials scrambled to find additional attractions to draw audiences back to the prison stadium. Women became increasingly featured to offer a "pleasant break in our rough and rugged rodeo."[171] In 1968 the first Miss Prison Rodeo contest was held, featuring the daughters of prison officials.[172] Most importantly, in 1972, incarcerated cowgirls were finally given an opportunity to compete. The women's events operated as pieces of sexualized humiliation. Dressed in tennis skirts utterly unsuited to the muddy arena, they caught greased pigs, chased calves, and rode donkeys. Most of the women in the rodeo were African American, though promotional materials still routinely portrayed "Goree cowgirls" as white. While women had petitioned to be included in previous rodeos, cowgirl labor remained largely invisible until the 1970s. In 1973, the program chuckled that the new programming was a score for "Women's Lib."[173] This shift from erasure to hypervisibility characterizes both a desire to keep audiences engaged with new forms of entertainment and a mockery of the rights-based language of "inclusion." By serving as expendable fodder for unnecessary injuries, men and women of color, often hailing from urban areas, became the backbone of the entertainment juggernaut of the Texas Prison Rodeo in the last stage of its development. People enjoyed the "slapstick humor" of women chasing slippery pigs and men chasing angry bulls, and the narrative of social salvation dissipated.[174]

Ultimately, the communal narrative of the rodeo failed because imprisoned people reclaimed their labor from an exploitative system. During the 1960s and 1970s, the War on Crime and then the War on Drugs offered law enforcement an expanded toolkit that ranged from military-grade weapons to mass arrests. Instead of ending the social disorder of the 1960s, these aggressive police tactics merely created new forms of distrust and fear between communities and police departments, often creating a cycle of brutality.[175] In the 1970s, draconian drug laws increased nationwide and harsh sentencing practices led to an ever-increasing prison population. Between 1965 and 2000, prisons populations nationwide grew by six hundred percent; in Texas, the population grew by twelve hundred percent.[176] The worsening of prison conditions, from crowded living spaces to unimaginable violence, and the activist traditions of the 1960s laid the foundation for Texas's prisoners' rights movement.[177] While national leaders focused on "law-and-order" programs to control urban riots like those in Watts and Detroit, Texas prison officials worked unsuccessfully to inhibit prison populations from revolting against the labor regime.

In 1972, David Resendez Ruíz submitted a handwritten petition stating that the abuses of the Texas Department of Corrections, including physical assaults by guards, overcrowding, lack of medical care, and unsafe labor conditions, violated his constitutional rights. By 1974, Ruíz had gathered enough support from other racially diverse incarcerated men to file a class action suit against the department. In particular, these men hoped to expose both the larger labor regime and especially the internal prison economy, based on sexual and physical violence, to the public's attention. Drawing on the civil rights and labor rights experience of many of their leaders, in 1978, they organized a ten-day nonviolent labor strike in order gain public sympathy for the lawsuit.[178] The testimony of over a hundred inmates who had been horrifically brutalized swayed public opinion and helped shape the course of reform.

In 1979, the US District Court for the Southern District of Texas ruled that the department practiced cruel and unusual punishment. *Ruiz v. Estelle* would go on to have far-reaching effects for the everyday lives of imprisoned Texans. It mandated the hiring of an expanded guard force, the building of more housing structures, and the end to the use of trustee, or inmate, guards. Particularly, *Ruiz* threatened to move Texas prisons completely away from isolated plantations and toward more urban, industrialized areas with treatment-focused programs.[179] The prisoner-led agitation of the late twentieth century exposed the disjuncture between the realities of prison violence and the rhetoric of prison reform. Countering the narrative of decades of prison and prison rodeo officials, inmates argued that the abuses they suffered did not render them productive citizens.

As the public scrutinized the system as a whole, the prison rodeo in Texas ended amid criticisms and scandal, seen as a vestige of a prison past best forgotten. Inmate activists' revelations of the horrors of the system implicated prison rodeo audiences as complicit. Declining interest was compounded by fewer prominent celebrities, persistent bad weather, and high gas prices.[180] In the 1980s, the rodeo also garnered extensive criticism for its inappropriate use of funds and its exploitation of prisoners, especially as injury rates were more widely publicized. In 1985, a *Wall Street Journal* article called attention to the audience's enjoyment of an inmate's broken jaw and also informed the public that thirty-nine of the one hundred participants were treated in the prison emergency room. The article went on to quote Harry Whittington, a former corrections board member, who explained that inmates "will take any kind of risk, from getting their eye punched out to death, to get that tobacco sack off the bull—while the crowd laughs and eggs them on."[181] In 1987, with growing public criticism for the prison labor regime and the rodeo that had once advertised its supposed successes, the Texas Department of Corrections did not even have the money, the support, or the unpaid labor force to tear down and rebuild its condemned rodeo stadium.

The disappearance of a moral impetus for the rodeo ultimately rendered the gladiatorial spectacle of the Texas Prison Rodeo void and the heroics of the convict cowboy impotent. As the prison population grew, cowboy convicts represented a shrinking proportion of incarcerated men and could no longer be glorified as real cowboys. Civil rights activists condemned the pastoralized vision of slavery the rodeo had once portrayed. When prison officials turned instead to an image of the bumbling urban convict, desperate for money, it was the officials' desperation that became visible.

While prison rodeo ended in Texas, it did not die out nationally. As ethnographers have shown, today, prison rodeo audiences express less interest in the violence of the arena producing rehabilitated and productive men and more interest in inmate riders as "inept objects deserving of punishment."[182] Louisiana State Penitentiary, or Angola, created its rodeo during the final decades of the Texas Prison Rodeo. Staging events similar to Hard Money, which emphasize rider inexperience, current performances of punishment demonstrate the widespread embrace of the spectacle of the desperate inmate and the rejection of midcentury beliefs about redemptive prison labor. While incarcerated outriders can continue to resist a simple narrative of humiliation and exploitation, using rodeo to gain public recognition and render themselves heroic, prison rodeo also continues to allow prison officials to use socially sanctioned violence to brutalize incarcerated people.

CHAPTER 3

History Unedited

Black Rodeo, Progress, and the Performance of Heritage

"I DIDN'T KNOW WE HAD BROTHER COWBOYS," MUHAM-
mad Ali remarked during his surprise appearance at a rodeo in New York
City in 1972. Captured on film by white director Jeff Kanew in his documentary *Black Rodeo*, released the same year, Ali articulated the core
premise of Kanew's portrayal of black cowboys: they were unexpected.[1]
The film began with rolling sepia-toned photographs of famous white
cowboys accompanied by a stilted version of "Home on the Range." Sud-
denly, as the beat shifted to soul music and color bled into the picture, the
bustling streets of New York appeared on screen. Contrasting the clichéd
cowboys of the immediate postwar era with the "hipness of the '70s black
funky sound," Kanew portrayed a stereotypical urban summer—the crush
of busy people, the heat radiating from the concrete, the constant blare of
horns—using each of these images to highlight the incongruity of saddled
horses lining the streets of Harlem.[2] Children beamed in delight and older
folks reminisced about their own youth, expressing the feeling that Harlem was excited to see a rodeo. Dubbing them "atomic age cowboys," film-
makers, journalists, and white cowboys portrayed black rodeoers as new
products of a new age, a hip twist on tradition.[3] Yet black rodeo organizers
hoped to assert the very opposite: black cowboys were not new and should
not have been unexpected. Black rodeo represented history, not hipness.

By the mid-twentieth century, American popular culture had almost
erased three centuries of black rangeland labor. In a former Spanish and

99

Mexican colony and a former slave state, nineteenth-century Texan cowboys were highly likely to be of Mexican, Native, or African descent.[4] As early as the eighteenth century, large, often mission-based, herding operations sent tallow and hides from Texas to other areas of the Spanish Empire. Many black or mixed-race families, while at the bottom of the intricate racial hierarchy of the Spanish colonies, found the northern borderlands to be less socially restricting and often took advantage of the increased economic opportunities found in the borderlands.[5] But black, Mexican, Native, and mixed-race landowners saw their property rights diminish as Anglo-American and enslaved black populations increased in the nineteenth century.[6] Between 1850 and 1860, the enslaved population tripled in Texas, growing from 58,000 to 182,000.[7] Having been driven themselves as chattel overland in chains or brought from the West Indies in ships, most bonded drovers worked initially on foot, as was common in the American South. Increasingly, however, American herdsmen adopted the *vaquero*, or Mexican, style of herding cattle with horses.[8]

Over the nineteenth century, free and enslaved black men and women worked as breeders, trainers, drovers, traders, and cattle-drive cooks.[9] After the Civil War, cowboys like Daniel Webster "80 John" Wallace and Nat Love left the places of their former enslavement as teenagers, seeking work along the cattle trails.[10] Love, known as "Deadwood Dick," recounted his larger-than-life tales of work on the cattle trails in his self-published autobiography in 1907.[11] Few of the thousands of cowboys of color, whether Hispanic, Native, or black, ever became famous, however.

In the early twentieth century, black performers like the famed Bill Pickett, inventor of the rodeo event bulldogging, and Herb Jeffries, star of 1930s cowboy films like *Harlem on the Prairie*, fought against the solidification of the cowboy as a white icon.[12] Yet even as they told their stories, the role of these cowboys was often diminished in popular culture. In 1910, early folklorist and musicologist John Lomax traveled widely to collect folk music, published in *Cowboy Songs and Other Frontier Ballads*. A black cook who had worked the Texas cattle trails provided one of the most famous of these songs, "Home on the Range." Lomax often drew connections between cowboys and a romanticized Anglo-Saxon past, calling these men "bold young spirits who emigrated to the West for the same reasons that their ancestors had come across the sea. They loved roving; they loved freedom; they were pioneers by instinct."[13] Even as he noted that

African American men also commonly worked as cowboys, Lomax separated "negro" and "cowboy" songs, effacing, in the words of music historian Robert Cantwell, the collaborative culture "the black and white working classes in the south and midwest had created and shared throughout the nineteenth century."[14] At the very moment of collection and classification, "Home on the Range" became a cowboy, and thus white, song, allowing director Jeff Kanew to select it to communicate quintessential whiteness in 1972. In the 1960s, television westerns showed gallant white men fighting off savage Indians and news programs covered civil unrest in Newark and Detroit, writing African Americans into the urban North and out of the rural West. From Oklahoma to Oakland, however, community organizers in the 1960s, 1970s, and 1980s used the cowboy as a tool to resist the persistent whitewashing of their regional past and to promote black heritage, civic pride, and community education.

Black outriders re-narrated not only their participation in the settlement of the regional West, but also their long and complex histories with Native Americans. As scholars of black western culture have illustrated, nineteenth- and early twentieth-century African American settlers often advanced stories of the vanishing Indian and national progress to promote theories of racial uplift grounded in economic independence and political self-determination.[15] For instance, the most successful African American filmmaker of the early twentieth century, Oscar Micheaux, homesteaded an allotment on the Rosebud Sioux Reservation in South Dakota. In his 1915 novel *The Forged Note*, Micheaux describes the West as "perhaps, the land of the future; a land in which opportunity awaits for courageous youths, strong men, and good women."[16] African Americans' complex relationship with the West as a place of both aspiration and violence continued well into the late twentieth century. As civil rights activists won battles for political and social representation, particularly the Civil Rights Act of 1964 and the Voting Rights Act of 1965, black cowboys and community leaders used rodeo to articulate an urgent need for African Americans to be remembered as active agents in America's history of continental conquest and settlement. As prominent black rodeoer Bud Bramwell said, "The black cowboy is part of America's heritage. And we're here to prove it."[17] Black rodeo outriders reminded all Americans that their ancestors were also explorers, settlers, Indian fighters, conquerors, and cowboys. Similar to white ethnic immigrants of the nineteenth and twentieth centuries who had participated in anti-black racism in order to define themselves as Americans, in the 1960s and 1970s, many black rodeoers emphasized their roles in Native dispossession as a crucial contribution to nation building.

As millions of African Americans migrated to cities for better social and economic opportunities over the twentieth century, rodeo was a key performance both for people who had been forced off the land and for those who remained behind. While many people desired to maintain a connection to their rural pasts through rodeo, Jim Crow segregation laws had an immeasurable impact on how African Americans could participate. As white women fought to stay on the program in the 1930s and 1940s, black and Native men experienced complete exclusion from mainstream rodeos in the midcentury. Like other sports leagues, cowboy unions never explicitly banned the participation of men of color, but custom did. In response, black, Native, and mixed-race men formed their own riding associations and rodeo circuits.[18] Often small and informal compared to the spectacles being staged in Cheyenne, Wyoming, or at Madison Square Garden, these ranch rodeos were held on weekends for mostly local people.[19] Rodeo associations, like the Southwestern Colored Cowboys Association and the Anahuac Saltgrass Cowboys Association, provided cowboys of color a place to demonstrate their skills, share a sense of camaraderie, and give the public a history lesson. Dozens of community leaders worked to bring these rodeos to their cities, towns, and ranches for the betterment of their black citizenry.

In the Black Power era, many Americans looked to "heritage" to personalize the past. Heritage and history have often been equated; yet while history connotes the examination of the past, heritage communicates a quantifiable connection to those bygone days, whether genealogical or cultural.[20] History and heritage occupied a significant place for many African Americans who were demanding political and social inclusion. One black cowboy wrote in a fund-raising letter that to "snuff out this history is genocide."[21] James Baldwin articulated this violence in 1965, "When I was brought up I was taught in American history books that Africa had no history and that neither had I."[22] Activists and writers like Baldwin expressed the growing sense that mere legislative change in the mid-1960s would not be enough to change racial inequality; instead white Americans needed to acknowledge black people's historical presence in the founding and the expansion of the nation.[23] While all forms of rodeo drew on glorified notions like "tradition" and "heritage," black rodeo did so with the explicit aim of gaining racial equality through the embodiment of heritage. Drawing on a multiplicity of tactics, including balancing Black Power ideas about self-determination and civil rights ideals of integration, black towns and neighborhoods all over the United States began supporting the expansion of black western performance as a way to reinsert themselves into a national narrative, resist the silencing of their own past, emphasize black education, and encourage civic engagement in local communities. By recovering their history and performing their heritage, rodeos could motivate progress through the past.

Places like Boley, Oklahoma, sat at the heart of this reclamation of western history and identity. Established in 1903 as a black town, Boley was a crossroads of the South and West, of indigenous peoples and black people, of hope and disappointment. From the moment of its founding, Boley relied on community festivals like rodeo to draw in settlers. Resisting both Jim Crow narratives of black inferiority and colorblind stories that erased injustice, Boley's leaders reestablished a town rodeo in the 1960s in hopes of inspiring a new generation of youthful settlement and investment in black communities. Even those rural Oklahomans who moved to urban centers like Oakland, California—home to the Black Cowboy Parade after 1975—continued to hold up the history of the black cowboy to create civic pride and educate young people, and the nation, on their right to claim western roots. As many communities searched for ways to encourage change during an era of increasing political and economic stagnation, the notion of "heritage" became a central tenet of progress. For many of these towns and neighborhoods, selling the idealized past seemed the most likely way to ensure survival in the present and hope for future successes.

Like other forms of marginalized western performance, black rodeo has been underdocumented in the white-dominant historical record throughout its existence. Even as rodeoers and organizers sought to fight against this historical silencing, their performances were often informal or auxiliary to main (white) events, which exacerbated their marginality. It took until 1970 for an African American cowboy, Bill Pickett, to even be inducted into the National Cowboy Hall of Fame, despite having pioneered a key rodeo event, bulldogging. Ultimately, communities served as their own historians, collecting town rodeo programs, promotional materials, and national news coverage. Places like Boley, Oklahoma, and Oakland, California, were home to community organizers who wrote letters to donors, solicited vendors, booked trick ropers, contracted stock, got parking permits, paid police officers, and communicated with contestants. Examining the stories of these places illustrates how black rodeo outriders from the 1960s to the 1990s exposed core tensions in the enactment of western history and the fraught potential of the cowboy icon. By staging centuries of forced and free range labor as a way to encourage racial pride and economic growth, these narratives also at times commemorated illegal settlement and anti-Native violence as a necessary step in nation building. Even as people protested national forgetting through the embodied performance of western heritage, their claims to a unique American identity were also imbued with a distinctly settler-colonial past, complicating any radical potential for racial equality.

· · ·

The story of Boley, Oklahoma, like that of Oakland, California, has been a story of movement, whether through forced displacement or optimistic migration. It is also the story of centuries of tense and intertwined relationships between black and Native communities. As some people of African descent arrived in the early nineteenth century enslaved to Native people, often alongside free black citizens of Native nations, others began arriving in the late nineteenth century eager to capitalize on Native dispossession. Exemplifying the changing racial attitudes of in the emergent Jim Crow West, the variety of paths people of African descent trod into Indian Territory in the nineteenth and twentieth centuries produced a place dedicated to promoting "progress," in terms of both the settlement of the territory and racial equality.

Distinct groups of black people helped create Boley. The first group were referred to as "Natives." These people were made up of both Afro-Indians and the Freedmen of the "Five Civilized Tribes," including the Creeks, Seminoles, Choctaws, Chickasaws, and Cherokee, who once held territory in today's southeastern United States. Prior to the Revolutionary War, these tribes routinely enslaved war captives, whether white, Native, or black. In the early nineteenth century, black chattel slavery solidified among the tribes, including the inheritance of enslaved status and the inability to become a citizen of the nation.[24] Enslaved black people and many of their free family members made the trek westward with the tribes after Andrew Jackson signed the Indian Removal Act in 1830.[25] In Indian Territory, present-day Oklahoma, enslaved people produced crops, often for export outside the territory. Working with little supervision, they farmed corn, rice, and wheat and raised hogs, cattle, and horses.[26]

During the Civil War, the Native nations of Indian Territory split between the Confederacy and the Union. The Creeks, Seminoles, and Cherokees preferred neutrality, while most of the Choctaws and the Chickasaws supported the Confederacy. Ultimately, many members of the Creek Nation fought for the Union.[27] With the Union victory, the Native nations signed new treaties in 1866, in part agreeing to free their enslaved populations, calling them Freedmen.[28] The Freedmen, as historian Gregory Zeller describes, "quickly established themselves on the lands of their former masters, where Creek laws recognized their rights to share in the Creek commonwealth, and developed as a stable class of yeoman subsistence farmers."[29] Alongside Afro-Creeks, or free Creeks of African descent, in the decades following the Civil War, freed black men and women worked hard to build homes, grow their families, and establish communities across Texas, Indian Territory, and Oklahoma Territory.

The opening of Indian Territory to outside settlement significantly impacted the Native Freedmen. After the Civil War, the Creek Nation alone lost three million acres and its members were forced to allow the building of two railroads across their territory.[30] The presence of transportation helped encourage white and black settlers to squat illegally on Native land and eventually led to the land rush of 1889. Between 1893 and 1907, the Dawes Commission worked to divide communal lands into allotments and sell additional lands to non-Native people, both black and white. The commission focused on assimilating Native peoples, forcibly sending young children to distant boarding schools, while segregating African Americans. As Gregory Zeller has observed, "The division of the tribal estate that began in 1899 not only divided Creek lands but also divided the Creek communities, African and Indian."[31]

The division and sale of lands allowed for the arrival of more and more "state people," or black settlers who came to Indian Territory from elsewhere. As legalized segregation and terror drove thousands of black people out of the South in the 1890s and 1900s, eastern Oklahoma, then Indian Territory, offered a beacon of hope to black leaders all over the country. Like white Americans, African Americans were eager participants in the settlement of Indian Country. Black newspapers, such as the *Topeka American Citizen*, and land agencies, like the Oklahoma Immigration Association, urged black homesteaders to be prepared the moment the territory was opened in 1889.[32] The white press often accused African American leaders of trying to make Oklahoma an all-black state. While historians have shown that it would have been extremely difficult for a black population to maintain a political majority in the state, many people did dream that Oklahoma would become a place where the wave of southern people fleeing poverty, violence, and disenfranchisement could settle.[33] Between 1890 and 1900, the black population in Oklahoma surged from three thousand to nineteen thousand.[34] As historian Kendra Field explains, the encroachment of black settlers into Indian Territory continued to divide people less in terms of race and more in terms of "nation," resulting in often uneasy relationships between new arrivals, Afro-Indians, and Freedmen as immigrants sought to gain rights to Native land. Yet, it also laid the groundwork for the racialized violence, disenfranchisement, and dispossession of the twentieth century.[35]

In 1903, the Fort Smith and Western Railroad Company gained permission to construct a route from Fort Smith, Arkansas, through Indian Territory to Guthrie, the capital of Oklahoma Territory. Legally, the railroad was not allowed to buy land to build towns, but it was allotted land to build stations. Railroads sought to encourage town growth at each of these stations to boost their profits. One often retold story of Boley's founding frames the town as the result of a bet between two white men. Supposedly, Lake Moore, commissioner to the Indian Tribes, and a white railroad employee, William Boley, disagreed about whether black men could govern themselves. So they encouraged their African American acquaintance Tom Haynes to undertake a community that would prove or disprove black people's natural abilities. In reality, Moore and Boley formed a townsite company to make money developing land along the railroad line. Haynes had experience as a town promoter, and he was most likely recruited to sell the venture to other African Americans.

Thomas Haynes emigrated from Texas in 1869. In 1903, he worked to lease the land of James Barnett, a Native Freedman with Creek allotments in his children's names, in order to establish the town of Boley.[36] Freedmen and women could sell their land much more easily than "full blood" Native people. Seeking the best possible chance of making some profit from his daughter Abigail's allotment of poor farmland, James Barnett sought to lease and eventually sell the land to Moore and Boley.[37] The location of Boley on a railroad line, unlike Langston City and other black towns, facilitated promotion and settlement. In the summer of 1903, Moore leased eighty acres of Barnett land and had it surveyed. In September 1903, just as the railroad started to operate, Boley officially opened for settlement.

Promotions for the town in southern papers painted a glorious image of Boley as a place of opportunity. The *Boley Progress* sang, "Oh, tis a pretty country / And the Negroes own it, too / With not a single white man here / To tell us what to do—In Boley."[38] Town pioneers often did not describe migrating westward but instead heading "North to Boley," a place of potential safety after southern terror.[39] Many settlers arrived prepared to work but with little ready capital. Many lived in tents and boardinghouses for years until they could buy land, sending their children into the woods to forage berries and nuts.[40] Others arrived as professionals ready to establish businesses. During its first years the town grew steadily and proudly boasted, in addition to several cotton gins and a newspaper, an accredited high school, water mains and electricity, a telephone company, restaurants, general stores, and hotels. The town also built a Masonic Hall, which attracted Masonic men of color from all over the nation. Incorporated in 1905, by 1907 the town itself held about eight hundred residents, with hundreds of families filling the farmland around the town.[41] Unlike other communities that demanded people "Come Prepared or Not At All," Boley leaders reportedly welcomed and even aided struggling families.[42]

Boley's leaders had a vision of racial equality grounded in middle-class respectability politics. In 1908, Booker T. Washington described Boley as a youthful, striving experiment in black self-governance. Most importantly, Washington reiterated that while it was a "rude, bustling Western town," it drew "not a helpless and ignorant horde of black people, but land-seekers and home-builders, men who have come prepared to build up the country."[43] Boley and other black towns could not simply be havens against oppression; they needed to be actively contributing to the economic development of previously "unsettled" or even "savage" lands. Washington and many other black leaders espoused the "gospel of the toothbrush," which promoted "racial uplift," or the social progress of African Americans. Many people defined uplift as impeccable personal presentation, middle-class respectability, ardent Christianity, and economic self-sufficiency.[44]

Economic independence and self-governance for African American settlers shaped the appeal of black towns. As literary scholars like Daniel Moos and Michael Johnson have noted, black western authors often portrayed the West as a land of masculine opportunity, a place where African American men could earn recognition as full American citizens through their self-sufficiency on the rugged "frontier."[45] Clearview, a town settled at the same time as Boley, was the proud birthplace of the Patriarchs of America, an organization that sought to encourage racial uplift through political organization and civic engagement. One article from the *Clearview Patriarch* insisted that manners "unconsciously acquired" under slavery must be eradicated because "slavish habits, customs, manners and dispositions are objectionable to free people the world over regardless of race or color."[46] Segregationists and Progressives alike celebrated black towns, as they both rid white neighborhoods of supposed undesirables and provided opportunities for economic advancement and self-determination to African Americans. Boley and other black towns strove to demonstrate what black folks could contribute independently to the social and economic progress of the nation.

Boley, like many other western towns, attempted to stimulate economic and population growth through community festivals. Just as Buffalo Bill Cody organized his Wild West show as a Fourth of July celebration and town leaders in Pendleton, Oregon, planned their Round-Up around booster-ism, so Boley staged a town carnival and rodeo in 1905. Scheduled to coincide with Juneteenth, the holiday celebrating the reading of the Emancipation Proclamation in Texas on June 19, 1865, this carnival situated cowboy games within a wide array of entertainments.[47] The Fort Smith and Western Railroad Company offered discounted fares, and the *Boley Progress* declared that "this is the homeseeker's opportunity to secure a good home in a Negro town."[48] Like other early rodeoers who performed alongside dancing dogs and acrobats, bronco busters and calf ropers at the June carnival in Boley could also watch a ballgame between Creek and Seminole men, purchase sweets from street vendors, and listen to a brass band from Okmulgee. Both residents and potential newcomers were treated to speeches, recitation competitions, and business souvenirs. The carnival was a rousing success, attracting thousands of visitors, often men who had traveled ahead of their families to search for a suitable place to settle. Thomas Haynes and other land agents ensured that many visitors left with an idea to return.[49] Boomtowns at the turn of the twentieth century depended on American leisure pursuits like baseball and rodeo to communicate welcome, promote civic pride, and, hopefully, attract settlement.[50]

The five decades between Boley's carnival and the creation of an annual rodeo were not easy times for the community. While Boley swiftly grew to be the largest all-black town in America, it also began suffering political and economic setbacks. Oklahoma gained statehood in 1907, stripping all members of the Five Civilized Tribes and the Freedmen of their tribal citizenship, which had guaranteed fundamental rights like voting and land ownership. Instead, all residents of Indian Territory were converted into second-class citizens of the United States, subject to Jim Crow segregation and voter restriction laws. With statehood, divisions between Creek Freedmen, Afro-Creeks, and black migrants were, in the words of Kendra Field, "quickly flattened, effectively racializing the whole."[51] Boley leaders fought the retraction of their state and national voting rights, but in 1910 white Democrat state legislators ensured that African American men could only vote locally.[52]

In fact, Boley experienced the rising tide of Jim Crow violence beyond the Deep South. While many people of color migrated north to Boley for safety for themselves and their children, white people still terrorized the town. In 1911, a group of fifteen families arrived from Alabama having fled a white mob, among them a young girl named Ora Spears. Shortly after their arrival Spears and her family were forced to bear witness to the same terror they had escaped in Alabama. In May, a lynch mob kidnapped a mother, Laura Nelson, her young daughter, and her teenage son, L. D., from the county jail in Okemah, a white town near Boley. The mob raped, tortured, and hanged mother and son from the John Earnest Bridge, taking photos of the atrocity and leaving Laura's young daughter on the bridge until a neighbor found her. When news reached Ora Spears's parents, "who had come so far in search of freedom," they simply uttered: "Not yet."[53]

Continuing migrations also destabilized the town's population and economic growth. Chief Alfred Sam, a congregational minister with the Akim Trading Company, came to Boley in 1913 and led as many as a third of the forty-two hundred residents on a trek toward the West Coast of

Africa. Although Chief Sam actively discouraged people from selling property at a loss or rushing to migrate until he could guarantee passage, the withdrawal of thousands of dollars from Boley's bank caused significant damage to the town's financial stability.[54] Boley suffered the boll weevil in the 1920s and national financial collapse in the 1930s. In 1940, Boley native Velma Dolphin-Ashley noted in her dissertation on the town's history that after "practically starving" through the early years of the Depression, "Boley [was] almost ninety per cent 'New Deal.'"[55] With government relief checks sustaining most families, alongside employment at Works Progress Administration sewing rooms, many residents, especially younger people, chose to move westward to urban centers like Oklahoma City and the San Francisco Bay area in hopes of finding work. Disenfranchisement, violence, and economic struggles aged Boley considerably over four decades. Instead of representing energetic strides toward future progress, the community of Boley began drawing strength from looking backward.

● ● ●

The narrative of decline pervaded national media coverage of Boley during the mid-twentieth century. *Life* and *Ebony* continued to write about Boley, once the largest all-black town in the country, as a model black community. In 1964, an article in the *New York Times* titled "A Dream That Faded" painted the town as a relic of a bygone era: "Today, as integration has become the guiding star of the Negro and as economic independence has become almost impossible, the town is an anachronism that is slowly fading away."[56] According to this article, the ideal of segregated, self-governing communities belonged in the past, not as part of the modern civil rights movement. Labeling Boley a "town without a future" and claiming that "passivity on racial matters characterizes most of the town," the *New York Times* dismissed any efforts town leaders were making to invest in their home. "Her young leave and her older citizens remain in apathy," with "a sense of hopelessness in the face of social and economic forces that are little understood and completely beyond control." Town leaders did not simply passively await the death of their town, though. Instead, they hosted rodeos.

By the mid-1960s, the myriad actors who had made up the civil rights movement were increasingly addressing income inequality, women's rights, welfare reform, and the Vietnam War. The Black Power movement critiqued the notion of integration, understanding it as the forfeiture of black peoples' own vibrant culture and thriving institutions in order to be accepted by white society. As people's frustration with the slow pace of change increased, a right-wing response gained strength in the early 1970s. White people all over the country, many of whom had benefited from government assistance through the Homestead Act, land-grant colleges, New Deal legislation, and the GI Bill, began to agitate against programs like busing and affirmative action, which supposedly only benefited African Americans. Turning instead to "colorblind" policies, politicians like Richard Nixon and later Ronald Reagan presented voters with the idea that the work of civil rights had been achieved, even as communities of color continued to fight.

As Americans grappled with the realities of race in every aspect of American life, rodeo became a crucial battleground for the meaning of an American icon. The engineers of black rodeos argued that these performances served not just to celebrate black westerners' pioneer ancestors but also to recognize the collective participation of African Americans in building the United States. After decades of struggling to stay economically viable and socially engaged, Boley maintained a strong sense of pride—anchored in its past. While the town had hosted rodeos sporadically throughout the 1940s and 1950s, it was not until the 1960s that the rodeo truly coalesced as a Boley tradition every Memorial Day weekend.

As Henrietta Hicks, unofficial town historian, described, in the late 1960s rodeo became a way to invite people back to Boley for "fun, frolic, friendship."[57] In 1964, *Ebony* magazine lauded the event, saying, "For those two days the town really wakes up. It's Boley Round-Up Time—a whoopin', hollerin' 48 hours of rodeoing, parading, tons of good barbecue and plenty of beer."[58] The chamber of commerce worked on promotional activities, selling advertisement space, creating the program, enlisting vendors, and organizing the parade, while a professional production team staged the rodeo. As an amateur rodeo outside the Professional Rodeo Cowboys Association (PRCA) system, Boley and other local rodeos could be more selective about which events they included on the program. In 1966, only the most exciting roping and rough stock events made the cut, including tie-down roping, bareback bronc riding, bull riding, and bulldogging. In 1974, Boley added women's barrel racing.[59] With visitors coming from all

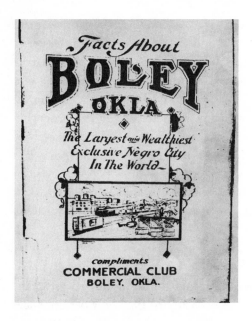

Boley always used the rodeo to promote town pride and encourage more visitors and potential settlers. *Facts about Boley: The Largest and Wealthiest Exclusive Negro City in the World* (pamphlet), 1977. Courtesy of Oklahoma State Historical Society.

over the state, attendance at the two-day festival ranged between ten thousand and fifteen thousand in the mid-1970s, often causing serious traffic problems along State Highway 62.[60] The rodeo also drew famous personalities like comedian Flip Wilson to the small community. In 1974, he "adopted" the town and was subsequently named Honorary Police Chief.[61] As the rodeo brought in money, the chamber of commerce promoted the event as a fund-raiser to "build recreational facilities for Boley kids." Most importantly, however, the rodeo was viewed as a way to generate general interest in the town. As chamber president M. W. Lee Jr. said: "We're just getting ready for the day when Boley really begins to boom."[62]

At the rodeo, Boley invited visitors to share in their triumph and grief as the community's yearly highs and lows graced the program pages. Memorials to loved ones and prominent figures accompanied heartfelt congratulations for hometown success stories. Young people especially received a significant amount of attention for scholarships won or degrees earned. Chamber of commerce members, employees at the Boley State School for Boys (previously known as the State Training School for Negro Boys), the Cub Scouts troop, and high school sports teams all prominently featured in programs designed for hometown pride.[63] In 1974, the program also detailed the dedication of Boleyites to the town's physical renaissance as the new city hall was built. "This is truly a community effort, as all labor for its construction has been donated by Boley citizens."[64] This building was designed to contain a fire station, a police station, a courtroom, and a jail. The rodeo, as a community festival as well as an invitation to visit, showcased the very best of Boley.

Boley was not the only rural community building pride through western historical performance. Clearview, another all-black town near Boley, started its own rodeo in 1980. Like Boley, Clearview promoted its history as crucial to its future. In 1983, the rodeo program called Clearview a "legacy" that would "never fade," stating, "Other men dream of things that never were and ask why not. [. . .] At Clearview, we can reminisce over the way Clearview was and say, *why not again*" (emphasis in original).[65] Featuring reproductions from the town's original newspaper, the *Clearview Patriarch*, the program highlighted Clearview's contribution to a century of debate about racial uplift and black people's ability to socially and economically advance in American society. According to the program, town leaders clearly stated that self-determination was key to overthrowing the "vestiges of slavery" and refused to believe themselves "innately inferior." Reproducing the middle-class Progressive-era views of the town's founders, the rodeo was designed to "call Clearviewites home" and marketed a history that "should serve as a catalyst for self-improvement, racial pride, town loyalty."[66]

Designed for the benefit of the small farming community, Boley's rodeo also helped expand a growing circuit of black rodeos. Black rodeo was not intended to discourage white participation, and some white, Mexican American, and Native American men did participate. Instead, it simply ensured that black participants could compete unmolested. Jim Crow segregation prohibited African Americans from participating in rodeo throughout the mid-twentieth century, with the problematic exception of prison rodeos. For instance, in 1905, Knox Simmons, later described as "nearly white," won the calf roping title at the St. Louis World's Fair. Once rodeo officials discovered his African blood, however, they disqualified him and stripped him of his title.[67] These barriers persisted into the late twentieth century. A. J. Walker, a Texas cowboy, described the hardships of trying to participate in PRCA rodeos as a black man during the 1960s. Growing up, Walker explained, most working cowboys were black: "The only white was the boss man [. . .] the only white boys we saw were his sons [. . .] Them white boys would get on the horses after you got them broke."[68] While mainstream rodeos often discouraged black participation, they capitalized on black labor. Walker recalled helping lead a string of one thousand horses through the streets of Manhattan for the Madison Square Garden rodeo.[69] Living in the basement of the venue for over a month, black cowboys were allowed to compete during the "slack," meaning after the regular show had finished and the audience had left. When Walker joined the PRCA in 1964, he observed, "White cowboys didn't really like having the black cowboys around. They look at you crazy. They do anything they could to you. We stayed out of their way."[70] As many had discovered before him, the rodeo road was harsh and unforgiving. With a construction job and property, Walker found it difficult to travel, pay fees, deal with injuries, and still meet his responsibilities at home in Texas. Instead he chose to focus on providing ranch rodeos at his Circle 6 Ranch, opening it to the public in 1967.[71]

Like Walker, other cowboys strove to create spaces where black men and women could rodeo. In Oklahoma, men like Roy Edward LeBlanc helped create and promote local rodeos all over the state, particularly in Okmulgee and Clearview. His son, Clarence LeBlanc, turned professional in 1975, winning the Rodeo Finals Championship in 1978.[72] In 1981, Clarence LeBlanc explained that rodeo was cost-prohibitive for many young people, saying that not many African Americans turned professional because "so few blacks can afford to start at a young age in rodeo—to afford a horse and a saddle and a trailer to cart your horse around." The long hours and small winnings made traveling a long distance for an amateur rodeo difficult for working people. He, on the other hand, "was lucky. My father had those things because he had worked on ranches, and he staked me to them."[73] Oklahoma State University provided rodeo scholarships to African American students in the 1960s, a rare chance for black men in a white-dominated collegiate sport. These scholarships helped launch the professional careers of such men as Cleo Hearn and Bud Bramwell.[74] Together these men created the American Association of Black Cowboys, a small group of rodeo performers mainly from Texas and Oklahoma.[75] Hearn and Bramwell staged rodeos in New York, New Jersey, Washington, DC, and many other places in the 1970s. In 1971, Hearn started the Texas Black Rodeo, changing the name to the Cowboys of

Boley Rodeo Parade, the *Daily Oklahoman*, May 31, 1982. Photograph by George Wilson, courtesy of Oklahoma State Historical Society.

Color in 1995 to be more racially inclusive. Other national black circuits, like the Bill Pickett Invitational, emerged in the 1980s.[76] Black rodeos in Okmulgee, Boley, and Clearview provided small communities of color the opportunity to participate in the expansion of these black rodeo circuits. Additionally, as magazines like *Ebony* pointed out, people of all races came from the surrounding area to watch the Boley rodeo and white cowboys increasingly entered the competition.[77] The rodeo operated as a way to bring people together to celebrate a shared past across racial lines.

Civil rights activists often framed historical recognition as vital to social progress. Until the postwar period, white historians often constructed nonwhite cultures as "fundamentally non-historical."[78] As academic disciplines like anthropology and history produced historical knowledge with embedded racial attitudes, they often labeled people of color as primitives without histories of social, economic, or political development. The persistent notion that African American history was separate from American history defined the core problem between white and black America for writers like James Baldwin: "Until the moment comes when we, the Americans, are able to accept the fact that [. . .] I am not an object of missionary charity, I am one of the people who built the country—until this moment comes there is scarcely any hope for the American dream."[79] Throughout the civil rights era, key historical works like C. Vann Woodward's *The Strange Career of Jim Crow* and Lerone Bennett's *Before the Mayflower* helped frame the particular institutions of racial segregation as historically contingent and therefore changeable.[80] Black Power activists, many of them young, also increasingly established their own Freedom Schools, or "independent black institutions." These schools sought to build community by instilling pride through black history.[81] As discrimination continued in people's everyday lives despite legislative change, many people demanded that America reckon with both the individual and collective histories of black Americans.

Rodeo organizers often focused on the need to uncover this history and denounced the grievance of national forgetting. "The black cowboy is one of America's forgotten pioneers. [. . .] Many of the best riders, ropers and wranglers were black cowboys. They ate, slept out, worked and died alongside Whites, Mexicans and Indians but were almost thoroughly excluded from the glorious image of cowboys portrayed in the movies and on TV screens."[82] Jim Crow also took its toll on rodeo riders of color as they "were relegated to competing against one another in amateur tournaments," earning hundreds instead of thousands of dollars in prize money. The 1987 Boley rodeo program credits the civil rights legislation of the 1960s with the opening of white rodeo to black contestants again; yet black rodeoers still were not fully welcomed in white-dominated rodeo associations, ensuring their continued marginalization in professional sport and the need for Boley's outrider rodeo.[83]

Town leaders framed this erasure of black men from the cowboy mythology of America as a form of violence that black cowboys battled: "For nearly a century, they were never acknowledged. Although their skills and accomplishments played a major role in the development of the American West, history has generally forgotten or obligingly ignored them. Yet these strong, rugged and fiercely independent men have endured and survived. They are cowboys, and they are black."[84] Boley's rodeo, like other black rodeos, urged for reclaiming history as an act of resistance. Unlike many white cowgirls in the 1910s who assured their audiences that their performances were not explicitly political statements, organizers of black western performance in the 1970s and 1980s saw rodeo as an inherently political act—claiming space and asserting their rights to history.

More than just history, however, personalized and quantifiable "heritage" became a national obsession in the mid-1970s. Alex Haley's popular book *Roots* and the subsequent television series epitomized the growing feeling that the nation could never hope to move forward if it did not first look backward. *Roots* effectually linked the notion of historical silence to black people's "long-denied knowledge of heritage" and African ancestry.[85] Published in 1976, during the US Bicentennial, *Roots* quickly became a multimedia phenomenon with a million and a half hardcopies sold and a twelve-hour televised miniseries that aired only three months later. For media scholars at the time, the miniseries exemplified "the persistence of identity despite the obliterating impact of slavery."[86] The miniseries ended with the author Alex Haley narrating his quest to trace his roots back to Africa, optimistically communicating the idea that "those roots have made him free."[87] According to an NAACP survey, *Roots* deserved credit for "reviving and strengthening the black-history offerings in schools and colleges" and "enlightening whites about the black heritage."[88]

Yet the need to recover and be proud of one's family heritage also drove a popular fascination with white ethnic heritage, creating a boom in genealogy kits and "Kiss Me I'm Irish" pins. In Prague, Oklahoma, located near Boley, the Kolache Festival celebrated the town's settlement by Czech immigrants with traditional dances, a parade, and thousands of kolache pastries. As Matthew Frye Jacobson has demonstrated, the white ethnic revival "blunted the charges of the Civil Rights and Black Power movements and eased the conscience of a nation that had just barely begun to reckon with the harshest contours of its history forged in white supremacism."[89] For example, corresponding with the release of *Roots* in 1976, *Rocky*, the story of a hardworking Italian American pitted against an arrogant black man, became a national hit film. White people began to commit themselves to a narrative of mutual suffering.

Haley often stressed that *Roots* was meant to be meaningful for all African Americans, a "story of our people," despite its inaccuracies and idealistic visions of an untouched Africa, in part because it empowered people to discover their own heritage. Heritage could supposedly offer an embodied connection to the distant and potentially unknowable past. Scholars have noted that *Roots* was "acceptable to white audiences because of its essential conservatism; it unabashedly celebrated the family."[90] Yet many black Americans simply did not have the same access as people of European descent to documentation concerning their ancestors, let alone the time and money required to search. Author Lauret Savoy lamented in her recent work *Trace: Memory, History, Race, and the American Landscape*: "Bridging the distance between history and the particularities of family seemed an impossible task given the erosive and estranging power displacement could wield. Circumstances leaving no trace could outweigh any longing to remain in a homeplace."[91]

The enactment of the cowboy provided one avenue for coping with the silence of individual records by constructing not only a shared historical experience but a shared cultural heritage that could be recovered and leveraged for the betterment of the future. As scholar M. J. Rymsza-Pawlowska has argued, people in the 1970s were interested in not just consuming or reflecting on the past, but actively engaging with it and placing themselves within it through "logics of reenactment."[92] Many people looked to quilting, wagon train reenactments, and personal pilgramages to ancestors' homelands as a way to interact with the past. Unlike war or wagon train reenactments, however, rodeo operated as a place where the contemporary and the historical intertwined.[93] By enacting a collective imagined past and demonstrating their individual ability to compete in a modern sport, people of color used rodeo to perform both their national heritage and their future place in American society—making meaning not only through thinking about history but by embodying it as a way to improve the future.[94]

Boley's rodeo demonstrated the ways in which a sense of collective "western heritage" operated as a pathway to national inclusion, even if one's ancestors did not own a ranch or work the range. In her 1940 dissertation, Velma Dolphin-Ashley described cotton as the heartbeat of the town's economic life.[95] During the 1920s, the town's merchants would count the bales being transported from the gins to the railway, depending on these counts to predict their own daily business.[96] While many people would have owned and worked with stock, Boleyites historically identified as farmers, not ranchers. But their rodeo was never meant to embody a fictionalized ranching past; rather, it was meant to represent Boley's pioneer spirit.

In Boley, rodeo symbolized the history of western settlement, not just cowboy games. In the 1970s and 1980s, official programs told visitors that "Boley's history parallels that of the old west" and that "the black cowboy is closely tied with the history and development of Boley."[97] The historical ties between Boley and the cowboy were not defined by the cattle trails or small family ranches, but by its status as a boomtown where the founders "dreamed of a great future."[98] Briefly covering the town's founding, the 1987 program's "History of Boley" section focused on promoting the contemporary town, with Boley's new water system, federal investment in public housing, and expected industrial growth. Echoing the advertisements placed in southern newspapers during its early years, the rodeo program exclaimed, "Because of Boley's pastoral and peaceful atmosphere, many people find it an excellent place to live, and many former citizens have expressed a desire to return to Boley." With the rodeo, new leaders perceived themselves to be following in their ancestors' footsteps: "Years ago our forefathers extended a hand of welcome to one and all and practiced the spirit of togetherness. You are just as welcome today."[99] The retelling of Boley's history at the annual rodeo served as a bullhorn to remind people that Boley still existed and was on the cusp of being a thriving community again.

Boley's leaders also situated their town in the mythology of the lawless frontier. Rodeo programs recalled the 1932 bank robbery of Boley's Farmers and Merchants Bank by members of the Pretty Boy Floyd gang. During the shootout, gang members shot several people, including the bank president, D. J. Turner.[100] The story was legend in town. In 1980, as part of a larger push to highlight Boley's Wild West history, a local man detailed the event in his book *High Noon at the Boley Corral*, advertised as "a Native Oklahoman's Over-due, True Story of His Town's Victory over the Notorious Pretty Boyd Floyd Gang."[101] By highlighting Boley's trials and triumphs, the rodeo programs crafted an image that placed Boley at the center of both the lived and the mythological West.

In the 1980s, Boley's rodeo programs not only linked rodeo with Boley's pioneer heritage, but also, like most rodeo promotions, described it as the live performance of all Americans' heritage. "Rodeo is the All-American Sport. Not just a game, but a contest of actual working skills that are part of America's heritage." This collective, national heritage represented heroism in the face of a harsh environment: "Cowboys worked the open ranges in bitter cold and blazing sun: doctoring, roping, wrestling, and breaking the magnificent wild horses and savage cattle."[102] Asserting the right to call themselves pioneers, and thus cowboys, Boleyites staked their claim to the heroic past that had been denied to them.

Boleyites invested in heritage partly because it could potentially provide economic stability and encourage population growth. While the American Revolution Bicentennial Commission, an organization that provided public programming on American history, failed to provide sufficient focus on African American history, the Bicentennial offered African Americans and many other minoritized groups the opportunity to challenge these Eurocentric accounts of early American history and nation building. The Afro-American Bicentennial Corporation worked with the National Park Service in the early 1970s to reevaluate many places considered to be important national heritage sites and suggest new sites for consideration. "The national assumption that the history of white men in America is synonymous with American history, instead of just a part of it, has robbed the majority of Americans of any knowledge of the part that black, brown, yellow, and red men have played in this country," the corporation stated.[103] As celebrations of America's political, military, and economic place in the world exploded around the Bicentennial, African American people were determined to explain that Anglo-American history represented only a small portion of American history. As cultural historian Christopher Capozzola has noted about the Bicentennial, "Celebrating a community's past, or a family's history could help Americans negotiate the tensions they felt between their local and their national identities."[104] As the largest black town in the country, Boley occupied a role in these discussions, especially as "westward expansion" represented a key theme covered by the National Park Service.

People in Boley were enthused about the potential designation of their town as a historic landmark. In 1974, the *Kansas Star* reported, "A pride in the town's heritage has remained with its residents," even through "economic decline and flight of most of its younger residents." Lovingly describing their town as a place where "you don't have to draw up because you bump up against someone white," Boleyites touted the town as a history-rich area that had "shown what blacks can do by themselves." Events and monuments honoring this heritage of self-reliance could potentially revitalize the community. As one local noted, "Any attraction which would draw tourists would be a big help." As an enduring heritage, often epitomized by the rodeo, became integral to the national story of Boley and its economic vitality, performing the past offered a pathway forward: "Today, past and future stand side by side in Boley."[105]

Black rodeos also illustrated growing concern about black people's erasure from not only the history of the cowboy and the pioneer, but also from rural America altogether. The importance of land ownership for black migrants to Oklahoma was plainly visible in African American periodicals of the early twentieth century, such as the *Clearview Patriarch*. Advertising "room for a thousand homeseekers," a 1911 *Patriarch* article gushed: "The soil is the best, to say the least, one bale of cotton per acre can be raised every year and corn produces in abundance. The climate is mild and the winters are short, thereby making it possible to raise all kinds of produce, fruits and vegetables."[106] Oklahoma drew settlers because of the rich agricultural potential, but as farms failed and King Cotton fell, people looked to cities for survival. In 1985, *Ebony* articulated a deep concern about the increasing distance between black folks and the land in Thad Martin's "The Disappearing Black Farmer," which detailed how discriminatory practices by white landowners and local, state, and federal government had stripped black people of their land over the twentieth century. The article stated that in 1920, almost a million African Americans had defined themselves as farmers, owning roughly fifteen million acres. In 1978, fifty-seven thousand black farmers held only 4.5 million acres.[107] Many people felt that they were being denied their historical place in the soil-based American memory.[108] As millions felt the loss of a connection with the land and the ancestors who labored on it, rodeos allowed for larger audiences to invest in a collective memory.

Media coverage often undercut the efforts of rodeo organizers to reinsert African Americans into America's rural present, however. The urban unrest of the 1960s in dozens of cities around the country resulted in media and governmental reports on black "inner-city" delinquents and hoodlums. The equation of blackness with urbanity meant that news articles, even in the black press, persistently labeled black cowboys as "urban cowboys." Yet these same articles wrote that most of the rodeo competitors hailed from rural areas of Texas, Oklahoma, or Arizona.[109] Historian

Laura Barraclough notes that white suburbanites outside Los Angeles also classified Mexican American *charreadas* (rodeo-like events) as "urban" in the 1970s, equating "urban" with "people of color and immigrants."[110] As in Kanew's documentary vision of black cowboys in Harlem, black cowboys were continually being presented as unexpected. Because rurality has often defined authenticity in the imagined American West, this dissociation of African Americans from the land and rural lifeways discredited black claims to the settler past.

Reporters often obsessed over black riders who were raised in cities. Charlie Sampson, a champion PRCA bull rider, grew frustrated with people's constant questions about his childhood in Watts, California. After first riding a horse on a Cub Scouts field trip, Sampson worked at a local boarding stable in order to be closer to horses. He was one of only six black PRCA members in the early 1980s. Mentored by Myrtis Dightman, a prominent black rodeoer who had been denied titles because of his race, in 1982 Sampson became the first African American to win the PRCA bull-riding championship. The constant attention on his childhood persisted: "'Tell us about Watts, about the ghetto.' I'm no ghetto child, I'm a cowboy."[111]

In many ways, black cowboys were co-opted into the modernization of the cowboy image. While traditional cowboy television and films began to slip in popularity in the 1970s, new cowboy imagery, especially the urban cowboy and the rodeo cowboy, began to rise in prominence.[112] Framed around working-class men struggling to find freedom in a modern world of suburban constrictions, post-1970s cowboys did not need to prove their stock-raising credentials. As consumers across the globe embraced mechanical bull riding and western wear in the 1970s and 1980s, many people argued that all American men should be able to play cowboy.[113] Films like *Urban Cowboy* and *8 Seconds* helped establish the cowboy as a modern character, not one relegated to the nineteenth century. By focusing solely on black cowboys' urbanity, real or imagined, however, the American public also continued to imply that African Americans, more than other racial groups, needed to defend their claims to the cowboy icon. Yet, once again, community organizers would not stand for these types of exclusions.

•   •   •

Like the Boley rodeo, urban black western performance in the Black Power age blossomed because of a desire to reconnect with an idealized rural past, a concern for civic pride, a claim to national inclusion, and a dedication to educating young people. Cities like New York, Philadelphia, and Oakland each had black riding clubs and stables focused on teaching young people how to work with and care for horses.[114] Individuals and organizations had to work hard to create and defend these spaces. Madison Square Garden refused to host a black rodeo in 1971, saying it would not be popular enough.[115] And, as other marginalized groups like gay rodeoers experienced, municipal land was not always made equally available, either. The racial geographies of rodeo in this era can be seen in the history of Mexican American riders, who tied rodeo to a sense of nationalism and racial pride. Charro associations exploded in popularity alongside the Chicano movement of the late 1960s and 1970s. As Laura Barraclough explains in her work on the charros in suburban Los Angeles, historical, physical, and political geographies came into play for *charreadas* during the 1970s. Barraclough found that places where Mexican Americans had political representation at the local level provided more municipal support for these events.[116] Likewise, black rodeos thrived in places like Boley, where African Americans controlled public grounds and private capital, as well as Oakland, California.

The railroad made Oakland in much the same way it made Boley, creating a place that presented a beacon of migratory hope. As the terminus for the nation's first transcontinental railroad, the Central Pacific, Oakland provided both jobs and opportunity for new industry in the late nineteenth century. While the population remained predominately white until the postwar period, West Oakland in particular was home to a growing black community of railroad workers, longshoremen, and professionals. Like many others, cowboy Nat Love gave up the range and became a Pullman porter in 1889. Although the railroad paid low wages, it did offer job security, social status, the opportunity to travel, and a sense of shared identity. The city became the regional headquarters for African American organizations like the Brotherhood of Sleeping Car Porters and Marcus Garvey's United Negro Improvement League.

In the 1940s , Oakland was a bustling industrial city that housed a diverse group of working-class people, small business owners, and a growing middle class. As places like Boley struggled to keep their young people employed, war industries drew over 250,000 people to the Bay area. Oakland's population grew from 8,500 to 47,500. Between the 1950s and 1980s, Oakland went through several painful urban revitalization spurts. City planners and investors hoped to boost property values through the destruction of low-income homes and the construction of major highways and rapid transit. The Cypress Freeway, which connected the Bay Bridge to the Nimitz Freeway, cut Oakland in half and isolated West Oakland from downtown. These changes further segregated and disenfranchised the city's black working class. As Oakland's high black unemployment rate ravaged the community, groups like the Black Panther Party formed to advocate for Pan-African pride, community self-determination, and black self-education.[117]

Nestled against hills covered in an increasing number of ranch-style homes but few remaining ranches, local organizations worked to alleviate poverty, end racial segregation, and produce a new generation of educated young people. In the mid-1970s, city historians, officials, educators, and business leaders used Oakland's pioneer past to create pride in their city and to promote historical figures as role models for young black men. In 1977, just after winning Oakland's mayoral race with the help of the Black Panthers, the city's first black mayor, Lionel J. Wilson, issued a proclamation stating: "Black Americans have contributed much to the growth and development of the City of Oakland, the State of California, and to other States of the West." This proclamation set aside October 22 as Black Cowboys Day in Oakland, to be marked by an annual parade.[118]

The Black Cowboy Parade was first created and sponsored in 1975 by the Oakland Museum's Cultural and Ethnic Affairs Guild as a tribute to Oakland settlers and in conjunction with the exhibit "Blacks in the Westward Movement."[119] It was such a big success that the following year a group of civic-minded businessmen, the Oakland Traders, sponsored the parade, which wound its way from Tenth and Market Streets to the Oakland City Center Plaza. Complete with "Northern California's top black cowboys on horseback," marching bands, drill teams, community groups, and "colorful parade units in old west theme," the parade inspired several members of the community to found an organization promoting the history of the black cowboy, the Black Cowboy Association (BCA).[120] For four decades, this association, now called the Oakland Black Cowboy

Man riding in Oakland Black Cowboy Parade as onlookers stand on the sidewalk, 1980. Item 017, Oakland Black Cowboy Association Records, MS 190. Photograph courtesy of African American Museum and Library at Oakland, Oakland Public Library, Oakland, California.

Association, has fund-raised, organized, and promoted not only the parade but also a rodeo, roller skating outings, trail rides, and a Juneteenth celebration.[121]

Most of the executive members had longstanding investments in their community as members of other civic and religious organizations, such as Blacks United to Motivate Progress (BUMP) and the Good Samaritan House. As scholar Robert Self has demonstrated, Oakland in the Black Power era had a robust range of organizations that looked to change their community using tactics like Afro-centrism, militarism, black capitalist investment, and War on Poverty programs. Each group focused on a different combination of strategies, but most stressed education and economic development as vital to the community's survival.[122] While some of these organizations adhered to cultural nationalism, fostering an explicit relationship to an imagined Africa through clothing, food, and music, many, including the leaders of the Black Panthers Party, looked to ground black pride in American history.

Oakland leaders invested in African American cowboys as crucial representatives of both a larger American history and a specific regional past. As BCA chairman Booker T. Emery wrote in 1980, "The goal of the Parade is to have all Americans, regardless of color, understand our common heritage and appreciate our history."[123] For these men and women, the cowboy crossed color lines and brought people together, in terms of both shared cultural heritage and physical landscapes. Oaklanders also used the cowboy to commemorate more recent black migration to California. As the *San Francisco Examiner* noted in 1975, "Like many middle-aged urban black folks," Larry Scoggins, founding member of the BCA, traced "his roots to farm life in the South." In the 1940s he had worked on ranches in Arizona, Arkansas, and Texas. Scoggins left the land during World War II. He moved to California, where he worked as "a carpenter, fork lift operator, general laborer, and more recently as a truck driver."[124] While "most of the riders never rode the range," many of the older generation of Oakland residents had followed similar journeys.

Although African American cowboys sought to be included in national history as a way to gain full citizenship, they did not always want simply to integrate into white country western culture. Oakland's parade demonstrated the ways in which black western performance both asserted a shared past with white Americans and acknowledged that because of cultural segregation, black cowboy culture developed in unique ways. Similar to Boley's founders, but also influenced by Black Power's ideals of black nationalism and self-determination, black cowboys in the post–civil rights era stressed pride not only in their western roots but also in regional black music, foodways, and organizations. In 1978, for instance, the Oakland parade was followed by a "Country Western Soul Dance" that featured "both old time western music and modern soul music."[125] Likewise, Boley's festivities of the same era not only included a dance, but also a barbeque festival, which helped draw surging crowds to town. As the mayor of Oakland noted in 1978, the Black Cowboy Parade demonstrated a "spirit of community, bringing a sense of history and ethnic pride to our civic affairs."[126]

The depth and breadth of black rodeo roots was evident in the inclusion of zydeco bands and dances. Zydeco, a form of country music in which French lyrics accompany the accordion and rubboard, grew out of black Creole culture in southwestern Louisiana. While largely denigrated by whites as illiterate, ignorant, and lazy during the early twentieth century, Creole culture attracted a massive resurgence of interest during the ethnic revival movement of the 1960s and 1970s, when "exploration of ethnic roots and heritage" were becoming "downright chic."[127] Zydeco trail rides through the countryside of Louisiana and Texas became especially popular in the 1970s. Dressed in western wear, riders spent weekends traveling the countryside with a zydeco band playing in a wagon or truck bed. Hogs' cracklins, boudin, and beer energized the riders as they sang, danced, and rode. Commemorating the legacy of Louisiana's cattle industry and racehorse circuit, Creole cowboy culture fed directly into the heritage-centered black rodeo circuit. Zydeco made inroads into Oakland culture as small waves of Louisiana immigrants arrived in Northern California during the postwar period, bringing their own brand of country music and dance with them.[128] With such performances of heritage, black rodeos and parades functioned to teach young black children that they deserved a just a place, but a distinctive place in American cowboy history.

Influenced by Freedom Schools and the Black Panthers' work with youth, parade and rodeo organizers continually reiterated the need to teach young people about the contributions of black cowboys, explorers, and scouts as a way to encourage personal success and protect civil rights. In 1991, the Northern California Black Horsemen's Association described themselves as "an ethnically mixed group who feel that the history of the real west has not been taught."[129] As they promoted their growing circuit of black rodeos, Bud Bramwell and Cleo Hearn told reporters, "You talk about cowboys and most black children think about white people."[130] By allowing black youth to reclaim their right to be cowboys, organizers and participants hoped to instill a sense of collective identity. Actor Danny Glover, as grand marshal for the 1986 Bill Pickett Invitational, explained that the rodeo provided people, especially children, with "a sense of history and a perception of who they are and what they're about."[131] The BCA routinely set up school events to teach children about black western history and even provided small college scholarships.[132] Groups like the Oakland Museum and BCA used the black cowboy icon to inspire collective betterment through education.

Young African American men in particular were often the focus of these history lessons. Like the Clearview Patriarchs and Boley boosters, black rodeos promoted masculine independence and strength as the key to racial equality. Black rodeoers disclaimed the notion that black men could not be cowboys: "A man is a man, no matter what color he happens to be. That horse don't care what color you are. Are you man enough to ride him?"[133] For Bud Bramwell, the cowboy as a masculine icon was central to his mission to stage black rodeo: "Americans have always idealized the cowboy as a symbol of manhood, strength and courage. But what about Black children? How can they identify with this symbol of manhood when they've never seen a black cowboy—when they know of no black pioneers, no black western explorers—To Black children the cult of the cowboy is no source of pride because they've been left out."[134] Black rodeos sought to hold up the cowboy as a role model for all boys, not just white boys.

In the years following problematic studies like the Moynihan Report, which blamed black family "dysfunction" on female-headed households and black men's emasculation, many black leaders sought to encourage a

A young man keeps his seat as his horse rears in the Oakland Black Cowboy Parade, 1980. Item 026, Oakland Black Cowboy Association Records, MS 190. Photograph courtesy of African American Museum and Library at Oakland, Oakland Public Library, Oakland, California.

vision of black male strength.[135] In 1981, Joan Burt, a lawyer educated at Howard University, worked hard to bring the National Invitational Black Rodeo to Washington, DC. Having seen a black rodeo on a visit to Texas, she enthusiastically embraced cowboys as role models: "Most blacks don't go to regular rodeos because they don't figure there'll be any blacks in it, so I started thinking about the kids in D.C. and what a terrific image this would be. We're talking about independent, self-made men."[136] Like the founders of Boley in the early twentieth century, organizers of black rodeo desired a future in which black men could claim American masculine values like economic independence and pride.

This emphasis on black masculinity did not fully acknowledge the realities of female organizational labor. Joan Burt in Washington, DC, Henrietta Hicks in Boley, and hundreds of other women were instrumental in planning these events. Of the nine executive members of the BCA, four were women. These women were seen as valuable assets to the organization because of their community connections and "expertise in putting a social gathering together." The two female social coordinators were "responsible for all social events" and fund-raising for the association. While Mabel Dedeaux was "one of the few women horseback riders in our Parade," Betty Alcutt, parade coordinator, communicated with all participants, organized them into categories, started the parade, and kept it moving.[137] Women also barrel raced in rodeos, marched in dance troupes, and appeared as queens in parades. Yet, even as women were integral to these events, they were also at times left out of the historical glorification of the great explorers and cowboys of African descent in both popular and academic renderings. As scholar Bruce Glasrud noted, few women have been celebrated as cowboys because few would have been counted in the census as working hands. Instead their labor was located on family farms and ranches.[138] As Cleo Hearn once explained, "Everybody could be a cowboy, except a black person."[139] Black women, especially, felt the weight of this statement. Although rodeo was often couched in the language of masculinity, women were vital to the black cowboy movement.

As popular and academic writing on black cowboys began to appear and black cowboy performances grew in the 1960s and 1970s, a hopeful notion of rewriting the national narrative took hold.[140] Starting in the late 1960s scholars such as Philip Durham, Everett Johns, William Loren Katz, and W. Sherman Savage began publishing histories of the African

American experience in the West and especially in the cattle industry. These academic histories became foundational tools for promoters of black rodeo. Rodeoer Bud Bramwell rejoiced, "Soon, with friends telling friends, America will again remember the heroes it has forgotten—the black men and women [who] play[ed] such an important role in discovering and taming the West."[141] As children in Kanew's *Black Rodeo* documentary stared in awe at both the horses and the cowboys, adults praised the instructive aspects of the rodeo, saying, "We were out in the West, too. We helped put it together."[142] Watching black men perform the cultural ideals of the "Old West" allowed many people to feel that the time had finally come when black people could "make a place for [themselves] under the sun equal to all men."[143] Equality could be found through social and historical representation and performance, an admission by white Americans that black folks had been present during the process of continental conquest.

• • •

While men like Ronald Reagan increasingly appropriated the cowboy icon in the late twentieth century as a mascot for militant stances on the Cold War and the welfare state, black outriders from the 1960s to the 1990s in both rural and urban spaces used cowboy performance to argue for social equality through historical representation. Rodeo vendors sold Black Power buttons and Oakland educators listed black cowboys alongside the Black Panthers and the NAACP as community leaders.[144] Rodeo producers, chamber of commerce members, and working cowboys believed that the futures of their children could be improved through an embrace of history, without "any of it edited out."[145] While attending a Washington, DC, black rodeo in 1985, one clinical psychologist dubbed black cowboys "positive role models" because "it is good for kids to know that we are part of the making of American history in all its facets."[146] This narrative of progress through history, however, demanded that black western performance at times re-narrate black participation in Native American dispossession and death, drawing on popular ideas of the noble savage and exciting frontier violence.

In their recovery of black pioneering tales, rodeo programs often celebrated western characters famed for their violent interactions with Native peoples. Nat Love, a favorite historical character for academics and rodeo organizers alike, only considered himself a true cowboy after his first gun battle with Native Americans. Having survived the fight, he exclaimed that he and the other men had the "satisfaction of knowing we had made several good Indians out of bad ones."[147] Playing on the notion that the "only good Indian is a dead Indian," Love imbued his narrative with wooden Indian stereotypes, painting them as brave yet savage, the natural enemies of both white and black Americans. In line with Love's tale, Boley's 1982 rodeo program referred to the Buffalo Soldiers as "a very effective peace keeping force in Oklahoma Territory."[148] "Buffalo Soldiers," the popular nickname attributed to the Twenty-Fourth and Twenty-Fifth Infantry Regiments and the Ninth and Tenth Calvary Regiments, were all-black troops who participated in the expansionist wars of the late nineteenth centuries, including the campaigns against the Cheyenne and Comanche, and the Philippine-American War.[149] The description of them as "peace keepers" glosses their state-sanctioned role in fighting to expand American empire through the slaughter and imprisonment of indigenous peoples.

The glorification of historical figures continued well into the twenty-first century, even after black rodeo associations became more racially inclusive, welcoming Native and Latino members. In 2014, the Cowboys of Color circuit, for instance, lauded unintentional explorers of African descent like Estevanico, a Moroccan bondsman shipwrecked with Cabeza de Vaca off the coast of present-day Texas. After an eight-year, thousand-mile trek to Mexico City, Estevanico reported rumors of cities made of gold and helped lead a Spanish expedition northward. While he found no gold cities and was slain by unfriendly "Indians," the program explained, Estevanico had "discovered something much more valuable: the land we now call Texas and New Mexico."[150] By emphasizing the heroic contributions of these explorers, cowboys, and soldiers, black rodeo organizers continue to problematically invest in US expansion and forced removal of Native peoples as a site for racial pride.

These violent interactions carried forward into the performance of black cowboys on the screen and in the arena. Woody Strode, himself the son of an African Creek and Blackfoot father and an African Cherokee mother, articulated black violence against Native peoples as a powerful image for young people.[151] In the 1960 film *Sergeant Rutledge*, directed by

John Ford, Strode portrayed a man wrongly accused of the rape and murder of a white woman. Initially, he runs because he knows he will be unjustly convicted of the crime and that it will taint the reputation of the Ninth Calvary. Yet he returns to fight renegade Apaches, who have "broken out" of their reservation. Freed momentarily from his bondage in order to fight to ensure the reincarceration of the Apache, Rutledge barked at his cheering men to "stop yelling and start shooting. Squeeze them triggers." When a fellow soldier dies in his arms, lamenting his part in a "white man's war," Rutledge responds: "It ain't a white man's war. We're fighting to make us proud." Like the character of Sergeant Rutledge, for Strode, this film articulated the pride African Americans should feel about their participation in the history of westward expansion. Referring to the film during his interview in *Black Rodeo*, he said, "It was the first time blacks ever saw themselves fight the Indians." Indeed, he continued, racial tensions had only increased over the twentieth century because television and films showed black people in "competition against the white. Instead of showing how we helped build the country."[152]

Black western performance often defined Native peoples as noble savages—good, nonprejudiced people woefully inadequate for civilization. As a University of California, Los Angeles, graduate, with a bachelor's degree in history, Strode explained that "the Indian was never prejudiced. It's just a shame that they had to be conquered to develop the country." Black rodeos were expanding at the same moment Native activists founded the American Indian Movement (AIM) and other Native civil rights organizations. AIM leaders led delegations to Washington, DC, and occupied culturally significant places like Wounded Knee to protest for their educational, economic, and cultural rights, which had continued to be systematically violated through the breaking of treaties over the twentieth century. Refusing to acknowledge Native activists' claims that they had not vanished into the mists of time, prominent men who identified as black, like Strode, continued to narrate the Native past as inevitable conquest for the sake of national progress.

These distinctions between black and Native communities reflected centuries of enslavement, warfare, dispossession, segregation, and violence, as well as the vestiges of Progressive-era racial science. In 1908, Booker T. Washington wrote: "Boley, although built on the railway, is still on the edge of civilization. You can still hear on summer nights, I am told,

the wild notes of the Indian drums and the shrill cries of the Indian dancers among the hills beyond the settlement."[153] Townspeople, mostly black
immigrants, complained of drunken "Indians" and Freedmen riding
through town shooting up houses for entertainment. The racial mixture of
many Freedmen, or at least their socialization with Native people, often
led black migrants to characterize them as part of the untamed West.
Washington and the patriarchs of Boley were civilizing savage land, ways,
and people as Boley sought to prove "the right of the negro, not just as an
individual, but as a race, to have a worthy and permanent place in the civilization that the American people are creating."[154] Rodeo organizers
reached back to the actions of their forefathers to urge white Americans to
remember that they had participated in this taming of savage people
alongside Anglo settlers.

Despite their efforts, African Americans still felt frustrated at the persistent erasure of their existence in favor of a white cowboys and Indians
narrative. Cleo Hearn recalled his mother's annoyance at a Denver reporter
who focused heavily on Hearn's Native ancestry instead of his blackness.
Criticizing both her son and the reporter, Hearn remembers her observing, "He grew up here all his life and he goes up there and wins all that
money. Now he's an Indian."[155] By privileging his Native bloodline, the
media inserted Hearn's rodeo success into an already established mythology, ignoring the struggles of he and his family endured as black westerners. Failing to tell complex stories about Native and black communities
forced cowboys of color to be black or Indian but never both.

Indeed, as James Baldwin articulated, the racialized violence of cowboy versus Indian structured many African Americans' everyday experiences. Growing up on Hollywood westerns, Baldwin described national
exclusion in terms of being an "Indian": "It comes as a great shock around
the age of 5, 6, or 7 to discover that the flag to which you have pledged allegiance, along with everybody else, has not pledged allegiance to you. It
comes as a great shock to see Gary Cooper killing off the Indians, and
although you are rooting for Gary Cooper, that the Indians are you."[156] By
engaging in popular spectacles that celebrated violence against Native
people, African American outriders at times refused to critique the Gary
Cooper visions of the West or identify themselves with Indians.

Likewise, the emphasis placed by rodeo organizers on the benefits of
historical representation in education often outweighed critical engagements

with these stereotypical portrayals of the heroic cowboy and the savage Indian. As literary scholar Blake Allmendinger observed in 1993, much of the work on black cowboys popularized in the 1960s targeted children. Yet he notes that even the scholarly work refused to engage critically with the violence encoded in Nat Love's seemingly colorblind adventures on the American frontier. Allmendinger writes: "So far, *The Life and Adventures* [*of Nat Love*] has escaped attention (and slipped through the theories) of high culture's critics. But low culture's minions have hog-tied it, confining the retelling of Love's life to the pages of coloring books and children's short stories."[157] Love's story was also told and retold in rodeo programs to bolster the narrative that future equal opportunity could be achieved by memorializing the past conquests of men of color in the West. Programs did not necessarily emphasize the realities of Love's life as a black man relegated to black working-class servitude to white bosses on the cattle trail or the railroad, but instead, like Love's narrative itself, simply frames him as a colorblind cowboy. Unlike men such as Malcolm X, Love and other black cowboys failed to fully embody a revolutionary moment of civil rights or Black Power, simply operating to further a claim to national inclusion through mutual exclusion.

In 1997, Toni Morrison published *Paradise*, the story of an all-black town determined to protect its western paradise from the dangers presented by mysterious women living together just beyond the social and geographical boundaries of the town. Morrison describes the sense of agony the founders feel as they doggedly trod their way from Louisiana to Indian Territory, the shame of being turned away by "rich Choctaw and poor whites, chased by yard dogs, jeered at by camp prostitutes and their children." Most significantly, they are unwelcomed by black people in black towns, being told to "come prepared or not at all."[158] These Old Fathers laboriously "cut Haven from the mud," but their children suffered as they watched the town decline from "a dreamtown in Oklahoma Territory" to "a ghosttown in Oklahoma State." Sons grieved to see "Freedmen who stood tall in 1889 dropped to their knees in 1934 and were stomach-crawling by 1948."[159] The New Fathers migrated again, founding Ruby and promising "to make sure it never happens again. That nothing inside or out rots the one all-black town worth the pain." Convinced that only an external threat could cause the corruption of their new haven, the men of the town do not welcome these bruised and broken women. They respond not with "fellowship or love," but with violence, attacking what threatens their gendered and racialized paradise. Morrison illustrated that, in the late 1990s, tales of black western success could no longer be told without attention to the mythologies they perpetuated and the problematic narratives of masculinity, self-sufficiency, and violence they ultimately crafted.

Black rodeo organizers sought to create progress through collectively reminding the American public of the black western past. In 1934, at the 30th Anniversary town celebration, the souvenir program stated: "Boley will always stand as an attestation of sacrifices and untiring efforts of the early pioneers and serve as a symbol of progress and an inspiration to future generations."[160] As media scholar Nicole Fleetwood argues, black cultural production carries a great "weight" to "produce results, to do something to alter a history and system of racial inequality that is in part constituted through visual discourse."[161] Communities like Boley and Oakland put forth a great deal of time, money, and effort to stage black western performance in the Black Power era. Reiterating their participation in the history of nation building, including western exploration, cowboying, and the taming of both the savage land and savage people, rodeo organizers hoped to rejuvenate their towns, neighborhoods, and cities. As outriders, both marginal and yet invested in the forward movement of western mythologies, black cowboys could prove, once and for all, that black men were as masculine, heroic, and American as white men and deserved to be treated accordingly. With their efforts on education, traits like self-determination and economic independence could be passed to young men. Yet, by the close of the 1980s, Boley had yet to boom and the black cowboy had not yet entered the national consciousness. As one observer noted in 1989: "There is an aura of patient waiting for the return of better times."[162] Despite the radical potential of black western performance to use the past to create a better future, black cowboys remained unexpected.

CHAPTER 4

Camp and the Cowboy

The Serious Fun of Gay Rodeo

AT TIMES, SOME SAID, GAY RODEO COULD BE TOO GAY.
Greg Olson, future seven-year all-around champion of gay rodeo, expressed
disappointment with the first National Reno Gay Rodeo he attended in
1977. "It wasn't anything like the normal rodeos we always went to and
watched back home."[1] Raised on a Nebraska farm, Olson critiqued the
emphasis placed on campy fun. Greased-pig chasing and wild cow milking seemed more popular with the crowd than traditional events like bull
riding and calf roping. Luckily for Olson, many other cowboys and cowgirls felt the same way. He noted that as the annual National Reno Gay
Rodeo gave way to the International Gay Rodeo Association (IGRA) circuit in the 1980s, with standardized rules and member associations, gay
rodeo began to be "taken more seriously by competitors." After Olson won
five consecutive years of all-around titles from 1987 to 1993, other members of IGRA complained that gay rodeo was becoming too professional
and no longer open to amateurs. "We do take it seriously," Olson admitted,
but insisted, "we still make a lot of fun of it." The desire to be joyful and the
need to be serious illustrated the precarious position of gay rodeoers from
the mid-1970s to the late-1990s.[2] These men and women articulated larger
debates about the role of play in American gender, rendering visible America's growing need for hard-line, authentic masculinity and allowing this
desire to be openly debated.

In the late 1970s, cowboys were becoming chic again. The beginnings of gay rodeo coincided with a boom in country western music, mechanical bull riding, western wear, and cowboy politics. Presidential hopefuls like Jimmy Carter and Ronald Reagan constantly reiterated their rural predilections, with Reagan posing for routine photoshoots on his California ranch. After winning the presidency, he often sent out thank-you cards that featured himself in western wear standing in front of a White House miraculously transported to sit under the Hollywood sign in the Los Angeles foothills.[3] Designers like Ralph Lauren and Calvin Klein spent a good portion of the next decade selling western-themed dresses, jeans, and jackets. Television, too, shifted away from nineteenth-century westerns and instead showcased the new Wild West of oilmen and wealthy Texans. Forty million Americans watched *Dallas* every week for over a decade.[4] People could even play cowboy at bars with the first installation of a mechanical bull for entertainment purposes at Gilley's Bar in Pasadena, Texas, in 1976.[5] The popularity of the cowboy across mediums in the late 1970s reiterated the longstanding tradition by which most white American men had the ability to adopt and discard a cowboy identity at any time due to their inheritance of a uniquely American form of masculinity. In 1989, *Esquire* ran a western wear photo spread declaring, "You work in a city. You live in a suburb. [. . .] But if you're an American male, buried somewhere deep in your soul is a little bit of cowboy."[6] Politicians and fashion designers alike framed playing cowboy as an expression of an inborn American identity, rendering it open for all white men.

This upwelling of cowboy kitsch explicitly linked cowboy masculinity to an emerging desire to reassert American global dominance after the supposed effeminizing effects of the 1960s. Contrasting themselves with the image of the self-absorbed, whining protesters of the counterculture, Black Power, feminist, and civil rights movements, Reagan's supporters heralded the return of the "hard line." Exemplifying the masculine angst of the era, *Esquire's* April 1980 cover featured an image of John Wayne with the headline, "Somewhere the Duke is Smiling."[7] This cover article chronicled the death of the "soft-line" days of the 1960s and early 1970s. Deploying the cowboy, symbolized by the cowboy-performer John Wayne, as the definitive mark of American masculinity, independence, and dominance, the magazine joked that the soft-line era had been overly sensitive: "We trembled, we shook, we wore clogs." But "people didn't want a president saying that he was having a crisis-of-confidence," as Carter had done on live television. Thus, in rejection of Carter's sensitivity, Reagan was ushering in "tough-guyism," which held the "hard line."[8] Make-believe cowboys in politics, the fashion industry, movies, and mainstream rodeo were widely considered to be "genuinely authentic."[9] The performative qualities of their cowboy masculinity were rendered invisible.

Simultaneously, gay men increasingly faced their own crisis of masculinity. Gay male subcultures celebrating hypermasculinity developed rapidly after 1945 with the emergence of motorcycle gangs and sadomasochist communities. After the late 1960s, gay men also felt the growing cultural pressures of Reaganite masculinity. By 1982, books like *Real Men Don't Eat Quiche* and *The Butch Manual* gained popularity among gay men, and the term "straight acting" gained traction as a desirable trait. Leathermen, bears, and cowboys became sexual icons for gay men fighting against the "assumed effeminacy" stigma of homosexuality.[10] This cult of the masculine operated within gay rodeo, and, as white men dominated the association, white hypermasculinity defined the association's cultural image in the early years.

Gay rodeo illuminated these deep anxieties erupting around masculinity and play. In the late twentieth century, as cowgirls were frozen out of rough stock riding and black rodeo expanded to provide safe spaces for cowboys of color, gay men wanting to play cowboy needed to cater to the accepted forms of white masculinity that defined mainstream rodeo by the 1970s. Adhering to a commitment to "tradition" and "heritage" helped combat the considerable homophobia they faced, including the accusation that "they're making a fiasco of the cowboy [. . .] They're making fun of our heritage."[11] Yet, precisely because they were already pushed to the edges of the country western world, gay rodeoers also used the concept of "fun" to set themselves apart as different from "traditional" cowboys. Even as IGRA celebrated hypermasculinity as a way to prove gay people's authentic place in cowboy culture and dedication to professional-style rodeo, they also used "camp" as a way to promote their form of rodeo as inclusive, caring, and, most importantly, enjoyable.

Beginning in 1980s, IGRA promoted fun by officially sanctioning three unique camp rodeo events. While gay rodeo otherwise resembled a mainstream rodeo, with speed, rough stock, and roping events, camp events were explicitly framed as amateur contests in which anyone could

IGRA's cultural image often balanced a celebration of both serious masculinity and campy fun. Rocky Mountain Regional Rodeo Program Cover, 1985. Illustration by Leon Marfell, courtesy of Leon Marfell and the Colorado Gay Rodeo Association.

participate. Performed on foot, with little experience needed, these events were considered to be the most entertaining of the day. One rodeo drag queen explained camp in the context of the rodeo as "seeing things in an unordinary fashion and being able to laugh at it." She, and many others, described the creation of these events as what defined gay rodeo as a potentially radical queer space: "I think you best beat back the misunderstanding and the ugliness with humor. So I think the gay rodeo beats back that oppression with funniness, with clever funniness."[12] As scholar Sara Warner has demonstrated in her seminal work, *Acts of Gaiety: LGBT Performance and the Politics of Pleasure*, frivolity is "an important but neglected political affect" that can "create a pleasurable and empowering experience out of an event or situation that is hateful or painful."[13] Gay rodeoers used fun and gaiety to distinguish themselves from mainstream rodeoers. Seriousness and fun became a gendered spectrum in gay rodeo, with individuals attempting to navigate and narrate this duality.

While previous studies of 1980s gay rodeos have emphasized its resistance to hegemonic masculinity, I argue that these complicated spaces both celebrated and threatened established forms of white masculine performance.[14] To men like Ralph Lauren and Ronald Reagan, playing cowboy was a masculine birthright. Gay rodeo, which invited cowboys to play feminine as well as hypermasculine, disturbed notions of American masculinity not only because it threatened to overthrow serious cowboy tradition with frivolous gay fun, but also because it threatened to demonstrate publicly the constructed nature of gender and sexuality in general. Americans could play cowboy in the political arena and fashion world, yet gay cowboys who at times wore dresses threatened to expose all cowboyness as a gendered performance.

The history of IGRA has been meticulously preserved by dedicated members, including posters, programs, news articles, correspondence, internal documentation, and oral histories.[15] Gay rodeo outriders, in their own debates on the performance of hypermasculinity, exposed the critical overlaps between the fun and the serious, the authentic and the inauthentic, the real and the fantastical, and the masculine and the feminine. Building a place where thousands of people found family and a wider community who shared their love of a "country-western lifestyle," IGRA also forced members to examine the meaning of inclusivity and trouble the assumption of authenticity in American masculinity in the age of Reagan. Competing desires to be both authentic cowboys and a joyously accepting community made the separation between the real and the imagined in the performance of gender and sexuality more difficult in the late twentieth century.

· · ·

Over the forty years of its existence, gay rodeo has fought for a safe space to inhabit. Born at the dawn of the age of Reagan, surviving the AIDS epidemic, and persisting into a new century, gay rodeo's birth and expansion were fueled by questions of what it meant to be masculine and gay in America. Most importantly, gay rodeo has knitted together diverse subcultures and offered people a place of belonging, even as it maintained associations of the West with white masculinity.

Gay rodeo got its start as a fund-raiser for local charities. The first gay rodeo was organized in 1976 by a Reno businessman named Phil Ragsdale.

At the time, Ragsdale was serving as Emperor I of Reno's Imperial Court System, a philanthropic organization that was first established in San Francisco's drag bars by José Sarria in 1965.[16] As emperor, Ragsdale proposed hosting an amateur rodeo in order to raise money for the local senior center and, later, the Muscular Dystrophy Association. He was able to secure the county fairgrounds for October 1976. Local stock contractors were reluctant to rent him animals so he proceeded to round up "wild" stock. By 1981, the National Reno Gay Rodeo had become an annual weekend-long festival accompanied by a parade and a plethora of cowboy-themed parties. Over the first five years, donations for the Muscular Dystrophy Association raised at the rodeo surged from a couple hundred dollars to over forty-thousand dollars per year. Attendance reached ten thousand spectators, and Joan Rivers grand-marshaled the parade.[17] Growing out of a longer tradition of LGBTQ+ civic engagement and coinciding with a major surge in country western trendiness, Reno's early gay rodeos provided participants with a place to line-dance, cruise, and raise money for charity.

As the annual western celebration drew together many people wanting to rodeo in a nonthreatening atmosphere, pressure to create a new rodeo circuit and standardize rules increased. Slowly, in the early 1980s, dedicated contingents from Denver, Houston, and Los Angeles added their own gay rodeos and Colorado, Utah, and California created their own associations. Many rodeoers, however, felt that rules were not fairly applied and should adhere to the standards of "real" rodeo.

Finally, in 1985, the National Reno Gay Rodeo folded. Gay rodeo enthusiasts like Wayne Jakino and others in Colorado, Texas, and California worked to establish a new umbrella organization. The newly birthed IGRA knit together local associations by managing membership requirements, seeking large sponsorships, sanctioning rodeos, training officials, reviewing formal complaints, and standardizing all rodeo rules. While gay rodeoers were still required to join specific local associations—no one is technically a "member" of IGRA—they found a national, and even international, community through IGRA. The association rapidly grew. By the 1990s, state associations were reporting eight thousand members, though active members in good standing were closer to three thousand.[18] In 1986, IGRA hosted its first official royalty competition and in 1987 its first dance competition. These events helped raise roughly two million dollars for a variety of charities, notably AIDS research and care, over the next several decades. At its peak, IGRA hosted more than twenty annual rodeos, with the number of rodeos doubling between 1991 and 1994.[19]

This rapid expansion ceased in 1996, which was the first year to cancel instead of add rodeos to the circuit. By 2013, IGRA had more defunct associations than ones still in operation. The product of a particular historical moment that created a crisis in masculinity, a boom in western chic, and the gay equal rights movement, today IGRA is now struggling to reinvent itself after a decade of declining participants and rodeo numbers. Importantly, the tone of gay rodeo increasingly emphasized the "serious" business of rodeo as it moved from an offshoot event of the Imperial Court to an association in its own right.

Even as it became a self-sufficient organization in the 1980s, gay rodeo depended on the institution of the gay bar to grow its membership. As a former IGRA president noted, gay rodeo emerged at a time when "country music was all over the place, big country bars were the thing."[20] The ability of gay cowboys to organize, form associations, and plan rodeos in the early 1980s was due in large part to the growing popularity of the urban cowboy and the presence of gay country western bars. Bar owners such as John King recognized the profitability of cowboy chic. His bar, Charlie's of Denver, would offer a home to the rapidly growing Colorado Gay Rodeo Association, especially as his business partner Wayne Jakino worked to promote gay rodeo.[21]

Likewise, in towns all over the West, bars like the Barn, the Bunkhouse, and the Rawhide provided the gossip networks, dance floors, and alcohol necessary to bring crowds out to party, if not to rodeo themselves. One reporter claimed, "A first-timer at a gay rodeo will find that the parties surrounding the event may well be his greatest adventure. [. . .] Whatever your choice, leather Levi disco - piano bar - country/western dance-bar, all will be running full tilt and the tone is total party."[22] Indeed, throughout IGRA's history, bars that were not primarily country western consistently catered to gay cowboys when the lucrative rodeo was in town. Often these bars used sexualized cowboy imagery in order to temporarily transform their image and draw in rodeo customers. One 1996 advertisement from the Venture Bar in Tucson shows a stern, muscular, and shirtless cowboy brandishing a lasso from his pelvis as a surrogate penis—presumably to "rope in" customers—and the tagline promises a night of "Groovin,

Cruisin, and Boozin."[23] Deeply connected to other forms of LGBTQ+ organizing and entertaining, gay rodeo actively used bars and the sexual culture surrounding them to build new communities.

Bars facilitated the growing ability of gay rodeo to gather a spectrum of interest groups and gay-identified people. Charlie's of Denver provided a meeting space not only for the Colorado Gay Rodeo Association but also dance groups like the Denver Country Cloggers and the Mile High Squares. Thus, the diverse and intersecting social world of gay rodeo continued to expand through the 1980s and 1990s. As of 1987, gay rodeos included an official dance competition, with gay square dancers, cloggers, and two-steppers becoming increasingly involved. In 1990, the dates of the Rocky Mountain Regional Gay Rodeo were shifted in order to coincide with a week of Pride Fest activities, as were several other local rodeos. This not only gave the rodeo a boost in attendance but also helped assert IGRA's place in an often alienating queer urban culture.

Similarly, in 1990, IGRA was considering participating in the Gay Games in Vancouver, British Columbia. Started in San Francisco in 1982 as a way to promote inclusion and encourage athletic participation among LGBTQ+ people, the Vancouver Gay Games drew thousands of competitors and spectators worldwide.[24] Sporting culture, along with ideals of "western heritage," made up an integral aspect of gay rodeo culture. These junctures of shared interest with other gay organizations, including dance, politics, and athletics, helped draw in both dedicated members and casual attendees and kept widening the space of gay rodeo. For many gay rodeoers, rodeo was the hub of a much larger wheel of gay life and activities.

As gay rodeo grew, however, it also existed as a contested space between the political right and left. Shaping gay rodeoers' desires to be accepted into mainstream cowboy culture and a larger gay community was the rejection of the very notion of "gay cowboys" by a variety of groups. Blatant homophobia was the most recognizable form of exclusion. As one Alberta professional cowboy claimed, "Well, I've rodeo-ed for 25 years and I don't think I've ever come across a queer cowboy at a real rodeo."[25] Hate mail was often sent to IGRA, questioning if gay rodeoers "can ride bulls when you can't even ride a woman" and asserting that "rodeo is a sport for men." Hateful, epithet-filled letters told IGRA participants that they would "burn in hell."[26] From 1975 to 1985, the National Reno Gay Rodeo was plagued with everything from slurs to refusals to rent stock. For instance, in 1981, Commissioner Belie Williams of Washoe County, Nevada, attempted to stop the National Reno Gay Rodeo because he believed that it only encouraged a gay "lifestyle" and generated "unfavorable publicity" for the city. Lieutenant Governor Myron Leavitt of Nevada threw in his support for the commissioner, stating, "I'm strongly opposed to queers using public property."[27] Prominent IGRA member John King described anti-AIDS sentiment as a key aspect of a larger homophobia, making it difficult to get business licenses as community members labeled gay spaces as inherently diseased.[28]

While the 1981 rodeo went on as scheduled, several gay rodeos were canceled or had to move venues in the late 1980s and early 1990s. In 1988, for instance, the IGRA Finals Rodeo, scheduled to take place outside Reno at a private arena, was canceled after the local district attorney filed an injunction against the rodeo because of supposed concerns about public health, traffic, dust, and fire safety. The decision to ban the rodeo was immediately appealed by the American Civil Liberties Union to the Nevada Supreme Court but was upheld due to unexplainable clerical errors. Police staked out the area over the weekend to ensure no rodeo was held. All vehicles and individuals seen entering or leaving the property were photographed and videotaped.[29]

Similarly, in 1991, the *Wichita Eagle* published a friendly article on plans for the first Kansas gay rodeo. IGRA president Linn Copeland stated that while local support had been necessary only a few years earlier, membership in the organization was strong enough that more conservative, rural areas could host events and members would travel to them. She also mentioned that she would not be surprised if controversy surrounded the rodeo. Unfortunately, Copeland underestimated the need for local support or at least tolerance. This article ultimately incited other organizations, like the American Quarter Horse Association, to pressure the Penny Kaye DeBoer arena into canceling its contract with IGRA or lose their business. The owners offered Linn Copeland money and equipment to help set up another rodeo arena, but that aid never materialized. The loss of the arena cost the Kansas state association an estimated sixteen thousand dollars, and the last-minute changes also resulted in lost ticket money, with attendance down by almost two thousand people.[30]

The Wichita case and other such incidents helped prompt intense scrutiny of who could and should speak to the press on behalf of the organization. In a 1992 Arizona Gay Rodeo Association (AGRA) bid to host the finals, AGRA insisted that IGRA board members comply with the local association's media regulations. Explicitly, this meant that "no I.G.R.A. Board Member or Officer shall grant an interview or discuss the 1992 Rodeo Finals with a regular newspaper, radio station, or TV station without prior approval of the A.G.R.A Board." The desire to control information also resulted in more professionally styled media packages. The 1992 Bay Area Regional Association produced a three-page media sheet that outlined the history, goals, and popularity of gay rodeos, emphasizing the commitment to charitable fund-raising and alliance with major sponsors.[31]

The mainstream media's attempts to put gay rodeoers on display was often a more insidious form of degradation. During the 1980 National Reno Gay Rodeo, Phil Ragsdale invited a film crew from NBC's reality talk show *Real People*, known for often displaying its subjects as sideshow oddities. One gay rodeoer found the presence of film crews insulting and exploitative, saying, "We had paid to come here, paid to enter and then upon entering were told we had just joined the circus."[32] After IGRA was founded, a member had the choice to remain anonymous by providing an alias when they enrolled in their local association. Photos of competitors were allowed only with express permission from the individual and most community advertising was limited to a network of gay bars, allied organizations, and the gay press.

Another media crisis arose in 1993 when members were invited to appear on the *Jerry Springer Show*. The now-notorious talk show was only two years old and had not yet gained its nationwide reputation for vulgarity and belligerence. Unaware of its combativeness, several members of IGRA appeared on the show, hoping to share their experience as rodeo cowboys. Members of the Professional Rodeo Cowboys Association (PRCA) were also invited in order to denounce gay rodeo as a "circus" that "makes a joke of real rodeo." The PRCA members spouted homophobic stereotypes that were shared by many in the audience. One man even referred to a rodeo royalty member dressed in drag as "it." Overwhelmingly, however, audience members supported the notion of a segregated gay rodeo, telling the straight men to simply "look away."[33] The gay rodeoers asserted numerous times that they had no intention of asking for integration into mainstream rodeos. Gay cowboys could be accepted in the early 1990s, as long as they advocated for their own amateur, niche status. The mainstream public at times consumed gay rodeo as a type of sideshow with the assumption that all gay men were effeminate and therefore could not possibly engage in the masculine performance of rodeo. The desire to be considered real rodeoers by a larger audience often led to public exploitation and sensationalism.

Rejected by a politically conservative mainstream, IGRA also had a complicated relationship with LGBTQ+ rights as a political and cultural movement. For some outriders of the gay rodeo, the country redneck or hick has existed as external to and incompatible with "the gay community" because of the association of rurality with political conservatism. Taken aback by the solemnity with which gay rodeoers sang the national anthem and prayed, a reporter lamented the need to prove their allegiance to a country that had largely rejected them. "Here they were—big town, cow town, redneck, white collar, liberal, Baptist—singing their allegiance with their hats over their hearts, the most denied, the most legislated against."[34] Some people from urban-dominated gay communities wondered if rodeo was a place for gay people at all.

Gay rodeoers, too, were split on the topic of the rodeo's place in gay rights activism. An *In Touch for Men* interviewee at the 1980 National Reno Gay Rodeo was asked, "A lot of cowboys are right-wing, but I wonder if this applies to gay cowboys. Are you right-wing?" The contestant responded, "Sometimes I find myself in the middle. But it's a real world, and we have to start living in it." He continued, "We have to deal with it and say, I'm gay, I'm bigger and more understanding. Separatism didn't work for the Jews or the Blacks; it's not going to work for the Gays."[35] Many members even saw formal politics as a waste of time in comparison to building their own community, with comments like, "To me it's better than the Gay Pride march. Don't misunderstand me, I respect the march. But this isn't political; this is what gay life is all about. The rodeo draws men closer together."[36] Gay rodeoers were not unilaterally dedicated to political revolution; instead, many rodeoers were attempting to assimilate into an already established, and often idealized, western lifestyle.

For many progressives, animal rights constituted a particular source of concern. Rodeoers have always negotiated the line between being animal lovers and animal abusers in the public eye. As a sport, rodeo has contended with animal rights activists since the early twentieth century. Tex

Austin, a noted organizer of rodeos in Chicago, London, and New York City during the 1920s, had major publicity problems as the Humane Society agitated against rodeos as an "Orgy of Brutality" and a "barbarous and cruel form of so-called entertainment." In 1922, in New York City, the Society for the Prevention of Cruelty to Animals had twenty cowboys arrested on charges of animal cruelty, only to have them acquitted after the judge watched a rodeo. Indeed, in 1925, despite a large campaign against the rodeo by the local Humane Society, it gained sanction from the national Humane Society's secretary and chairman of the rodeo committee, George A. H. Scott. He expounded to skeptics, "The sport is more dangerous to the man than the animal."[37] There was an assumption that anyone who opposed the rodeo had never seen one, which was not strictly true. Eulalia Bourne, who raised cattle on a remote southwestern ranch during the 1930s and 1940s, noted in her memoir that she found rodeos to be outdated modes of cowboy spectacle that did not reflect modern ranch work and were disrespectful to the animals.[38]

Gay rodeo suffered from an additional dose of public scrutiny because as an oppressed population, gay people should have "known better." Tracy Reinman, the head of the Gay and Lesbian Animal Rights Caucus for People for the Ethical Treatment of Animals (PETA), led the charge against gay rodeo, stating, "It glorifies a time when violence against women, ethnic minorities, and gays was accepted. The way I think about it, human domination over animals is the same as human domination over other people," and "we should know about oppression."[39] In 1994, a PETA letter-writing campaign delivered dozens of anti-rodeo letters to IGRA headquarters. While a form letter was the most popular correspondence, other rhetorical tactics were used by those dedicated to animal liberation. In some cases, PETA supporters' letters betrayed their homophobia. Anna Moretto handwrote at the bottom of her form letter, "Gays are not to be sympathized with, they choose their lifestyle—in my opinion they are an abomination on the earth and have created all too much sickness and disease. Animals cannot choose and are to be treated humanely."[40]

IGRA has consistently denied and resisted the notion of being abusive to animals. Past IGRA president Roger Bergmann, like hundreds of rodeoers before him, responded to accusations of animal cruelty by saying that the events cause only "mild irritation" for the animals, like "grabbing and tickling someone."[41] IGRA also attempted to ensure animal safety by creating a committee to discuss animal welfare in 1994. The committee created new rules that required a veterinarian to be onsite and laid out procedures for removing injured animals.[42] These arguments and actions did not fully appease organizations like PETA. Seen by many progressives as overly religious, hyperpatriotic, and even downright cruel, gay rodeoers faced organized protests from both sides of the political spectrum.

In its struggle to establish itself, its interactions with other LGBTQ+ groups, and its need to defend itself on many political and cultural fronts, gay rodeo crafted a particular membership base and audience that was interested in issues of hypermasculine presentation, the heritage of the American West, and athletic prowess. Leathermen, two-steppers, and equestrians all found a common ground at the gay rodeo. Legitimacy and authenticity, however, were paramount to gay rodeoers in constructing a space that bridged the radical and the reactionary.

• • •

Caught between a political left that accused them of orchestrating an "orgy of brutality" and a conservative mainstream that perceived an orgy of sin, gay rodeoers ultimately embodied a common yet often unacknowledged tension of the imagined West. Namely, gay rodeoers expressed both the desire to be seen as authentic and therefore legitimate participants in cowboy culture and the desire to be recognized as different, and even better, than the original. Gay rodeo participants used "seriousness" to claim "realness," primarily through the language of masculinity. Simultaneously, gay rodeoers used "fun" to mark themselves as an improvement on mainstream rodeo, often by staging femininity.

Throughout gay rodeo's existence, several hard-line contestants openly questioned the rest of the community's ability to rodeo earnestly, assuming an incompatibility with fun and seriousness. For instance, in 1995, an equine disease outbreak prevented out-of-state contestants from bringing their horses into New Mexico, and some rodeoers felt that the rodeo should have been relocated to a different state. One irate contestant wrote to the association:

> When did we forget why we started IGRA in the first place? Yes it was a time of good clean cowboy fun, a hate free place where gays could

compete without the hassle of the straight world. But then we got into the mode of party-time. Now don't get me wrong I have no problem with that, but when we make that our main reason for putting on a rodeo, I believe we have gone astray.[43]

This member narrated the decline of IGRA from genuine rodeo that only took part in "clean" fun, to "party time." In contrast, other members, like Greg Olson, narrated the trajectory of gay rodeo as a move away from campy playtime to focused and determined competition. When asked if most rodeo attendees felt that the rodeo was a big party, one cowboy noted that "the serious contestants are real serious about rodeo, and that's what they think about until after the end of the rodeo and the awards are done."[44] For some people, dedication to the rodeo, and not the party, marked the line between the committed cowboys and the weekend wannabes.

When IGRA's own members critiqued gay rodeo as less serious than "real" rodeo, these doubts joined the deafening roar of disbelief by the

Steer Riding at the Windy City Rodeo, Chicago, Illinois, August 2005. Photograph by Frank Harrell.

larger population. Joan Rivers, when serving as grand marshal for the National Reno Gay Rodeo in 1982, asserted to the gay press, "I take the rodeo seriously because I take gay people seriously. The mainstream press wanted me to make isn't-it-a-hoot disparaging comments. I refused to talk."[45] As gay rodeo outriders were continually prompted to narrate themselves as authentic cowboys, they at times helped police the boundaries of the cowboy even as they attempted to expand it.

In an effort to sell gay rodeo to the larger public and prove the seriousness of gay rodeo, both journalists and some gay rodeoers drew lines between the authentic and inauthentic cowboy, which often hinged on the physical presentation of cowboyness. In 1980, during the National Reno Gay Rodeo, *In Touch for Men* asked one contestant, "You're a real cowboy, huh?" The man responded, "In the realest sense of the word, yes. A cowboy is a man who works with horses and cows." The magazine then asked what his response was to "pretend cowboys." He expressed his frustration at the idea of "tricking" people. He explained, "They're not being themselves. [. . .] If I see a San Francisco businessman in a cowboy outfit, I think he should dress and act like a business person. [. . .] I'd like them to appreciate me for who I am, and me to appreciate them for who they are." This gay cowboy saw his identity as grounded in his work with horses and cows, and yet dress and occupation were intimately related. When asked how to spot a faker, he quickly noted, "The way they walk, the way they dress and the way they put their hat down." All of these tell-tale signs privileged bodily presentation over employment, lifestyle, or personality traits. "Fake cowboys just don't move right. They wear Lees, Wranglers or some of those other form fitted jeans that are coming out. Cowboys wear one brand: Levi Strauss. [. . .] The third thing is the hat they wear. Wearing it back on your head is fake."[46] For this man, despite his initial definition of a cowboy as a profession, performing cowboyness depended on knowing which clothing brands were "real" cowboy gear.

Similarly, in 1987 the *Los Angeles Times* wrote, "Their hands were calloused, their muscles tough, and they wore the sweaty, stained clothes and frayed chaps of people who have spent much of their lives on ranches and farms. [. . .] No urban cowboys here. No electronic bulls. No designer jeans, satin shirts, shiny new snakeskin boots or fancy suede Stetsons to complete the effect."[47] Unlike the larger rodeo community, gay rodeoers did not see sexuality as a key aspect of cowboy authenticity; instead, they drew the line between "genuine" and "fraud" with the bodily presentation of manly ruralness. These descriptions of masculine cowboy authenticity did not differ greatly from assertions that straight urban cowboys in Gilley's honky-tonk wore "the real thing, thank you, none of those faggy designer jeans."[48]

For gay rodeoers, as with other marginalized cowboys, western heritage operated as a crucial pathway to legitimacy. In order to prove one's seriousness, one had to demonstrate an almost spiritual commitment to the arena as a place that revealed the true self. As one rodeoer asserted, "More than anything, gay rodeo is a chance to bring our community together for a celebration of our western heritage, which we all feel a part of."[49] This western heritage was experienced as the discovery of an essentialized identity. Another participant observed, "Your heritage comes back to you, it lets you know this is you. Can't paint a picture, but I can ride a bull, and I can wrestle a steer."[50] Migration to cities may have been the only option for LGBTQ+ rural folks to openly express their sexuality in the 1970s and 1980s, but rodeo allowed them to reclaim their rural authenticity. Specifically, competition in the arena drove the recovery of this heritage: "The rodeo brings you into a more real area. Going into that arena to compete gives you the chance to be you—just you. And if you're lucky enough you come out understanding more of yourself—the real you."[51] Performing one's rural past in potentially dangerous ways forced the revelation of one's true self.[52]

In the interest of maintaining rodeo tradition, IGRA also focused more attention on gay people's rights to be a part of a longer cowboy history. Western heritage was not only a personal experience in the arena, but also the recovery of the history of same-sex relationships on the nineteenth-century cattle and mining frontiers.[53] Extensive information on same-sex practices in the "Old West" became highly sought-after pieces in gay rodeo programs and magazines. This historical recovery project was used to bolster the claim that gay men and women belonged in the western imaginary. For instance, American historian Jim Wilke wrote several articles in *Roundup* and other magazines covering incidents of cross-dressing, all-male stag dances, and the importance of partners in cowboy culture. These past perspectives lent respectability to the gay rodeo project. Like African American rodeoers, gay outriders used to rodeo to invest in history and heritage as pathways to social inclusion, at times refusing to fully analyze the violent realities of settler colonialism.

Building on the inherent masculinity of cowboy imagery, histories printed in IGRA programs often re-narrated the myth of the cowboy. At its foundations, IGRA did not question the place of the cowboy as a masculine hero in American culture, but instead inserted its members into the cult of the cowboy. The 1989 Arizona Roadrunner Regional Rodeo program dedicated the rodeo to all patients struggling with "AIDS, cancer, and other medical problems." A quote by Teddy Roosevelt, one of the original make-believe cowboys, on the same page stressed western values of masculine determination and endurance: "The credit belongs to the man who is actually in the arenas—whose vision is marred by the dust and the sweat and the blood . . . if he fails, at least he fails while daring greatly so that his place shall never be with those cold and timid souls who know neither victory nor defeat."[54] Reminiscent of Frederick Jackson Turner's "frontier thesis," according to which American character was bred through steady conquest of the western frontier, gay rodeo histories retold how rodeo evolved from the "hardworking lifestyle of the American cowhand. The hard life of the Old West developed a character and an attitude that would become legendary." "Independent and bold" people of the American West shared their "spirit of freedom" through rodeo competition.[55] By embracing and reiterating the glory of "western heritage," particularly the image of the daring and unquestioningly white cowboy, IGRA helped elide centuries of land dispossession and violence toward Native peoples.

Many gay rodeoers embraced cowboy culture because it provided a space to perform hypermasculinity and resist the "pansy" stereotype that haunted gay men in the late twentieth century. While *Esquire* was writing about the need for a hard line in politics and culture, gay cowboys struggled against a long history of "assumed effeminacy."[56] The advent and expansion of gay rodeo coincided with a crisis in masculinity in both the gay and straight worlds. Adoration of young, sleek, muscle-bound men was a staple among affluent and white gay communities, like those who frequented the high-end New York vacation destination Fire Island.[57] Gay cowboys, both men who grew up in rural areas and urban men drawn to cowboy culture, significantly overlapped and interacted with these other forms of hypermasculine gay subcultures.[58]

Gay rodeo contributed to a growing sexual culture around hard masculine homosexuality. In the 1950s and 1960s, gay illustrators such as Tom of Finland had started publishing suggestive images of leather-clad cops, soldiers, and cowboys in magazines like *Physique Pictorial*. These images, which became increasingly pornographic as the Supreme Court struck down anti-obscenity laws, offered "a sharply contrasting image of homosexuality to the one that was considered—even by most gay men—universally valid. He invented a (pretty butch) fairy-tale gay universe in which masculinity was held up as the highest ideal."[59] Indeed, in the burgeoning soft- and hard-core gay pornography industries of the 1970s and 1980s, cowboy-themed plots were highly popular alongside other hypermasculine characters like construction workers, athletes, and cops.[60] For many gay men, leather was both a piece of clothing used for safety while riding motorcycles or horses and a fetishized cloth that implied solid masculinity. As sexuality scholar Mark Thompson has remarked, "The look, scent, and feel of black leather sexualizes everything it comes in contact with."[61]

Arguably, the most visible group with which gay rodeoers overlapped was leathermen. After World War II, many men refused to simply return to the restrictive heteronormative suburban dreams of the 1950s. They created a thriving network of leather clubs, biker bars, and sadomasochistic relationships. While men were organizing leather sex parties by at least the 1940s, it was not until 1954 that the first gay motorcycle club, the Satyrs, was established in Southern California.[62] Throughout the 1980s and 1990s, these hypermasculine gay subcultures overlapped and interlaced at various venues. A 1990 ad for the Phoenix club the Bum Steer featured a well-endowed anthropomorphized man-bull, with pierced nipples and snout, a leather harness, and elongated horns. The ad noted that this is "THE place to meet a man's MAN," and asserted that leather, Levi, or western attire was required for entrance.[63]

In addition to these commercial advertisements, members of the rodeo and leather communities often interacted. From the earliest days of IGRA, Mr. Leatherman and similar fund-raisers gained coverage in local associations' newsletters. In 1995, gay cowboys and a leather club in Minneapolis co-hosted a fund-raiser with one man suggesting that the rodeo entertainment committee "beg" Mr. Minnesota Leather 1995 to perform his whip-cracking routine at the next rodeo.[64] Exemplifying this growing affiliation between the leatherman and the cowboy, the American Brotherhood, a leather competition established in 1989, added an American Cowboy title in 1994 as a "means of bringing together the leather and Western communities and organization from around the continent."[65] The materiality of leather and denim stitched these two groups of men together. As one gay horseman asserted, "I like the look, smell and feel of a good man in levis and leather."[66]

Similarly, gay cowboy culture has intersected with the emergence of the bear subculture. Bears developed as a response to hypermasculine leathermen in the 1980s. Wanting to distinguish themselves from both effeminate homosexuality and unemotional hypermasculinity, men began to place teddy bears in their pockets, resisting the clone hanky code and denoting a desire to cuddle. Combining masculinity with nurturing, bears celebrated large, hairy bodies and encouraged emotional as well as sexual intimacy among manly men. The bear subculture exploded in 1986, with the Lone Star Saloon in San Francisco being the hotly debated epicenter of the subculture's newfound popularity. By 1987, self-identified bears were organizing private parties and creating community bulletin boards. *BEAR* magazine began publication in 1987 and slowly formalized bear beauty standards. Bears shared the blue-collar "everyman" mentality of cowboys. Before the establishment of beauty hierarchies and exclusive members-only clubs, bear bars drew in an eclectic mix of queer nonconformists. According to scholar Les Wright, both urban and rural blue-collar men, including chubbies, bikers, farmers, and cowboys, were welcomed under the banner of "come-as-you-are," contesting the hyperstylization of leather and clone culture. After the formalization of bear and cowboy subcultures the two groups continued to overlap.

IGRA as an organization had fewer official events with bear clubs than with leather clubs, but many members of bears clubs were interested in mingling with cowboys. In 1994, members from the Bears Club UK sent letters to IGRA asking for opportunities to make personal connections with cowboys because they were quintessential "American guys." Along with invitations to be "pen pals, friends, and hopefully more," these men repeatedly invited IGRA members to the United Kingdom for visits. While the idealized image of the gay cowboy tended more toward hard-bodied clones, this did not mean bear-bodied men were not cowboys. And the lack of a bear body did not preclude cross-pollination between the groups.

As one bear said, "I would prefer you to be hairy," but if not, it did not "really matter."[67]

These groups, alongside mainstream urban cowboys, used fantastical trips into the Old West as one way to participate in an imagined past of masculine American dominance. As a Guess fashion book profiling Texas stated, "Women are treated with great respect [in Texas], but it is assumed they know their place, which is supportive, and their function, which is often decorative."[68] For both gay and straight men, western identity was crafted as essentially masculine. Ultimately, performing masculinity bolstered claims of the cowboys' authenticity and the rodeo's legitimacy, even as cowboyness was also often acknowledged as drag and fantasy.

While leather and bear subcultures provided comfortable overlaps, for some men who grew up in rural settings, all forms of urban LGBTQ+ culture made them distinctly uncomfortable. As Will Fellows noted in his oral histories with rural gay men, "Some disapproved of gay pride parades or other highly visible events, and of gay men who are drag queens or who behave in flamboyantly effeminate ways." Many men felt that men should act like men on farms, that is, as men. One man pondered, "I wonder if there aren't other people out there who are like me, more quiet and more private, not like the gay mafia that you see so much of—the outgoing, outspoken, socialistic, activist, flamboyant and fast-paced, dishing, camping-it-up type of people who seem to dominate when gays come together in urban areas."[69] Men who rose to prominence in IGRA, like 1995 president Roger Bergmann, also expressed concern upon entering a larger gay community, narrating their initial fear of going to gay bars.[70]

The idea of flamboyant gay culture even kept people away from the rodeo because of their assumption of what a "gay rodeo" would entail. Bruce "Grumpy" Roby, originally from rural Idaho, explained that he was not initially interested in attending a gay rodeo because he thought it would be "pink pansies, purple horses." When some friends dragged him to Friday night dance before the Los Angeles gay rodeo, he was overwhelmed by three thousand gay men and women dancing: "It's men, it's, like, regular guys. [. . .] They are just regular people that happen to be gay and that's kind of where I really wanted to find life. And I called in sick the next day and went to the rodeo. I called in sick the next day and went back. It was like, I found a life."[71] Part of the appeal of the gay rodeo was the presence of the "regular guy" instead of gay stereotypes.

Women, gay and straight, interested in pursuits deemed masculine often found acceptance and encouragement in IGRA. When asked if she found it frustrating that she could not bronc ride at mainstream rodeos, longtime competitor Ann Kinney responded, "Had I been younger I would have been quite frustrated."[72] Kinney, who at first did not even realize she could participate in a gay rodeo, helped train a new generation of bronc riders. Other women did start younger, turning to gay rodeo as a place to ride. Jeannine Tuttle, a respected IGRA cowgirl, described how her only option for riding bulls in college was to ride in exhibitions, rather than competitions. She explained, "You see there weren't many women bull riders around, so they would advertise on the rodeo posters that they were having an exhibition bull ride by a woman, hoping to draw a bigger gate. I was like a freak show, but it was the only way I could ride, so I let them take advantage of my ability."[73] Many straight women began using the gay rodeo as a space to participate in rough stock events. Unlike their cowgirl foremothers, these women were either ostracized or ogled in mainstream venues. At the gay rodeo, in contrast, they were allowed to compete and celebrated for their skills, though still gender-segregated.[74]

Importantly, during the 1980s and 1990s, people who competed in the women's events still faced additional hurdles at the gay rodeo. Because the events remained separated based on gender identity, and because almost all associations drew fewer members who identified as women, the amount of money available to winners rarely matched the men's events. As in early rodeo, even if women posted higher scores and better times than their counterparts, they simply had a harder time recouping traveling and registration costs. The expense of participating therefore discouraged women from participating. This model also left non-binary people in limbo— ensuring that they needed to choose a gender under which to compete. Only camp events included both genders, with some remaining regulations for gender representation and performance.

The institutional preference for masculinity was a topic for debate in the early years of the association; as the *1986 Bylaws, Standing Rules, and Rodeo Rules* stipulated, "The word he or his shall mean both male and female gender."[75] This reference to pronouns and gender was almost immediately retracted the following year as many members voiced their opposition.[76] Both the local and international associations have persistently struggled to celebrate the masculine meanings attached to rodeo and the imagined West while also maintaining a welcoming attitude toward women members.

While women were involved with gay rodeo on a number of levels, as both participants and organizers, the rodeo association and the gay press intentionally crafted an image of hypermasculine and hypersexual cowboys.[77] Photo spreads mostly included action shots of the rodeo events or still shots of well-muscled men, often shirtless, with jeans, chaps, and cowboy hats. One member being interviewed by the press described being together as men and "doing manly things, being hypermasculine," as the most alluring aspect of the gay rodeo.[78] Advertisements for bars featured in the programs featured a heavily mustached, pant-less cowboy offering his posterior to the camera, saying, "Come and get it, cowboys."[79] Promotional materials tended to draw solely from standard western themes, including boots, hats, bucking broncs, and western scenery. The rainbow flag was not regularly featured and the word "gay" was almost never used, often for safety reasons. Only rarely were more imaginative illustrations chosen, and these were still often hypermasculine. For instance, Chicago's 1994 gay rodeo was advertised with the image of a satyr cowboy riding a centaur cowboy with the moon and the city skyline behind. While this publicity image broke the common tropes of western heritage, it still celebrated a masculine mythology of animalism in gay rodeo.[80]

Gay rodeoers also referenced the sexual power of cowboy physicality, giving credence to cowboyness as an essential mythology of American manhood. As one rodeoer observed, "A man is referred to as 'a stud,' 'a horse,' 'a cowboy.' The cowboy is the American macho, but I think it's good. It gets to the origin of America, the pioneer."[81] Gay rodeoers and journalists not only marked the cowboy as the primogenitor of American masculinity, but also often framed the cowboy as an origin story of gay male sexual awareness.[82] As a leatherman said about cowboys, "I personally think that a great deal of our hero worship is also erotic."[83] For instance, in a *4 Front Magazine* interview, a thirty-four-year-old rodeo contestant narrated his first cowboy experience when, as a seven-year-old, his father had taken him to the Houston Rodeo.[84] He reminisces, "And the next thing you know, I was surrounded by cowboys [. . .] Those Stetson Hats. Those beat-up Levis. Those worn boots. Those flannel checkered shirts." The materiality of cowboy sexuality, like leather and Levi's, served repeatedly as common links to manliness. An article discussing Roger

Bergmann's interest in the rodeo explained, "He knew what he liked about rodeo: the excitement, the challenge, the leather, the smell, the outfits, the jeans, the cowboys, the ruggedness, the men."[85] The portrayal of gay cowboys routinely reveled in gay rodeo as a space that drew together hypermasculine men in a web of sexual fantasy focused on the physical presentation of manliness, even as the association encouraged women to join.

Particularly in the mainstream press, gay rodeoers continually reasserted that the inherent masculinity of the cowboy negated the assumed effeminacy of gay men. As one leatherman said, "We don't have a song of Roland, we don't have Beowulf, but we do have stories of the cowboys on the cattle drives."[86] When speaking with the *Albuquerque Tribune*, one gay rodeoer celebrated the chance to break the "sissy" stereotype: "Now they know we're not just a bunch of pansies."[87] Comments about gay rodeo being "just as dangerous" and disproving the "fag" and "limp wrists" stereotypes appeared repeatedly as participants attempted to sell their sport to a prejudiced nation.[88] One member told the *Reno Evening Gazette* that the rodeo was full of men whom you "wouldn't recognize" as gay on the street because they were "still men," designating "straight-acting" as a key aspect of the gay rodeo. This mediated battle to prove that gay people were not "flighty, mostly city-dwelling creatures of the night" problematically cast effeminate gay men as the outcasts of gay rodeo.[89]

The cowboy's relationship to danger was explicitly eroticized and intertwined with hypermasculinity in the age of AIDS. Rodeo has always included a high number of participant deaths, a particularly alluring aspect for many contestants, and the gay rodeo community at times experienced loss of life. For instance, in 1994, a novice bull rider named Gary Gilchrist was thrown at the Atlanta gay rodeo and died of his injuries several weeks later.[90] Yet, in this era death in the gay rodeo community was much more likely to be caused by AIDS than a bull, as the epidemic wrought incalculable changes on people's rodeo family. Most charitable donations were redirected to hospice care, information hotlines, safe sex campaigns, and AIDS research funding. The rider-less horse ceremony, when a saddled horse is led across the arena in remembrance of lost riders, was added to most rodeos as a public form of grief. Gay Rodeo Hall of Famer and past IGRA president Brian Helander described the toll of AIDS on the association: "If you look at pictures from the early days the stands were packed with guys and that audience was decimated by HIV and we've really struggled to get that audience back. They're not there. That audience, the people of my ilk, my age, the western cowboy kind of lifestyle, I'm not sure we're there anymore."[91] Gay rodeoers described being forced back into the closet not because of blatant homophobia but because of anti-AIDS discrimination. Within the tragic shadow of these experiences, some gay men also began resisting the emergence of a safe sex regime in the late 1980s and 1990s by turning toward "barebacking," or the practice of intentionally unprotected sex.

In gay cowboy culture, the risk of the rodeo and risk of unprotected sex became enmeshed. As sexuality scholar Thomas Linneman noted, "Making sex safer, by definition, reduces the risk involved in the sexual activity, thus demasculinizing it. Some gay men engaging in unsafe sex even refer to the act as 'barebacking,' making an allusion to the days of the risk-taking, masculine frontier cowboy."[92] Gay cowboy erotica celebrated this risk-taking mentality in both the arena and the bedroom: "In every town, no matter how big or how small, Justin Longacre always found a good ride. Sometimes it was a horse named Diablo, Crazy Eight, or Snake Eyes, and sometimes it was a man named Brogan, or Charles, or Thad. Justin didn't care which it was because he always rode bareback. He lived to take risks. It was the cowboy way."[93] The beauty and sexual potency of risk gave life meaning to many men. One bull rider asserted, "If there is such a thing as risk-free living, it certainly doesn't sound like much fun."[94] The hypersexual and hypermasculine image of the cowboy revolted against sexual politics in the era of Reagan as men attempted to navigate the AIDS crisis. While it is unclear how many active IGRA members actually practiced riding bareback at this time, the tension between proper sexual behavior and the wild fantasies of cowboy enthusiasts was palpable.

The element of fantasy coexisted with gay rodeoers' claims to masculine authenticity. As *Vanity Fair* wrote in 1988, Ralph Lauren's sprawling seventeen-thousand-acre Colorado ranch rebuilt the West as "the Old Frontier, reverently re-created and even improved upon. [. . .] Even more familiar and real than the original could have been."[95] Playing cowboy, which improved the historical reality of West, was "part of the Great American Tradition": "We believe we're given not only the right but the ability to play comfortably many different roles in many times and places." As one gay rodeoer explained, the embrace of play allowed gay rodeoers to see their performances as a form of enchantment: "I think it's much like the knights and ladies of the crusades. I think it's an image or it's an aspiration or an ideal that's going to continue in our culture for a long long time to come. It's always going to speak to people's experience and that mystique or the 'glamour,' we'll say, (put that in quotations marks) of the West."[96] For many gay rodeoers, there was as much glamour, or magic, in performing masculinity as femininity.

"Cowboy drag," or even "cowgay drag," quickly became a popular descriptor for western wear.[97] John Carroll's 1993 article "Rodeo Rookie or the Virgin Cowpoke" described performing self-conscious masculinity. He marveled how his cowboy costume helped him say words like "howdy," smoke cigars, and generally feel "rugged." Casually critiquing the notion that any cowboy of the modern age is authentic, his friend quipped about the rodeo cowboys: "These guys are the real thing. Just like on TV." Real cowboyness was a performance and one that could be discarded at will. After the rodeo, his friend demanded, "Hey, Lone Ranger, the rodeo is over. Next week is the Black and Tans Uniform Party. Throw that cowboy drag in the closet. We have to get a police uniform ready 10–4."[98] As film critic David Thomson noted, the conflation of western myth and reality made towns like Rawhide, Nevada, "so fake a name now, so camp, it might be set in neon above a gay bar on the outskirts of some military base." And range cowboys "hardly know if they're wearing their own clothes or are dressed in costume."[99] In naming cowboy masculinity as drag and linking it explicitly to camp and to effeminacy, gay cowboys cracked open larger questions about the meaning of gender and play, as their gender performance so readily mimicked and yet also mocked other masculinities as play.

The desire to be accepted as legitimate, however, often led advocates of the association to casually temper the truly campy aspects of hypermasculinity. For instance, common reassurances in the mainstream press calmed readers by stating that "transvestites, by the way, were few" and that "only a handful of drag queens and ass-less leather chaps showed up."[100] While cowboy drag was appropriate for the rodeo, extreme leathermen and flamboyant drag queens both were cast as too much for the mainstream.

Gay rodeo revealed and reveled in the fantastical nature of masculinity in the age of Reagan. Camp and drag were always integral to the performance of American hypermasculinity, but only at the gay rodeo was cowboyness as drag rendered visible, namable, and even debatable. Indeed, these questions of gender were hotly disputed. After an organizing mishap one member angrily wrote, "This was one chance for gays to show they can do more than just do drag and be hairdressers!!!! I guess rodeo is too masculine a sport for most of the gay community to handle." The recipient of this tirade responded sarcastically, "Women and less than butch men should be asked to leave. Maybe we could enact a basic membership requirement that you must be as butch as Dave in order to join an IGRA Association."[101] As the association attempted to sell gay rodeo to a wider audience, the danger of hypermasculinity lay in its easy polarization to drag queens and other "non-normative" forms of gender presentation. Hypermasculinity bolstered the serious, traditional, and professional claims of gay rodeo, but also threatened all cowboy masculinities if it was rendered too visible as a performance.

• • •

Many of the same gay rodeoers who invested in narratives of masculinity simultaneously aligned themselves with a larger sense of gay community through "gaiety." When asked what marked their rodeos as different from the mainstream, gay rodeoers have usually provided a similar answer: gay rodeo is more fun. Reasons for this fun have included inclusivity both in terms of sexuality and skill level, the willingness to share equipment and advice, and the simple fact that, as Brian Helander asserted, "We're funner people."[102] When confronted with a protester holding a sign stating rodeo was not gay, Bruce Roby scoffed:

When I was a young guy going to [PRCA] rodeos there was never a bunch of tighter butts in jeans in my life, and the women had hair to heaven. I'm sorry, we got the same thing at the gay rodeo. You've got drag queens with hair to heaven and you got men in tight pants. There's nothing different. Except we are actually a little more open and accepting and we have a lot more fun.[103]

Gay cowboy culture has been seen as inherently more joyful than straight cowboy culture. When describing his time at a gay rodeo, one reporter asserted that because it was a gay rodeo, the event was touched by humor.

He went on to joke that during his interview with an elderly lady, she explained that the word "gay" meant: "just a bunch of people having fun."[104] Gayness as a collective performance of liveliness was inscribed into the rhetorical narrative of the distinctiveness of gay rodeo.

While rural upbringings and landscapes often curtailed LGBTQ+ men and women's public displays of their gender and sexuality, at the rodeo, they were given the opportunity to engage in "acts of gaiety." Sara Warner notes that acts of gaiety were not necessarily an expression of inner happiness as much as a "theatricalization" of joy in the face of struggle. She explains, "Acts of gaiety facilitate a respite from the drudgery of daily life, provide escape from untenable situations, and enable the construction of alternate realities governed by values and aspirations obverse to (and despised by) mainstream culture."[105] Many contestants lived in rural areas of the country or simply felt out of place on the urban gay scene because of their rural upbringings. As sexuality scholar Colin Johnson has noted, "Metropolitan chauvinism is a normative force to be reckoned with in the lives of lesbians and gay men. Many people do feel humiliated because they feel that they are not doing homosexuality right, which is to say amid the bright lights of the big city."[106] Rodeos offered a cultural space that was familiar and safe to rural LGBTQ+ people, many of whom had spent years driving hundreds of miles to the nearest city to participate in a variety of queer subcultures. As gay outriders of the rodeo defined themselves against the mainstream through fun, and used fun to keep gay rodeo inclusive, many people also equated playing gay with playing feminine and staying amateur.

One crucial aspect of embracing gayness in gay rodeo was promoting the amateur status of the association. While gay rodeoers often wished to be viewed as legitimate participants in cowboy culture, they also argued that they were simply creating safe spaces for nonprofessionals "to escape the day to day pressures of life and to have some fun without fear of getting hit in the head with a horse shoe by people who don't approve." When hounded by the mainstream press for not being a "real" rodeo, one Canadian association asked, "Why must we justify our right to participate?"[107] The association emphasized that, never having professed to be a "professional" rodeo, it did not need to provide credentials. Similarly, one president explained that all the work that went into hosting a rodeo was worth it "to see people have fun in a setting that makes them comfortable."[108] Fun denoted safety and enjoyment, but also anti-seriousness and an amateur level of rodeo.

Gay rodeoers also valued sexual play as a key component of the larger gay rodeo culture. Gay rodeo was a space for people to "get together, have some fun, and maybe share in a fantasy or two."[109] The launch dances and post-rodeo parties, which surround most forms of rodeo, allowed gay rodeos to revolve around sex and sexuality in more ways than one, specifically by drawing on the sexual image of the cowboy and by providing an opportunity to engage in casual hookups. In 1978, a reporter for *In Touch for Men* commented that there was as much "greased pork" catching and "wild cow milking" near the darkened tennis courts as there was in the arena.[110] Taglines like "Come for the Rodeo. Stay for the Party" were used on promotional posters to draw in an enthusiastic audience, some of whom had little interest in rodeo. When skeptical about attending a rodeo, John Carroll's friend assured him that gay rodeo "has nothing to do with horses. You go to the gay rodeo to look at the stallions. [. . .] The cowboys. The Studs. The macho guys in their weathered chaps and wornout boots."[111] Party culture was considered by committed rodeoers as auxiliary to the rodeo, as sex over substance, yet the parties were the driving force for a larger audience who had no particular interest in rodeo, but plenty of interest in meeting cowboys and cowgirls. As one cowgirl explained, "The atmosphere at the gay rodeo is more laid-back than at the straight ones. When it comes time to compete, it's very serious, but away from the rodeo grounds, it's fun and relaxed."[112] Enjoyment was integral to gay rodeo culture, but often still external to the rodeo itself.

Three rodeo competitions called camp events allowed the gaiety of the larger community to infuse the rodeo itself. The "camp events" category makes up one of the four types of events at gay rodeos. The other categories include rough stock, speed, and roping events. In order to qualify for the "All Around" contest, a contestant must have competed in three of the four categories. This system of awarding significant points for events considered by many rodeoers to be "enjoyable" but not "serious" resulted in wide-ranging debates about the place and meaning of camp events in gay rodeo. The National Reno Gay Rodeo included events like greased-pig catching and wild cow milking, both of which were standard events at local rodeos throughout the twentieth century. As in prison rodeo, these types of events offered audiences endless amusement, though they were not sanctioned by the PRCA as one of the seven standard events. When IGRA formed, three camp events became sanctioned: steer decorating, goat dressing, and wild drag racing.

Camp events required little experience or expense because they were team oriented and were all conducted on foot. Steer decorating featured one team member holding a steer by a twenty-five-foot rope while a second team member attempted to tie a ribbon on its tail. The steer had to be pulled across a line marking ten feet from the chute, the rope removed from its horns, and its tail decorated before the timer could be tagged. Goat dressing, also a timed event, required a team of contestants to race toward a small goat, lift up his hind legs, and attempt to get jockey-style underwear onto the stubborn animal before racing back to the starting line. Lastly, wild drag racing involved a team of three people, including a male, a female, and a male or female member dressed in female-style drag. The female held the lead rope of the wild steer when it was initially released. The male had to help catch and direct the steer over the seventy-foot line

IGRA Hall of Fame Cowboys Brian Helander (back) and Chuck Browning (front) stare down an uncooperative steer in the campy wild drag race, Las Vegas, Nevada, April 2002. Photograph by Frank Harrell.

where the person in drag was waiting. The "drag" had to get astride the steer's back and stay on until all four legs recrossed the seventy-foot line.

The use of the word "camp" in the official event categories and descriptions encouraged the perception that these events were primarily for enjoyment rather than a test of skills. Camp, which is generally marked by a self-conscious and studied performance that exaggerates its gendered, racialized, and sexualized subject, in this context connotes humor, inclusivity, and pleasure.[113] The ability of camp to bridge the traditional and the playful in rodeo created tensions for members, as gay rodeoers struggled to engage gaily with cowboy culture while worrying that camp events were disrespectful and antithetical to the solemn tradition of rodeo.

For both contestants and spectators, camp events were often seen as the highlight of the gay rodeo. Often considered sheer entertainment rather than contests, the camp events were widely regarded as what made gay rodeo gay. As *Frontier* magazine wrote in 1996, "Sure, they have the rough stuff events with bulls, broncs, and steers, but like any good bunch of fags and dykes, they also hold what are known as 'camp events.'"[114] Wild drag racing and goat dressing in particular were promoted by association members as ways to build community and encourage novice participation. A common narrative of successful contestants included the admission that they first entered the competitive world of gay rodeo through the act of putting underwear on a goat.[115] Camp events functioned as "the open door for anybody that wants to play. For me that was my open door, putting panties on the goat."[116] Or, as another cowboy loudly lamented, "I can't barrel ride worth shit, but I can put panties on a goat."

Despite largely positive commentary to the press, debates about the necessity or desirability of camp events have persisted within the association from the 1980s to today.

These concerns were strong enough to induce many people to voice their displeasure with camp events on a questionnaire disseminated by IGRA in 1990. In the group of fifty-two completed questionnaires, forty percent of the participants stated that they began their gay rodeo circuit careers in camp events. Yet almost sixty percent were in favor of deemphasizing, limiting, or completely eliminating one or more camp events. One person claimed that camp events have "eliminated the real purpose of rodeo." Another gay rodeoer exclaimed, "Camp events have nothing to do with being a cowboy."[117] Similarly, in 1996, the Golden State Gay Rodeo

Association submitted proposed rule changes to IGRA suggesting the elimination of goat dressing, the implementation of time limits on camp events, and the removal of camp events from consideration for the All-Around title. For members of the California association, "The other 3 events are more traditional rodeo events deserving of an All Around title."[118] These comments reveal the association of the word "camp" with nontraditional, frivolous fun.

This perception of the frivolity of camp events was problematic in part because camp events were equivalent to "local events" at mainstream rodeos. Communities all over the West stage their own nonsanctioned elements, from chuck wagon racing to goat tying. In fact, two of the camp events were based on earlier rodeo events, steer undecorating and wild cow milking. These events were used throughout the early and mid-twentieth century to demonstrate a cowboy's dexterity and ability to herd. But because of a desire to establish distance between the supposed frivolity of effeminate camp and the seriousness of traditional rodeo, some rodeoers used the controversy of camp events to urge for a restricting and reduction of the boundaries of gay rodeo.

Although camp events have involved theatrically embellished gender performance, camp has not exclusively denoted drag in the rodeo. In fact, only one of these events included a drag element, and as one gay rodeoer explained, it is not "real" drag, but instead a man "just putting on a dress."[119] Gay rodeo capitalized on the image of hypermasculine cowboys in hyperfeminine dresses attempting to execute a difficult and dangerous task to bring pleasure to the audience through humor. The impulse behind this use of camp has been inclusive, using the frivolity of camp to make a serious statement about westernness. Simultaneously, however, the sheer hilarity of this event perpetuates the idea that cross-dressing and femininity are still inherently external to the enactment of rodeo, thus producing laughter. In fact, even if a female was the "drag," she was required to perform hyperfeminity, not hypermasculinity. The official rule book explicitly stated, "The drag must wear female-type drag clothing and a wig."[120] In "breaking stereotypes" about effeminate gay men, an explicit IGRA goal, generalizations about femininity and rodeo often persisted.

A few gay rodeoers at times directly attacked feminine drag as not compatible with rodeo. Similar to rodeo queens in mainstream rodeos, IGRA royalty members fulfilled important, but largely supplemental and supportive, roles in gay rodeo.[121] In the late 1980s and 1990s, IGRA's royalty team consisted of Ms., Miss, and Mr. titles, which went to a lesbian member, a female impersonator, and a gay male member, respectively. IGRA utilized its royalty members as fund-raisers and promoters, circulating through the crowd during the rodeo and holding shows during the evenings. Seen as spokespeople, instead of strictly as contestants, these members were supposed to add "a more glamorous aspect to the sport of rodeo" and also take "people's minds off the rough and tumble event in the rodeo arena."[122] As fund-raisers, the royalty members needed to have bubbly personalities that inspire laughter and gaiety among spectators. Antics like selling raffle tickets by inseam length allowed the royalty court physical access to the crowd and resulted in playful touching, measuring, and teasing. Many of these entertainers entered the IGRA royalty contest not through involvement with the rodeo, but instead through connections with the Imperial Court System and other charitable organizations.[123] Less integral to rodeo as a masculine sport, rodeo queens, both gay and straight, have been imagined as the feminine counterparts who soften rodeo.

Indeed, despite their large contributions to gay rodeo culture, drag queens have at times been denigrated or marginalized. In his experience of the gay rodeo in the late 1980s, Darrel Yates Rist described one man's negative opinion about the rodeo queens: "It makes me *sick* to see somethin' as nelly as that. I haven't got no use for it at all. People sees that kind of thing and they think all the queers are that ways. It's enough to make you stay in a closet. Pro'ly from California anyways."[124] Similarly, another man joked, "I don't know if putting on makeup is really a sport [laughs] [. . .] I don't think you're really fulfilling the mission of IGRA, which is to promote and preserve the Western lifestyle. Uh, obviously there were gay cowboys [during the nineteenth century], but I don't know how many of them, uh, were drag cowboys [laughs]."[125] Some cowboys complained about drag queens shouting back at homophobic slurs during the rodeo, referring to this behavior as "tacky."[126] Another cowboy wrote to IGRA condemning the organizer of an after-rodeo party for "subjecting" the audience to a "lengthy performance by female impersonators."[127] In searching for legitimacy as a "real" rodeo, some gay cowboys reiterated transphobic stereotypes that derided gender fluidity and questioned the authenticity of male-to-female drag.

Gay rodeos demonstrated how femininity was increasingly trivialized and pushed to the margins of the twentieth-century imagined West. While cowgirls in the 1920s depended on enactments of domesticity to remain in the rodeo arena, rodeo queens in the 1980s had embraced a new level of hyperfeminine presentation with big hair and flashy costuming. At a time when Miss Rodeo USA was first being aired on television, femininity's place in rodeo was to bring glamour to the arena and aid men in their athletic endeavors. In the early 2000s, rodeo anthropologists Craig J. Forsyth and Carol Y. Thompson interviewed a young woman who explained:

> Let's face it, women just can't and shouldn't ever be allowed to compete in the regular PRCA events. Like I said before, there are many other places where women are more useful in rodeo than in the arena . . . Look to the production side of things . . . without women secretaries, timers, producers, mothers, wives, and sisters our men wouldn't be able to rodeo anyways . . . making it happen so our men can go out and compete. Rodeo is about our tradition and our western heritage where a man was a man and a woman was a lady.[128]

While 1910s bronc rider Tillie Baldwin may have taken exception to this woman's statement about women "traditionally" not competing in rough stock events, many people still believed that women in rodeo needed to preserve their respectability. Even as the Girls Rodeo Association was rebranding itself as the Professional Women's Rodeo Association in the 1980s, strict dress codes, including a ban on jeans, were implemented to craft a particularly genteel image of women in mainstream rodeo. Campy femininity belonged on the sidelines of rodeo, keeping time and waving to the crowd. Gay rodeo, which invited men to wear dresses and gaily camp it up, ultimately surfaced longstanding tensions around the inauthenticity of femininity in the imagined West.

Camp events staged gender-bending as humor, marked the rodeo as gay, and kept gay rodeo amateur. Their association with effeminacy, frivolity, and flamboyancy, however, could serve to mark the outer limits of gay rodeo's expansiveness. Sexuality scholar Daniel Harris argued in 1997 that by embracing the "costume dramas of the new machismo [. . .] we became our own worst enemies, harsh, homophobic critics of the campy demeanor of the typical queen."[129] The shift in gay culture to eschewing the "failed male" stereotype by overperforming masculinity interlocked with the overperformance of westernness by men like Ronald Reagan, Ralph Lauren, and John Travolta. In gay rodeo, the tensions surrounding fun and seriousness, femininity and masculinity, fantasy and camp, and professionalism and amateurism were self-consciously rendered visible and staged for an audience in a way that remained impossible in other arenas.

• • •

Gay rodeo not only peeled back the skin of fantasy that surrounded gay and straight masculinities in the late twentieth century but also posed a threat to gendered order, as its members used play to make all genders and sexualities visible as performance. By undoing the strict separation between the feminine and masculine, and the authentic and the inauthentic, gay rodeo troubled cowboy performance in new ways. Playing cowboy and playing gay may have existed as gendered sides of a spectrum, but the pendulum swung back and forth for many gay outriders as they searched for the meaning of their own idealized West. Particularly important to the rodeo has been the use of camp to transform "the serious into the frivolous." As Susan Sontag commented in her foundational "Notes on 'Camp,'" "The whole point of Camp is to dethrone the serious. Camp is playful, anti-serious. More precisely, Camp involves a new, more complex relationship to 'the serious.' One can be serious about the frivolous, frivolous about the serious."[130] If fun and seriousness could both define gay rodeo, then the hypermasculine West could be converted to frivolous and effeminate camp could be read as serious.

Gay rodeo breached the wall between fun and seriousness. In the face of stern debate, camp events survived because IGRA members maintained a desire to stay inclusive. Thus, while femininity and campy performance were often seen as unrelated to the cowboy, gay rodeo made space for the possibility of play.[131] Eventually, camp events came to be accepted as serious competitions, as well as good fun. While announcing a 2005 rodeo, the announcer stated, "Even though this is fun and a camp event, people take it *so* seriously."[132] The wild drag race rapidly gained a reputation for producing a high number of injuries as people were dragged, stomped, and pitched off the steer's back. In 1995, the Health and Safety Committee even recommended "the elimination and replacement of the Wild Drag

Race or at least look into ways of making this event safer. (This event has the highest injury rate!)."[133] Furthermore, due to their importance to the contestants' point tallies, the rules became increasingly clear and strict as to what "riding" a steer entails or how long a ribbon must stayed tied on the steer's tail. These seemingly frivolous events became very serious for many gay rodeoers.

Gay rodeoers also combined hypermasculinity with effeminacy in a space otherwise reserved for only masculinity. When asked if a transgender woman should participate in the male or female category, former president Roger Bergmann answered, "There's a lot of mythology surrounding cowboys and it's funny to see that some of our best cowboys are in reality the nelliest queens."[134] In this moment, the word "funny" marked the gap between performed femininity and the assumed masculine space of rodeo. This gap was routinely theatricalized in gay rodeo. In particular, IGRA newsletters and internal press coverage embraced gender-bending and flamboyant language in its descriptions of its own rodeos. Phrases like, "Well honey if you can't stand the heat get out of the kitchen. (Snap)!" were much more likely to appear in internal forms of communication than in interactions with mainstream journalists or even the gay press.[135] Affected effeminacy was perfectly acceptable, as was self-mockery. "It was obvious the gay rodeo was in town the moment we stepped off the plane; witness the memorable sight of a cowboy throwing a 'hissy-fit.'"[136]

Indeed, gay rodeo heroes were described in terms of both cowboy masculinity and campy effeminacy. As one journalist remarked about Greg Olson's Arizona ranch house, "The entire place could be the setting for some tough-talking fifties Western, especially the spacious living room with its rough-hewn paneling, lodge-pole furnishing, and trophy mounts and cowhide rungs. There's an unmistakable odor present; horses, leather, and men. You betcha Pardner, this is a real cowboy bunkhouse, just like in the movies." Like Ralph Lauren and Ronald Reagan, Olson built a home that celebrated the performance of western masculinity. Yet, as the magazine notes, "Only in the movies, the cowboys never called each other 'sister' and they didn't share their beds with other cowboys like they do at Greg's."[137] Within the gay rodeo community, the enactment of gender fluidity demonstrated the ways in which all masculinities were performed.

Some of the most significant orchestrators of confluence between the seriously hypermasculine and the frivolously effeminate at the gay rodeo were the rodeo clowns. Rodeo clowns, characters who have united fun and seriousness through camp and drag in mainstream rodeo for over a century, uniquely experienced the complexities of rodeo drag as both liberating and constraining in terms of gender and sexuality. One gay rodeo clown noted the change that came over him in his costume: "It requires a lot of energy to play with the crowd, and it brings out a part of me that you don't normally see. I'm a very quiet and retiring person, but under this make-up and in this costume, I can get away with anything I want." Specifically, this enjoyment and play was put into terms of anonymous sex, as he admitted:

> I enjoy molesting pretty men but I'd never talk to them if it weren't for this make-up. [. . .] Of course they like it. It embarrasses them but they don't take me seriously. I know now what it's like for people who do drag, because when I'm out there playing the audience and having a good time with them and embarrassing them to death, they don't know who I am—they know me as Bullshot, the clown, but not Dwight.

When asked if he had a good sex life as a clown, he answered, "No, absolutely not. Would you fuck with someone who looks like this?"[138] Clowns, also known as in rodeo as bullfighters, play both sides of the spectrum as they use hilarity to steadfastly protect the safety of contestant. In doing so, they are both hypermasculine and effeminate, serious and playful, and sexual and desexualized, providing for fluidity in gender and sexual performance rarely seen elsewhere in the imagined West.

For those straight American men who embraced the fantasy of playing cowboy in the late twentieth century, gay cowboys were troubling because they made their costumes too obvious and were too willing to publicly frolic and play. Playing gay revealed the performative nature of the allegedly authentic impulse to play cowboy. Gender and sexual fluidity within the gay rodeo community staged a collapse of the boundaries that separated feminine and masculine, urban and rural, gay and straight, and authentic and inauthentic. Even as gay outriders maintained racialized narratives of glorious conquest and individual members struggled to perform their competing desires, these collective debates destabilized the meaning of masculine authenticity.

Conclusion

Performance and Embodied Epistemologies

CLIMBING THE SWITCHBACKS OF RELIANT STADIUM IN Houston, Texas, on what seemed to me an unbearably hot and humid day in 2013, I could not help but be struck by the differences between the small, hometown rodeos of my childhood and the massive Houston Livestock Show and Rodeo. Taking my seat, perched at an alarmingly vertical angle above the dirt arena in a major urban stadium built for a capacity crowd of seventy thousand, I felt like many spectators in the early twentieth century must have felt—distant and disconnected from the scenes being enacted before my eyes.

I did not know these cowboys, their families, or their stories. I did, however, have the benefit of the thunderous sound system and twenty-foot jumbotrons providing me with interview footage, advertisements, and score rankings. Each rider's information, from height to hometown, was carefully packaged and presented to me in an attempt to emotionally connect me with the individual competitor. This rodeo proceeded much like any other you could attend today, with short rounds of bulls, broncs, and barrel racing. Yet it also included nonsanctioned events, largely because it now operates independently from the Professional Rodeo Cowboys Association. Watching performances like the calf scramble, which featured eager young people attempting to chase, tie, and lead a calf back to the starting line, the audience laughed and cheered. Despite the distance between the urban setting and enactment of rural lifeways, the contest between human and animal still provided pleasure.

As the rodeo action picked up, a mixture of pop, rock and roll, and country music blared from the speakers. People fluidly entered and exited the stands, watching a bit of rodeo and then stepping out to find other amusements. Coming from all over the state, metropolis and hinterland alike, two million people attend this monthlong fair, carnival, and rodeo annually. Large groups of Mexican American men in their starched western wear ate delicious fried foods, drank cold beer, and watched the rodeo side by side with white teenage boys wearing cargo shorts and flip-flops. The throb of excitement crescendoed as the final cowboys secured their times, the evening's winners were announced, and a massive mobile stage was rolled into the arena. Along with a rodeo ticket, spectators are treated to a special musical performance after each of the twenty days of rodeo in Houston. Country music favorites like George Strait and Garth Brooks draw far more spectators than the rodeo could hope to do alone.

As carnival rides whirled with squealing children, mechanical bulls bucked off overly confident challengers, and champion 4-H stock sold for hundreds of thousands of dollars, the Houston rodeo illustrated just how far American rodeo has developed in terms of technology and athletics, yet also how the spectacle of rodeo has remained largely the same.[1] Within this cacophonous space, the Houston rodeo continued to successfully sell spectators an experience that balanced the imagined past with present realities, imbuing urban landscapes with rural nostalgia. Sated on barbeque, filled with anticipation for the imminent concert, and thrillingly entertained by the rodeo show, I, like so many others around me, understood the deep satisfaction of investing in this collective celebration of an imagined West. As rodeo performances shift to serve new audiences, however, it is clear that urban rodeos do not so much perform the rural for the urban as create new hybrids of rurality and urbanity within an increasingly globalized West.

As rodeo persists, it continues to offer audiences, organizers, and participants the chance to render cultural ideals about the West into flesh-and-blood performances, creating new epistemologies about the West. Embodied epistemologies enable people to move beyond traditional modes of knowledge transmission. By performing the West, or at least the pieces deemed culturally valuable, people at the margins have been able to demonstrate their own claims to western identities. While these assertions remained contested, men and women risked injury and death in their struggle to be seen as legitimate cowboys and cowgirls.

Each of the community histories examined in *Outriders* demonstrates how, as the cowboy has gained and lost national admiration, mainstream symbols can be potent tools for marginalized people. Indeed, instead of simply asserting that anyone could be a cowboy, these communities made claims as to why they should be included in this larger tale of national belonging, exposing how people have both resisted and perpetuated persistently gendered, racialized, and sexualized images of the cowboy. Binding these narratives together, these stories reiterate persistent concerns about sexuality, coercion, humiliation, and violence within the imagined American West.

Investing in tradition, heritage, and authenticity, these men and women reconfigured the meanings of western identity as they sought to find a place for themselves as both westerners and Americans. As rodeo emerged as a sport in the early twentieth century, slowly distinguishing itself from other forms of popular entertainment, women like Tillie Baldwin rewrote themselves as cowgirls not because of their pioneer ancestors but because of their own daring conquest of western performance. In the midcentury, incarcerated men at the Texas Prison Rodeo participated in debates about the meaning of range labor and heroics of the cowboy. In the 1960s, even as the diverse regional West was becoming increasingly flattened into an image of a taciturn white man, new niche organizations like the Black Cowboy Association and the International Gay Rodeo Association provided succor to those men and women determined to cowboy. Rodeo, quite literally, saved some people's lives—giving them family, community, and a sense of fitting into a longer national history—while also reenacting centuries of violence.

Particularly, sex and sexuality informed both the everyday lives and the cultural image of rodeo cowboys and girls as they have fought for inclusion. Cowgirls in the early twentieth century were often drawn to the rodeo because of sexual relationships, anchored to the circuit through marriage and children, and also vulnerable to sexual assault or slander because of their tenuous positions as overly masculine performers. By the mid-twentieth century, however, women in mainstream rodeo no longer needed to defend their sexuality because their roles in rodeo had been reduced to gender-appropriate forms of performance, even as they were more often framed as sexual objects. Rodeo queens rose to prominence and female bronc riders were pushed to the sidelines. Mainstream rodeo, however, continued to operate through sexual relationships as buckle bunnies, wives, and girlfriends conducted the manual labor of driving, washing, and cooking for male competitors.

Within this emphasis on the sex, the conflation of gender and sexuality, or the idea that gender presentation and object desire were inherently connected, played a major role in the performance of the cowboy. Convict cowboys and gay rodeoers alike sought to use the masculine performance of the sport to distance themselves from the negative gendered assumptions of homosexuality. As the public panic around same-sex relationships reached new heights after World War II, Texas prison officials used the rodeo to reassert heteronormative structure through the inclusion of free-world women performers and by allowing cowboys, to a limited degree, the ability to interact with free-world women in the crowd. Officials also used the funds from rodeo to build new dormitories that they hoped would reduce the rate of same-sex encounters, both forced and consensual. Gay cowboys, especially, faced homophobia grounded in their assumed effeminacy and the supposed incompatibility of rodeo and femininity. At times, some gay rodeoers rebuffed and mocked effeminacy so thoroughly that they helped maintain gendered hierarchies within a space meant to be inclusive.

The gendered, sexualized, and racialized dynamics of marginalized rodeoers' lives also exposed the politics of power and humiliation in the performance of the West. In the arena, early cowgirls were often at the mercy of the men who paid their contracts or winnings. They were also subject to the whims of their audiences and the wills of their husbands. Events like the Chase for a Bride, with a cowgirl being happily captured by a man from a horde of whooping cowboys, played out these vulnerabilities to the glee of the crowds. Their precarious positions only increased in the 1930s when white male rodeo cowboys began organizing in order to ensure their rights to fair pay as performers. Women and people of color were often excluded from these associations by custom, leaving them to fend for themselves in terms of finding their own contracts, having the terms of those contracts fulfilled, or creating their own associations.

Coercion was particularly important in the case of prison rodeo, where many people in the crowd found humor in the excruciating pain of an injured inmate cowboy. Men of color, first imagined in the rodeo as the contented remnants of a pastoralized plantation system, were later cast as bumbling, inexperienced urbanites chasing bulls for a little cash. Incarcerated women were put in hypersexualized events that evoked hilarity at their ineptitude instead of respect for their skills. Organizers' attempts to create an atmosphere of humiliation and audiences' desires for blood sport, however, were often rejected by convict cowboy themselves. Like the gay cowboys who reveled in their own gaiety and laughed along with the crowd during difficult and dangerous camp events, many convict cowboys derived great pleasure and pride from their performances. As a negotiation between a promoter's wishes, an audience's expectations, and an athlete's interpretation, rodeo reveals the competing desires of all those involved, with no single actor's vision creating the final cultural product.

Within these negotiated imaginaries, rodeo also staged the complex racial histories of the borderlands. As black cowboys in the 1960s demonstrated, the West that rodeo claimed to portray was far more diverse than the PRCA's membership rolls. While noted cowboys like Will Rogers claimed their Native heritage, they also at times upheld racialized hierarchies of Progressive-era America. Likewise, as black communities used rodeo to urge for national remembrance and black pride, they often elided the centuries of intermarriage, enslavement, and cyclical violence between African-descended people and Native-descended people. As many rodeoers with both African American and Native American ancestors found out in the 1970s, being a black cowboy often meant you could not also be a Native cowboy, let alone just a "cowboy." The violent separation of communities that occurred in the late nineteenth century was often reflected in the continued expansion of niche rodeo circuits that served disparate communities. As the twenty-first century approached, however, more and more people strove to heal these breeches and re-expand rodeo membership. Organizations like the Cowboys of Color and the Professional Bull Riders (PBR) have reinvigorated racially diverse fan bases, drawing international participants and spectators.

These circuits, however, continue to ground acceptance in bodily suffering. The desire to see cowboys thrown continues to be present in all forms of rodeo. While few people would claim to want to see someone seriously injured, bad wrecks are almost as entertaining as a good ride. In fact, sound managers often play humorous sound effects or clips from songs that get the crowd laughing at a tossed cowboy. On PBR tours, animals are at times cheered more aggressively than cowboys and, according to interviews from PBR representatives, bull merchandise often outsells cowboy merchandise.[2] As the international rodeo community slowly begins to grapple with the meaning of brain injuries and chronic traumatic encephalopathy (CTE), athletes and audiences will be forced to ask what price people are willing to pay to continue to stage this form of spectacle.

As marginalized communities have continued to pursue rodeo, they have helped rodeo adapt to changing pressures. Entering its third century, rodeo's construction of multiple wests, especially global wests, continues today. The Cowboy of Color circuit often reiterates its commitment to racial inclusiveness, something mainstream organizations like PBR are increasingly committed to as well. Staging global tours and boasting major international viewership, the PBR circuit strains the correlation of rodeo with the United States as a nation. The linguistic, religious, and racial diversity of PBR contests demonstrate how American-style rodeo, which has always been staged internationally, is truly transnational. Just as Buffalo Bill staged riding competitions between numerous horse-based cultures at the end of the nineteenth century, so champions from Brazil and Australia reenact their own countries' herding pasts. These global performances therefore reinvest not only in an American narrative of conquest, but in global settler-colonial narratives rooted in the worldwide expansion of ranching industries and herding cultures during the eighteenth and nineteenth centuries. As rodeo has adapted to new realities, it has become in some venues part local carnival and part global sport, offering new points of contact between the rural and the urban, the local and the global, and the real and the imagined. Negotiated between an audience, an athlete, and an organizer, rodeos continue to allow the multifaceted complexity of western identities to be fully performed on a variety of stages.

While each of these individual rodeo histories provides a piece of the puzzle in understanding popular performance as a tool with which issues of authenticity, humiliation, and violence have been negotiated, told in conjunction with each other, these stories provide a larger image of the fluidity of western identity, how real people lived out shifting cultural ideals, and who continues to have unrestricted access to cowboy performance. Popular fiction and film of the twentieth century helped drive the emergence of the white, male, heterosexual cowboy image that grew to prominence in the mid-twentieth century. *Outriders*, however, shows that diverse groups of people participated not only in the increasingly mythic activity of rodeo, but also in the claiming of western identity. Through their bodily performances of the West they struggled to assert their place in America. By acknowledging the history of people's ability to write region onto their bodies and into their lives, *Outriders* upends a straightforward narrative of oppression or resistance of marginalized people in the American West. Outriders in rodeo demonstrate the radical possibilities and persistent limitations of repurposing a contested national icon like the cowboy.

NOTES

INTRODUCTION: RODEO AND THE OUTRIDERS OF HISTORY

1 Key works in these fields particularly grapple with the meaning of performance in the expansion of empire and settler colonialism. See for instance Philip Deloria, *Playing Indian* (New Haven: Yale University Press, 1998) and *Indians in Unexpected Places* (Lawrence: University Press of Kansas, 2004); Adria Imada, *Aloha America: Hula Circuits through the US Empire* (Durham: Duke University Press, 2012); Karen R. Jones, *Epiphany in the Wilderness: Hunting, Nature, and Performance in the Nineteenth Century American West* (Boulder: University of Colorado Press, 2015).

2 "Paniolo Joe" Rodriguez, interview with Rebecca Scofield, Gay Rodeo Oral History Project, September 10, 2016, Duncans Mills, Calfornia.

3 In the past thirty years, scholars have pushed our understanding of epistemologies to incorporate bodily ways of understanding, particularly with regard to race and gender. See Sandra Harding, *Whose Science? Whose Knowledge: Thinking from Women's Lives* (Ithaca: Cornell University Press, 1991); Linda Alcoff and Elizabeth Potter, eds., *Feminist Epistemologies* (New York: Routledge, 1993); Susan Wendell, *The Rejected Body: Feminist Philosophical Reflections on Disability* (New York: Routledge, 1996); Kathy Davis, ed., *Embodied Practices: Feminist Perspectives on the Body* (London: Sage, 1997); Patricia Hill Collins, *Black Feminist Thought: Knowledge, Consciousness, and the Politics of Empowerment* (New York: Routledge, 2000); Linda Alcoff, *Visible Identities: Race, Gender and the Self* (New York: Oxford University Press, 2006); Shannon Sullivan and Nancy Tuana, eds., *Race and Epistemologies of Ignorance* (New York: State University of New York, 2007); Miranda Fricker, *Epistemic Injustice: Power and the Ethics of Knowing* (New York: Oxford University Press, 2009); Daniel Wildcat, *Red Alert! Saving the Planet with Indigenous Knowledge* (Golden, CO: Fulcrum, 2009); Stacy Alaimo, *Bodily Natures: Science, Environment, and the Material Self* (Bloomington: Indiana University Press, 2010);

Alexis Shotwell *Knowing Otherwise: Race, Gender, and Implicit Understanding* (University Park: Pennsylvania State University Press, 2011); José Medina, *The Epistemology of Resistance: Gender and Racial Oppression, Epistemic Injustice, and Resistant Imaginations* (New York: Oxford University Press, 2012); George Yancy, *Reframing the Practice of Philosophy: Bodies of Color, Bodies of Knowledge* (New York: State University of New York Press, 2012).

For works explicitly on embodiment see bell hooks, "Performance Practice as a Site of Opposition," in *Let's Go Get It On: The Politics of Black Performance*, ed. Catherine Ugwu (New York: Bay Press, 1995), 210–21; George Lakoff and Mark Johnson, *Philosophy in the Flesh: The Embodied Mind and Its Challenge to Western Thought* (New York: Basic Books, 1999); Karen Barbour, *Dancing across the Page: Narrative and Embodied ways of Knowing* (Bristol, UK: Intellect Books, 2011); Jeff Friedman, "Muscle Memory: Performing Embodied Knowledge," in *Art and the Performance of Memory: Soul and Gestures of Recollections,* ed. Richard Candida Smith (London: Routledge, 2011), 156–80; James Jacobson-Maisels, "Embodied Epistemology: Knowing through the Body in Late Hasidism," *Journal of Religion* 96, no. 2 (April 2016): 185–211.

4 Kathy Davis details the debates about poststructuralism, feminism, and the body in "Reclaiming Women's Bodies: Colonialist Trope or Critical Epistemology?" *Sociological Review* 55 (2007): 50–64. Specifically she examines Donna Haraway's "The Virtual Speculum in the New World Order," in *Revisioning Women, Health, and Healing,* ed. Adele E. Clarke and Virginia L. Olesen (New York: Routledge, 1999), 49–96, as it critiqued gendered and racialized discourses about bodily exploration but also potentially dismissed or ignored the bodily experiences of women of color.

5 Nicole Fleetwood, *Troubling Vision: Performance, Visuality, and Blackness* (Chicago: University of Chicago, 2011), 2.

6 See Richard Slatta, *Cowboys of the Americas* (New Haven: Yale University Press, 1990); Paul Starr, *Let the Cowboy Ride: Cattle Ranching in the American West* (Baltimore: Johns Hopkins University Press, 1998); Simon Evans, Sarah Carter, and Bill Yeo, *Cowboys, Ranchers, and the Cattle Business* (Calgary: University of Calgary Press, 2000). For the ways these cultures influenced rodeo see Mary Lou LeCompte, "The Hispanic Influence on the History of Rodeo, 1823–1922," *Journal of Sport History* 12, no. 1 (Spring 1985): 21–38.

7 Jacqueline Moore, *Cow Boys and Cattle Men: Class and Masculinities on the Texas Frontier, 1865-1900* (New York: New York University Press, 2010); Dee Garceau, "Nomads, Bunkies, and Family Men: Cowboy Identity and the Gendering of Ranch Work," in *Across the Great Divide: Cultures of Manhood in the American West*, ed. Matthew Basso, Laura McCall, and Dee Garceau (New York: Routledge, 2001), 149–69.

8 See L. Logan, "The Geographical Imagination of Frederick Remington: The Invention of the Cowboy West," *Journal of Geography* 18, no. 1 (1992): 75–90; Thomas Lyon, "The Literary West," in *Oxford History of the American West*, ed. Clyde Milner, Carol O'Connor, and Martha Sandweiss (New York: Oxford University Press, 1994), 707–43; Anne Butler, "Selling the Popular Myth," in *Oxford History of the American West*, ed. Clyde Milner, Carol O'Connor, and Martha Sandweiss (New York: Oxford University Press, 1994), 771–802.

9 Richard White's "Frederick Jackson Turner and Buffalo Bill," in *The Frontier in American Culture,* ed. James Grossman (Berkeley: University of California Press, 1994), describes the simultaneous creation of the frontier myth in both popular culture and academia by Buffalo Bill, who imagined a violent west, and Frederick Jackson Turner, who imagined a peaceful, agrarian west. Also see Richard Slotkin's foundational works, *Regeneration through Violence: The Mythology of the American Frontier, 1600–1860* (Norman: University of Oklahoma Press, 1973) and *The Fatal Environment: The Myth of the Frontier in the Age of Industrialization, 1800–1890* (Norman: University of Oklahoma Press, 1985).

10 Michael Allen, *Rodeo Cowboys in the North American Imagination* (Reno: University of Nevada, 1998), 28.

11 Tracey Owens Patton and Sally Schedlock, *Gender, Whiteness, and Power in Rodeo: Breaking Away from the Ties of Sexism and Racism* (New York: Lexington Press, 2011); Cecil Johnson, *Guts: Legendary Black Rodeo Cowboy Bill Pickett* (Fort Worth: Summit Group, 1994); Ricardo Palacios, *Tío Cowboy: Juan Salinas, Rodeo Roper and Horseman* (College Station: Texas A&M University Press, 2007); Allison Fuss Mellis, *Riding Buffalos and Broncos: Rodeo and Native Traditions in the Northern Great Plains* (Norman: University of Oklahoma Press, 2003); Jan Penrose, "When All the Cowboys Are Indians: The Nature of Race in All-Indian Rodeo," *Annals of the Association of American Geographers* 93, no. 3 (September 2003): 687–705; Hugh Dempsey, *Tom Three Persons: Legend of an Indian Cowboy* (Vancouver, BC: Purich Books, 1997); Peter Iverson, *Riders of the West: Portraits from Indian Rodeo* (Seattle: University of Washington Press, 1999).

12 "Attendance at Rodeo Passes 100,000 Mark," *Chicago Daily Tribune*, October 26, 1936.

13 "600,000 Saw Rodeo: Set Crowd Record," *New York Times*, November 1, 1943.

14 Autry's role in the changing image of the cowboy, especially in terms of gender, has been discussed by many rodeo scholars, including Owens Patton and Schedlock, *Gender, Whiteness, and Power,* and Mary Lou LeCompte, *Cowgirls of the Rodeo* (Chicago: University of Illinois Press, 1993), 126–33.

15 Stanely Corkin, "Cowboys and Free Markets: Post–World War II Westerns and U.S. Hegemony," *Cinema Journal* 39, no. 3 (2000): 66–91; Russell Meeuf, *John*

Wayne's World: Transnational Masculinity in the Fifties (Austin: University of Texas Press, 2013).

16 Allen, *Rodeo Cowboys*, 49.

17 See D. K. Gauthier and C. J. Forsyth, "Buckle Bunnies: Groupies of the Rodeo Circuit," *Deviant Behavior* 21 (2000): 349–65.

18 Allen, *Rodeo Cowboys*, 31.

19 Neil Smith, *The New Urban Frontier: Gentrification and the Revanchist City* (New York: Routledge, 1996); Meeuf, *John Wayne's World*; Rebecca Scofield, "'Chaps and Scowls': Play, Violence, and the Post-1970s Urban Cowboy." *Journal of American Culture* 40, no. 4 (December 2017): 325–40.

20 I would argue that those taking the drag position were marginalized people who have continued to participate in mainstream events instead of joining fringe associations, literally staying within the cattle drive, prodding along stragglers, and eating dust for their efforts. Drags often had to be the most talented cowboys because they needed to do both roping and doctoring, yet they had the worst jobs.

21 Patricia Nelson Limerick, "The Adventures of the Frontier in the Twentieth Century," in *The Frontier in American Culture*, ed. James Grossman (Berkeley: University of California Press, 1994); Richard White, *"It's All Your Misfortune and None of My Own"* (Norman: University of Oklahoma Press, 1991). See also Rebecca Solnit's essay on the simulacral West, "The Postmodern Old West," in *Storming the Gates of Paradise: Landscapes for Politics* (Berkeley: University of California Press, 2007), 22–40.

The historiography on the development of the frontier myth is extensive. The search for America's defining mythology first gained prominence with American Studies scholars, particularly Henry Nash Smith's *Virgin Land: The American West as Symbol and Myth* (Cambridge: Harvard University Press, 1950) and Leo Marx's *The Machine in the Garden: Technology and the Pastoral Ideal in America* (New York: Oxford University Press, 1964); both of these works draw on "high" culture and emphasize a vision of peaceful settlement of the continent. Richard Slotkin's *Gunfighter Nation: The Myth of the Frontier in Twentieth-Century America* (Norman: University of Oklahoma Press, 1992) continues to stand as the authoritative text on the myth of the frontier in the twentieth-century United States, especially western films. Slotkin maintains that savage warfare became a crucial metaphor in popular culture for America's place on the world stage in the age of imperialism and the Cold War. Also see Robert Athearn's *The Mythic West in Twentieth-Century America* (Lawrence: University Press of Kansas, 1986) and Blake Allmendinger's *The Cowboy: Representations of Labor in an American Work Culture* (New York: Oxford University Press, 1992). Will Wright in *The Wild West: The Mythical Cowboy and Social Theory* (London: Sage, 2001) and Louis Warren in "Cody's Last Stand: Masculine Anxiety, the Custer Myth, and the Frontier of Domesticity in Buffalo Bill's Wild West," *Western Historical Quarterly* 34, no.1 (Spring 2003): 49–69, also look at the social importance of narrating a mythological past. For other works on the popular portrayal of the West see Christine Bold, *Selling the Wild West: Popular Western Fiction, 1860–1960* (Bloomington: Indiana University Press, 1987); Marilyn Burgess, *Indian Princesses and Cowgirls: Stereotypes of the Frontier* (Montreal: Oboro, 1995); Peter Rollins and John O'Connor, eds., *Hollywood's Indian: The Portrayal of the Native American in Film* (Lexington: University Press of Kentucky, 1998); Peter Rollins and and John O'Connor, eds., *Hollywood's West: The American Frontier in Film, Television, and History* (Lexington: University Press of Kentucky, 2005). For a discussion of the racialized aspects of these performances, especially regarding Native American participants in Wild West shows, see L. G. Moses, *Wild West Shows and the Images of American Indians, 1883–1933* (Albuquerque: University of New Mexico Press, 1996). See also Lisa Penaloza's work on the marketing techniques used to sell the western myth: "The Commodification of the American West: Marketers' Production of Cultural Meanings at the Trade Show," *Journal of Marketing* 64, no. 4 (October 2000): 82–109, and "Consuming the American West: Animating Cultural Meaning and Memory at a Stock Show and Rodeo," *Journal of Consumer Research* 28, no. 3 (December 2001): 369–98. For the authoritative text on the shifting meaning of Wild West shows in the United States and Europe from 1860 to 1915, see Louis Warren's *Buffalo Bill's America: William Cody and the Wild West Show* (New York: Alfred A. Knopf, 2005). For an examination of how "frontier heritage" still impacts performance and tourism today, see Daniel Maher, *Mythic Frontiers: Remembering, Forgetting, and Profiting with Cultural Heritage Tourism* (Gainesville: University Press of Florida, 2016).

22 See Jones, *Epiphany in the Wilderness*, for the performative nature of hunting in the nineteenth-century American West. Also see Terence Young, *Heading Out: A History of American Camping* (Ithaca: Cornell University Press, 2017).

23 Warren, *Buffalo Bill's America*, xiii, xiv.

24 Frederick Jackson Turner, "The Significance of the Frontier in American History" (1893, repr. Eastford, CT: Martino Fine Books, 2014).

25 "Goree's All-Girl String Band," *Echo*, September 1940, 8.

26 Sally Friedman, "At South Jersey Rodeo, Cowboy Lives On," *New York Times*, August 8, 1993, 6.

27 The simultaneous feeling of being under siege and extremely popular has persistently characterized cowboy culture. See for instance Dirk Johnson, "Big Denver Cattle Show Reflects Sunset on West," *New York Times*, January 4, 1992, A16.

28 Authenticity has always haunted western cultural history. As Lee Clark Mitchell wrote, "The Western has so little to do with an actual West that it might better be thought of as its own epitaph, written by an exuberant East encroaching on possibilities already foreclosed because represented in terms of a West that 'no longer exists,' never did, never could." Mitchell, *Westerns: Making the Man in Fiction and Film* (Chicago: University of Chicago Press, 1996), 6.

29 Literary scholars William Handley and Nathaniel Lewis have argued, "As laden with meaning as it is difficult to define, authenticity is, like the American West itself, a hotly contested and widely deployable concept in American culture." See their introduction to *True West: Authenticity and the American West*, ed. William Handley and Nathaniel Lewis (Lincoln: University of Nebraska Press, 2004), 5.

30 Bonnie Christensen, *Red Lodge and the Mythic West* (Lawrence: University Press of Kansas, 2002), xvii, also see 101–2. Christensen explores the town of Red Lodge's creation of western authenticity as it catered to a mythic cowboy image with wooden building facades, annual rodeos, and dude ranches in order to draw in tourism over the twentieth century. This emphasis on a largely fictionalized pastoral ranching past at times obscured its immigrant, industrial mining past. As Christensen explains, flesh-and-blood cowboys, often Native, working class, or female, were systematically excluded in favor of white, masculine—and often movie—cowboys.

31 "The Dang Dude," *Echo*, March 1934, 3.

32 Some key works on the performance and nation outside of the US West include Paul Bouissac, *Circus and Culture: A Semiotic Approach* (Bloomington: Indiana University Press, 1976); Robert A. Orsi, *The Madonna of 115th Street: Faith and Community in Italian Harlem, 1880–1950* (New Haven: Yale University Press, 1985); Eric Lott, *Love and Theft: Blackface Minstrelsy and the American Working Class* (New York: Oxford University Press, 1993); Susan Anita Glenn, *Female Spectacle: The Theatrical Roots of Modern Feminism* (Cambridge: Harvard University Press, 2000); Kim Marra, *Strange Duets: Impresarios and Actresses in the American Theatre, 1865–1914* (Iowa City: University of Iowa Press, 2006); David Roman, *Performance in America: Contemporary US Culture and the Performing Arts* (Durham: Duke University Press, 2005); Jayna Brown, *Babylon Girls: Black Women Performers and the Shaping of the Modern* (Durham: Duke University Press, 2008); Robin Bernstein, *Racial Innocence: Performing American Childhood from Slavery to Civil Rights* (New York: New York University Press, 2011); Rebecca Schneider, *Performing Remains: Art and War in Times of Theatrical Reenactment* (New York: Routledge, 2011). For the development of performance studies see Diana Taylor's *The Archive and the Repertoire: Performing Cultural Memory in the Americas* (Durham: Duke University Press, 2003) and *Performance* (Durham: Duke University Press, 2016).

33 Classic New Western History includes Patricia Nell Limerick, *Legacy of Conquest: The Unbroken Past of the American West* (New York: Norton, 1987); White, *"It's All Your Misfortune and None of My Own"*; and Clyde Milner, ed., *A New Significance: Re-envisioning the History of the American West* (New York: Oxford University Press, 1996).

34 Dan Moos, *Outside America: Race, Ethnicity, and the Role of the American West in National Belonging* (Lebanon, NH: Dartmouth College Press, 2005), 11, 77. See also Sarah Deutsch, "Being American in Boley, Oklahoma," in *Beyond Black and White: Race, Ethnicity, and Gender in the U.S. South and Southwest*, ed. Stephanie Cole and Alison Parker (College Station: Texas A&M University Press, 2004), 99.

35 For histories of mainstream rodeo see Clifford Westermeier, *Man, Beast, Dust: The Story of Rodeo* (Kolkata, India: World Press, 1947); Kristine Fredrikson, *American Rodeo: From Buffalo Bill to Big Business* (College Station: Texas A&M University Press, 1985); Wayne Wooden and Gavin Ehringer, *Rodeo in America: Wranglers, Roughstock, and Paydirt* (Lincoln: University Press of Kansas, 1996); Demetrius W. Pearson and C. Allen Haney, "The Rodeo Cowboy as an American Icon: The Perceived Social and Cultural Significance," *Journal of American Culture* 22, no. 4 (Winter 1999): 17–21; and Joel Bernstein, *Wild Ride: The History and Lore of Rodeo* (Layton, UT: Gibbs Smith, 2007). Biographies such as Kim Turnbaugh's *The Last of the Wild West Cowgirls* (Nederland, CO: Perigo Press, 2009) also attempt to separate fact from fiction.

36 Gail Bederman describes Michel Foucault's foundational concept of discourse analysis in her introduction to *Manliness and Civilization: A Cultural History of Gender and Race in the United States, 1880-1917* (Chicago: University of Chicago Press, 1995), 24.

37 Foundational studies of cultural appropriation include Lott's *Love and Theft* and E. Patrick Johnson's *Appropriating Blackness: Performance and the Politics of Authenticity* (Durham: Duke University Press, 2003).

38 In particular, borderlands history, which argues that the West was a region of overlap and negotiation instead of neat and orderly frontier expansion, has allowed richer and more nuanced historical understandings of individual communities. See Gloria Anzaldúa, *Borderlands/La Frontera: The New Mestiza* (San Franscico: Aunt Lute, 1987); Richard White, *The Middle Ground: Indians, Empires, and Republics in the Great Lakes Region, 1650-1815* (Cambridge: Cambridge University Press, 1991); Susan Lee Johnson, *Roaring Camp: The Social World of the California Gold Rush* (New York: Norton, 2000); Nayan Shah, *Contagious Divides: Epidemics and Race in San Francisco's Chinatown* (Berkeley: University of California Press, 2001); Andrés Reséndez, *Changing National Identities at the Frontier: Texas and New Mexico, 1800-1850*

(Cambridge: Cambridge University Press, 2004); *Mae Ngai, Impossible Subjects: Illegal Aliens and the Making of Modern America* (Princeton: Princeton University Press, 2004); Juliana Barr, *Peace Came in the Form of a Woman: Indians and Spaniards in the Texas Borderlands* (Chapel Hill: University of North Carolina Press, 2007); Claudia Sadowski-Smith, *Border Fictions: Globalization, Empire, and Writing at the Boundaries of the United States* (Charlottesville: University of Virginia Press, 2008); Pekka Hamalainen, *The Comanche Empire* (New Haven: Yale University Press, 2009); Anthony Mora, *Border Dilemmas: Racial and National Uncertainties in New Mexico, 1848-1912* (Durham: Duke University Press, 2011); Rachel St. John, *Line in the Sand: A History of the Western U.S.-Mexico Border* (Princeton: Princeton University Press, 2011); Elliot Young, *Alien Nation: Chinese Migration in the Americas from the Coolie Era through World War II* (Chapel Hill: University of North Carolina Press, 2014); William Kiser, *Borderlands of Slavery: The Struggle over Captivity and Peonage in the American Southwest* (Philadelphia: University of Pennsylvania Press, 2017); Andrew Torget, *Seeds of Empire: Cotton, Slavery, and the Transformation of the Texas Borderlands, 1800-1850* (Chapel Hill: University of North Carolina Press, 2018).

39 Susan Gray and Gayle Gullett, eds., *Contingent Maps: Rethinking Western Women's History and the North American West* (Tucson: University of Arizona Press, 2014). Gray and Gullett are particularly critical about the role women's historians have played in keeping alive a Turnerian vision of exceptionalism, even within newer borderland perspectives, and the persistent isolation between western history and ethnic studies as disciplines. Classic works on women in the West include Elizabeth Jameson and Susan Armitage, *The Women's West* (Norman: University of Oklahoma Press, 1987); Mary Ann Irwin and James Brooks, eds., *Women and Gender in the American West* (Albuquerque: University of New Mexico Press, 2004); Laura Woodworth-Ney, *Women in the American West* (Santa Barbara: ABC-CLIO, 2008); Virginia Scharff and Carolyn Bucken, *Home Lands: How Women Made the West* (Berkeley: University of California Press, 2010).

40 José Esteban Muñoz, *Disidentifications: Queers of Color and the Performance of Politics* (Minneapolis: University of Minnesota Press, 1999), 11–12.

41 Muñoz, *Disidentifications*, 30.

42 Butler, "Selling the Popular Myth," 784. For Native use of "western" symbols see Donald Fixico, "From Indians to Cowboys: The Country Western Trend," *American Indian Identity: Today's Changing Perspectives*, ed. Clifford Trafzer (Sacramento: Sierra Oaks, 1985).

43 Sylvia Gann Mahoney, *College Rodeo: From Show to Sport* (College Station: Texas A&M University Press, 2004).

44 "Turnstile Tracker," *Sports Business Daily*, December 6, 2001, October 30, 2002, December 11, 2003, December 22, 2004; *2012 PRCA Media Guide* (Colorado Springs: PRCA, 2012); "Morning Buzz," *Sports Business Daily*, February 22, 2013.

45 See Fredrikson, *American Rodeo*.

46 See her letters to Freda Ashby in the Vera McGinnis Farra file, National Cowgirl Museum and Hall of Fame, Fort Worth, Texas. Also see Vera McGinnis, *Rodeo Road: My Life as a Pioneer* Cowgirl (New York: Hastings House, 1974), 182–86.

47 Renee Laegreid, "Finding the American West in Twenty-First-Century Italy," *Western Historical Quarterly* 45 (Winter 2014): 411–29. Also see Ruth Ellen Gruber, "The View from Europe: You Don't Have to Be American to Dream in Cowboy and Indian," *Convergence: Autry National Center Magazine* (Spring/Summer 2005), 30–34, and "Strum and Twang: Country-Western Music, Bluegrass and 'Wild Western Spaces' in Europe" (paper presented at the Autry National Center, September 2007); Sarah Sarzynski, "The Popular, the Political and the Ugly: Brazilian *Nordesterns* in a Comparative Cold War Context, 1960–1976," in *Rethinking Third Cinema: The Role of Anti-Colonial Media and Aesthetics in Postmodernity*, ed. Frieda Ekotto and Adeline Koh (Berlin: LIT-Verlag, 2009); Frank Christianson, ed., *The Popular Frontier: Buffalo Bill's Wild West and Transnational Mass Culture* (Norman: University of Oklahoma Press, 2017); Emily Burns, *Transnational Frontiers: The American West in France* (Norman: University of Oklahoma Press, 2018). Also see examples of Hebrew-language western pulp fiction in the IsraPulp Collection at Arizona State University, created by Rachel Leket-Mor in 2004.

48 "Questionnaire," MSA.26, box 4, questionnaires, 1990, International Gay Rodeo Association Institutional Archives, 1982–2009, Autry National Center, Los Angeles.

49 See Gauthier and Forsyth, "Buckle Bunnies," 349–65, and Craig J. Forsyth and Carol Y. Thompson, "Helpmates of the Rodeo: Fans, Wives, and Groupies," *Journal of Sport and Social Issues* 31, no. 4 (November 2007): 394–416.

50 Fredrikson, *American Rodeo*.

51 Rodriguez, Gay Rodeo Oral History Project.

52 Peter Applebome, "Last Roundup Feared at Texas Prison Rodeo," *New York Times*, March 19, 1987.

53 Susan Nance, "Outlaw Horses and the True Spirit of Calgary in the Automobile Age," in *Calgary: City of Animals*, ed. Jim Ellis (Calgary: University of Calgary Press, 2017), 15. Also see "A Star Is Born to Buck: Animal Celebrity and the Marketing of Professional Rodeo," in *Sport, Animals and Society*, ed. Michelle Gilbert and James Gillett (New York: Routledge, 2013), 173–91.

54 Mark A. Brandenburg, Dale J. Butterwick, Laurie A. Hiemstra, Robert Nebergall, and Justin Laird, "Comparison of Injury Rates in Organised Sports,

with Special Emphasis on American Bull Riding," *International SportMed Journal* 8, no. 2 (2007): 78–86.

55   D. S. Ross, A. Ferguson, P. Bosha, and K. Cassas, "Factors That Prevent Roughstock Rodeo Athletes from Wearing Protective Equipment," *Current Sports Medicine Report* 9, no. 6 (November–December 2010): 342–46. For more information on injuries see Dale J. Butterwick, Brent Hagel, Dexter S. Nelson Mark R. LeFave, and Willem H. Meeuwisse, "Epidemiologic Analysis of Injury in Five Years of Canadian Professional Rodeo," *American Journal of Sports Medicine* 30, no. 2 (March 2002): 193–98; Renée Crichlow, Steve Williamson, Mike Geurin, and Heather Heggem, "Self-Reported Injury Rate in Native American Professional Rodeo Competitors," *Clinical Journal of Sport Medicine* 16, no. 4 (July 2006): 352–54; D. J. Downey, "Rodeo Injuries and Prevention," *Current Sports Medicine Report* 6, no. 6 (October 2007): 328–32; M. C. Meyers and C. M. Laurent Jr. "The Rodeo Athlete: Sport Science, Part I," *Sports Medicine* 40, no. 1 (May 1, 2010): 417–31; M. C. Meyers and C. M. Laurent Jr., "The Rodeo Athlete: Injuries, Part II," *Sports Medicine* 40, no. 10 (October 1, 2010): 817–39.

56   Fredrick Errington examines different modes of masculine presentation between the wild, often younger, men willing to endanger themselves in rodeo, and the often older patriarchs who help organize local rodeos but deem them too risky for family men. See "The Rock Creek Rodeo: Excess and Constraint in Men's Lives," *American Ethnologist* 17, no. 4 (November 1990): 628–45.

57   Centers for Disease Control and Prevention, "Bull-Riding Related Brain and Spinal Cord Injuries—Louisiana, 1994–1995," *Morbidity and Mortality Weekly Report* 45, no. 37 (September 20, 1996): 796–98.

58   See Skip Myslenski, "Cowboy Had a Perfect Ride . . . Until It Ended in Death," *Chicago Tribune*, August 6, 1989. Also see "Rodeo Star Dies: Throng Mourns," *New York Times*, December 23, 1994. At times these deaths occur off the circuit, for instance, Gene Larson's death at a honky-tonk bull-riding exhibition in Texas; "Rider Thrown by Bull Dies of His Injuries," *New York Times*, May 23, 1997. Collegiate and amateur rodeos experience rider deaths as well, though these numbers are not well tracked. "Boy Trampled by Bull in Longmont Dies," *Denver Post*, June 29, 2009. In 2019, PBR rider Mason Lowe died with little media attention. "Bull Rider Mason Lowe, No. 18 in the World, Dies after Bull Steps on His Chest at PBR Event," *USA Today*, January 19, 2019. These deaths do not deter people from joining rodeo, as one rodeoer once told me: "The best way to create a hundred new bull riders is to kill one." There are, of course, also animal deaths yearly in rodeo, which are also rarely tracked or publicized.

59   Justin Sports Medicine Team, "27 Years of Statistics," *Justin Sports Medicine*. Retired sports medicine doctor Don Andrews, who led much of this research,

has spoken to the press extensively about the prevalence of brain injuries, particularly in bull riding. www.justinsportsmedicine.com/2011–2014-injury -study/.

60   "Bull Riders Struggle to Combat Concussions," *New York Times*, May 23, 2015.

61   Charlie Gillis, "Rodeo's NFL Moment," *Maclean's*, February 13, 2017; "B.C. Rodeo Star Ty Pozzobon Had CTE Brain Condition When He Died," *Global News*, October 11, 2017.

62   The centrality of violence to the history of what would become the American West is detailed in foundational works like Limerick's *Legacy of Conquest*; Karl Jacoby, *Shadows at Dawn: A Borderlands Massacre and the Violence of History* (New York: Penguin Press, 2008); Ned Blackhawk, *Violence over the Land: Indians and Empires in the Early American West* (Cambridge: Harvard University Press, 2006). Also, see Cynthia Skove Nevels, *Lynching to Belong: Claiming Whiteness through Racial Violence* (College Station: Texas A&M University Press, 2007), as a work that focuses on violence as the performance of belonging. For how rodeo sits within this violent past see Elizabeth Atwood Lawrence, *Rodeo: An Anthropologist Looks at the Wild and the Tame* (Knoxville: University of Tennessee Press, 1982); Beverly June Smith Stoeltje, "Rodeo as Symbolic Performance" (PhD diss., University of Texas at Austin, 1980).

1. COIFFEUSE TO COWGIRL: PIONEERING AND THE PERFORMANCE OF WESTERN WOMANHOOD

1   "The Champion Lady Broncho Buster: Mrs. William Slate of South Lyme," *Hartford Courant*, August 23, 1925, D2.

2   "The Champion Rough-Rider Who Never Saw a Ranch," *World*, September 3, 1916, National Cowgirl Museum and Hall of Fame, Fort Worth, Texas. Hereafter NCHF.

3   Jennifer Henneman, "Her Representation Precedes Her: Transatlantic Celebrity, Portraiture, and Visual Culture, 1865–1890" (PhD diss., University of Washington, 2016). Also see Henneman's "Annie Oakley and the Rise of Natural Womanhood in England," in *The Popular Frontier: Buffalo Bill's Wild West and Transnational Mass Culture*, ed. Frank Christianson (Norman: University of Oklahoma Press, 2017), 110–28.

4   See Joyce Gibson Roach's "Introduction: Cowgirls and Cattle Queens," in *The Cowgirls* (Denton: University of North Texas Press, 1977), 10–11.

5   Elizabeth Ludley, "Riding Man Fashion," *Oregonian*, morning edition, September 7, 1872, 4. In the 1890s, riding costumes were redesigned to allow for split skirts so women could ride astride—this was met with some shock in the

West. See "Ladies to Ride Horses Astride: Equestrian Dress Reform—Description of the New Garments," *Oregonian*, morning edition, March 18, 1890, 4.

6   Jacqueline Moore, *Cow Boys and Cattle Men: Class and Masculinities on the Texas Frontier, 1865–1900* (New York: New York University Press, 2010); Dee Garceau, "Nomads, Bunkies, and Family Men: Cowboy Identity and the Gendering of Ranch Work," in *Across the Great Divide: Cultures of Manhood in the American West*, ed. Matthew Basso, Laura McCall, and Dee Garceau (New York: Routledge, 2001), 149–69.

7   Gibson Roach repeats the popular story that Theodore Roosevelt used the term "cowgirl" first. *Cowgirls*, 84.

8   Henneman, "Her Representation," 3. Henneman notes that previous authors have cited usages as early as 1891. See Gibson Roach, *Cowgirls*, 90; Mary Lou LeCompte, *Cowgirls of the Rodeo: Pioneer Professional Athletes* (Chicago: University of Illinois Press, 1993), 36; Glenda Riley, "Annie Oakley: The Peerless Lady Wing Shot," in Glenda Riley and Richard W. Etulain, eds., *By Grit and Grace: Eleven Women Who Shaped the American West* (Golden, CO: Fulcrum, 1997), 104.

9   See the National Cowgirl Museum and Hall of Fame at www.cowgirl.net.

10   The complex gender performances of rodeo cowgirls demonstrated a form of female masculinity used by both rodeo cowgirls themselves and a larger public in service to an idealized domesticity. Jack Halberstam has argued, "By reading [female masculinity] as proto-lesbianism awaiting a coming community, we continue to hold female masculinity apart from the making of modern masculinity itself." *Female Masculinity* (Durham: Duke University Press, 1998), 46.

11   Buffalo Bill program, 1917, box 1, Wild West Show Collection (bMS Thr 586), Harvard Theatre Collection, Harvard Library, Harvard University, Cambridge, Massachusetts. Hereafter Harvard Theatre Collection.

12   See Renee Laegreid, *Riding Pretty: Rodeo Royalty in the American West* (Lincoln: University of Nebraska Press, 2006), and LeCompte, *Cowgirls of the Rodeo*.

13   As Gail Bederman has demonstrated in *Manliness and Civilization: A Cultural History of Gender and Race in the United States, 1880–1917* (Chicago: University of Chicago Press, 1995), gender and race worked in tandem in this period as white men were supposedly weakened through over-civilization. Masculine pursuits were thought to return white, Anglo-Saxon American men to their rightful places as the master race.

14   Gabriel Rosenberg, *4-H Harvest: Sexuality and the State in Rural America* (Philadelphia: University of Pennsylvania Press, 2016), 26–28. While Rosenberg notes that groups like 4-H created "agrarian futurism," with science as the way to reinvigorate rural places, cowgirls usually fit more solidly into a performance of a nostalgic past that was decidedly unscientific. These progress narratives were present in western narratives like Buffalo Bill's Wild West.

See Louis Warren, *Buffalo Bill's America: William Cody and the Wild West Show* (New York: Alfred A. Knopf, 2005), 256–81.

15 "101 Ranch Wild West to Appear Here This Month: Tillie Baldwin, Oklahoma Rough Rider, Will Be Feature of Interesting Show," *San Francisco Chronicle*, April 7, 1912, 49. Johnnie Baldwin also listed as a cowboy. "101 Ranch Spends Five Days in Frisco," *Billboard*, May 11, 1912, 63. Also see "Clever Ranch Girls, Real Cowboys and Bedecked Indians with Show," *Oregonian*, morning edition, July 2, 1912, 11.

16 LeCompte, *Cowgirls of the Rodeo*, 41.

17 Gibson Roach, *Cowgirls*, 82–84. Gibson Roach herself dubs her one of the "authentic cowgirls" in the show.

18 In many ways, Baldwin and other immigrant performers were the cultural equivalents of Mae Ngai's "impossible subjects," or people who should not legally exist yet do. See Ngai, *Impossible Subjects: Illegal Aliens and the Making of Modern America* (Princeton: Princeton University Press, 2004).

19 Ola Honningdal Grytten and Arngrim Hunnes, "An Anatomy of Financial Crisis in Norway, 1830–2010," *Financial History Review* 21, no. 1 (April 2014): 39.

20 Ingrid Semmingsen, *Norway to America: A History of the Migration* (Minneapolis: University of Minnesota Press, 1980), 99. Also see Karen Hansen, *Encounter on the Great Plains* (New York: Oxford University Press, 2013), 60–61.

21 *The Idaho Statesmen*, Woman's Edition, special issue, June 29, 1896, 13. Also see Aileen Kraditor, *The Ideas of the Woman Suffrage Movement, 1890–90* (New York: Columbia University Press, 1965); Ann Gordon, "Woman Suffrage (Not Universal Suffrage) by Federal Amendment," in *Votes for Women! The Suffrage Movement in Tennessee, the South, and the Nation*, ed. Marjorie Spruill Wheeler (Knoxville: University of Tennessee Press, 1996); Rosalyn Terborg-Penn, *African American Women in the Struggle for the Vote, 1850–1920* (Bloomington: Indiana University Press, 1998); Louise Newman, *White Women's Rights: The Racial Origins of Feminism in the United* States (New York: Oxford University Press, 1999). As Allison Sneider has shown in *Suffragists in an Imperial Age: U.S. Expansion and the Woman Question, 1870–1929* (New York: Oxford University Press, 2008), expansion, imperialism, immigration, and suffrage constituted overlapping conversations about national belonging and political rights.

22 There is a vast literature on the policing of bodies as immigration restriction tightened; see Matthew Frye Jacobson, *Whiteness of a Different Color: European Immigrants and the Alchemy of Race* (Cambridge: Harvard University Press, 1998), Margot Canaday, *The Straight State: Sexuality and Citizenship in Twentieth-Century America* (Princeton: Princeton University Press, 2009), and Nayan Shah, *Contagious Divides: Epidemics and Race in San Francisco's*

Chinatown (Berkley: University of California Press, 2001), for examples of how this played out in terms of race, gender, and sexuality. Also see Rosenberg's *4-H Harvest* for how rural communities fit into these eugenics debates.

23 Madison Grant, *The Passing of the Great Race: Or, the Racial Basis of European History* (New York: Charles Scribner's Sons, 1916), 210. Concerns over the racial makeup of America influenced the creation of the Dillingham Commission, which would help set immigration quotas in the 1920s.

24 LeCompte, *Cowgirls of the Rodeo*, 40.

25 "Circus Gossip," *Billboard*, August 12, 1911, 26.

26 Little documentation exists on Mrs. Sherry's life, with few photographs or news reports. See Tracey Owens Patton and Sally Schedlock, *Gender, Whiteness, and Power in Rodeo: Breaking Away from the Ties of Sexism and Racism* (New York: Lexington Press, 2011), 155, for a brief discussion of her career. See "Indian Squaws to Enter Races," *Kenosha News*, July 29, 1927, box 2, album 4, Tex Austin Collection, Museum of New Mexico, Fray Angelico Chavez History Library, Santa Fe, New Mexico (hereafter Tex Austin Collection). Women like Lillian Smith, who at times claimed to be part Native American, often used their unclear racial heritage to perform as "Indian Princesses." Smith's alter-ego Princess Wenona was quite popular with the 101 Ranch audiences. See "Princess Wenona and Other Hippodrome Indian Celebrities," *Commercial Tribune*, May 26, 1910, Mamie Francis Hafley file, NCHF; "Clever Ranch Girls, Real Cowboys and Bedecked Indians with Show," 11.

27 Indeed, as Louise Warren dscusses in his chapter "Cowboys, Indians, and the Artful Deceptions of Race," performers often played characters of different races—blurring the lines between white cowboy, Mexican vaquero, and South America gaucho. Pedro Esquivel, for instance, played all of these roles. See Warren, *Buffalo Bill's America*, 400–401.

28 Amy Ware, *The Cherokee Kid: Will Rogers, Tribal Identity, and the Making of an American Icon* (Lawrence: University Press of Kansas, 2015), 3–4.

29 See "Tillie Baldwin Weeps in Grief for Will Rogers: Noted Trick Rider, at Lyme for Show, Mourns First," *Hartford Courant*, August 17, 1935, 3.

30 As Philip Deloria has explained, the antimodern and the modern were two sides of the same coin: "Primitivism and progress defined the dialectic of the modern." Deloria continues: "And they both reflected the intuition that America had experienced a radical break in its history." Philip Deloria, *Playing Indian* (New Haven: Yale University Press, 1998), 100. Also see T. J. Jackson Lears, *No Place of Grace: Antimodernism and the Transformation of American Culture, 1890–1920* (Chicago: University of Chicago Press, 1994), for a discussion of the ways in which antimodernism bolstered the economic and cultural structures of modernism. Svetlana Boym in *The Future of Nostalgia* (New York:

Basic Books, 2001), 22, notes the codependence of "modern ideas of progress and newness and antimodern claims of rediscovery of national community and the stable past," which arose from a modern anxiety about a vanishing past.

31 "The Strenuous Life" (speech to the Hamilton Club, Chicago, Illinois, April 10, 1899), printed in *Theodore Roosevelt: Letters and Speeches,* ed. Louis Auchincloss (New York: Penguin, 2004), 755–66. Bederman, *Manliness and Civilization,* 184–85.

32 "Big Roping Contest" and "Contest for World Supremacy at Mulhall's Show Sunday," unidentified clippings, St. Louis, 1904, transcription from Georgia Mulhall's scrapbook, Lucille Mulhall file, NCHF.

33 Louis Warren notes how the racial frontiers of Eurasia and America were continually paired in late nineteenth-century popular culture, *Buffalo Bill's America,* 332. For analysis of Native Americans' roles in rodeos see Jan Penrose, "When All the Cowboys Are Indians: The Nature of Race in All-Indian Rodeo," *Annals of the Association of American Geographers* 93, no. 3 (September 2003): 687–705; Allison Fuss Mellis, *Riding Buffaloes and Broncos* (Norman: University of Oklahoma Press, 2003); Mary-Ellen Klem, *A Wilder West: Rodeo in Western Canada* (Vancouver: University of British Columbia Press, 2011); and Peter Iverson, *Riders of the West: Portraits from Indian Rodeo* (Seattle: University of Washington Press, 1999).

34 The mythology of the frontier was shaped by both entertainment and academia. See Frederick Jackson Turner, "The Significance of the Frontier in American History" (1893, repr. Eastford, CT: Martino Fine Books, 2014). The significance of Turner's thesis and its influence on the imagined West have been analyzed by western historians in the past several decades. See Richard W. Etulain, "Historians and the Turner Thesis," in *Does the Frontier Make America Exceptional?* (New York: Bedford/St. Martin's, 1999); Richard White, "Frederick Jackson Turner and Buffalo Bill," in *The Frontier in American Culture,* ed. James Grossman (Berkeley: University of California Press, 1994); Richard Slotkin, *Gunfighter Nation;* and Christine Bold, *Selling the Wild West: Popular Western Fiction, 1860-1960* (Bloomington: Indiana University Press, 1987).

35 Theodore Roosevelt, "Women's Rights: And the Duties of Both Men and Women," *Outlook,* February 3, 1912, 262–66.

36 George M. Beard, *American Nervousness: Its Causes and Consequences* (New York: G. P. Putnam's Sons, 1881). Also see Bederman, *Manliness and Civilization,* 85.

37 "Mamie Francis: Girl Who Rides Diving Horse," unidentified clipping, Mamie Francis Hafley file, NCHF.

38 Alice Greenough, "What a Cowgirl Wants from Life," unidentified clipping, Alice Greenough file, NCHF. This would be repeated by rodeo promoters like Tex Austin: "The girl of the west [is] the ideal woman." See "Women Never Fat

on Cow Ranch, Says 'Tex,'" *Chicago News*, May 26, 1925, box 1, album 3, Chicago scrapbook, Tex Austin Collection.

39   "What Do you Think of the American Girl?" *Chicago Tribune*, August 30, 1925, box 1, album 3, Chicago scrapbook, Tex Austin Collection.

40   Janet Owen, "Sports among Women: New London Woman Has Adventurous Career in Wild West Shows," *New York Herald Tribune*, July 19, 1936, C7, and "Champion Lady Broncho Buster."

41   Women's athletics were gaining popularity in the 1910s and 1920s, a trend cowgirls capitalized on; see LeCompte, *Cowgirls of the Rodeo*, 25–27.

42   "Convent Girl the Star of Wild West Show," unidentified clipping, May 15, 1910, Lucille Mulhall file, NCHF. "Beautiful but Brave These Cowgirls Here from the West," *Chicago Daily News*, August 15, 1925, box 1, album 3, Chicago scrapbook, Tex Austin Collection.

43   Lina Beard and Adelia Beard, *Girl Pioneers of America Official Manual* (New York: National Americana Society, 1914), 7.

44   Susan Miller, *Growing Girls: The Natural Origins of Girls' Organizations in America* (New Brunswick: Rutgers University Press, 2007), 9. In 1912, Dr. Luther H. Gulick and his wife Charlotte founded the organization. Gulick, a physician, was an early proponent of physical education for children and both worked to introduce children to the outdoors through summer camps. By the 1920s the organization flourished, with eight thousand camps and 125,000 members worldwide. See Helen Buckler, Mary Fielder, and Martha Allen, *Wo-He-Lo: The Camp Fire History* (New York: Camp Fire Girls, 1980) and the pamphlet *Camp Fire Girls* (New York: Camp Fire Girls, ca. 1922). The moto of Camp Fire Girls was "Wohelo"—meant to sound like a Native American word yet actually a shortening of the English words "Work, Health, Love." "The Law" of the organization included the following: "Seek Beauty; Give Service; Pursue Knowledge; Be Trustworthy; Hold on to Health; Glorify Work; Be Happy." And the "Seven Crafts" that were taught were Home Craft, Health Craft, Camp Craft, Hand Craft, Nature Lore, Business, and Patriotism. Americanizing foreign friends was an explicit goal of Camp Fire Girls by "teaching them American songs, games, customs; by reading American history with them."

45   Cited in Bucker, Fielder, and Allen, *Wo-He-Lo*, 66.

46   Teddy Roosevelt also adamantly encouraged women to undertake their own strenuous life, through childbirth. In a speech before Congress in 1905, he stated, "If the average family in which there are children contained but two children the nation as a whole would decrease in population so rapidly that in two or three generations it would very deservedly be on the point of extinction, so that the people who had acted on this base and selfish doctrine would be giving place to others with braver and more robust ideals. Nor would such a

result be in any way regrettable; for a race that practised such doctrine—that is, a race that practised race suicide—would thereby conclusively show that it was unfit to exist." Theodore Roosevelt, "On American Motherhood," National Congress of Mothers, March 13, 1905, printed in *Population and Development Review* 13, no. 1 (March 1987): 141–47.

47 Quoted in Glenda Riley, *The Life and Legacy of Annie Oakley* (Norman: University of Oklahoma Press, 1994), 113. Also see Warren, *Buffalo Bill's America*, 248.

48 Chris Enss, *Buffalo Gals: Women of Buffalo Bill's Wild West Show* (Billings, MT: TwoDot, 2015).

49 Patton and Schedlock, *Gender, Whiteness, and Power*, 23.

50 Other historians have claimed that Prairie Rose Henderson was the first to ride at Cheyenne; see biography, Prairie Rose Henderson file, NCHF. Mary Lou LeCompte details these debates in *Cowgirls of the Rodeo*, 40–41.

51 See LeCompte's *Cowgirls of the Rodeo* tables A.2–A.4, "Women's Participation in Professional Rodeos," 199–200.

52 "Fifth Pendleton Round-up to Be More Daring than Ever," *Oregonian*, morning edition, September 6, 1914, 1.

53 "Society Rides under 'Big Top,'" unidentified clipping, Eleanor McClintock Williams file, NCHF.

54 Vera McGinnis, *Rodeo Road: My Life as a Pioneer Cowgirl* (New York: Hastings House, 1974), 155–56.

55 Juanita Hackett Howell, interview with Kim Moslander, 1994, Juanita Hackett Howell file, NCHF.

56 Jill Charlotte Standford, *Wild Women and Tricky Ladies: Rodeo Cowgirls, Trick Riders, and Other Performing Women Who Made the West Wilder* (Guilford, CT: TwoDot, 2011), 26.

57 LeCompte, *Cowgirls of the Rodeo*, 28.

58 McGinnis, *Rodeo Road*, 154. These difficulties were experienced by many traveling shows, especially circuses and sideshows. See famous circus organizer C. W. Coup's *Sawdust and Spangles: Stories and Secrets of the Circus* (Chicago: H. S. Stone, 1901).

59 McGinnis, *Rodeo Road*, 170.

60 McGinnis, *Rodeo Road*, 152.

61 These stories had racial overtones as well, as Mamie Francis Hafley supposedly used her pistol to stare down a "black man" who had a knife on a train. This story, related in an oral history, was reminiscent of a racialized image used in the flyer for Hafley's show, in which three white women, including a young girl, take aim with guns at a man in blackface. Strong white femininity was often cast as fending off black masculinity. Mamie Francis Hafley file, NCHF.

62 The story of Goldie Griffith is told at length in Kim Turnbaugh's biography of Griffith, *The Last of the Wild West Cowgirls* (Nederland, CO: Perigo Press, 2009), 14–15.

63 Greenough, "What a Cowgirl Wants from Life."

64 Nomination Form, 5, and "A 98-Pound Heroine Who Trembles Only for Others," *Literary Digest*, August 1, 1925, Mabel Strickland Woodward file, NCHF.

65 Unidentified clipping, quoted in LeCompte, *Cowgirls of the Rodeo*, 102.

66 "The Champion Lady Broncho Buster."

67 She is repeatedly referred to as Johnnie's wife; see "International Rodeo," *Copper Era and Morenci Leader*, January 24, 1913, 8; "Thousands See Fair Second Day: Crowds Enjoy Midway Sights and Lunches, and Find Interest in All Exhibits," *Hartford Courant*, September 4, 1918, 6. "The Stampede," *Billboard*, September 6, 1913, 30, refers to Johnnie as her "her manager (and also her husband)." Janet Own, "Sports among Women," C7, notes that they were billed as the "Baldwin Twins."

68 "Champion Lady Buckaroo of the World," *Times-Gazette*, September 19, 1912, 1.

69 "Clever Ranch Girls, Real Cowboys and Bedecked Indians with Show," 11.

70 "Tillie May Be a Trifle Horsey but She Was Raised That Way: Girl 'Cowboy' Gives Ample Illustration," *Idaho Statesman*, July 20, 1913, 5.

71 When Will Rogers died in 1935 she told reporters, "Tillie Baldwin would never have been heard of but for Will." See "Tillie Baldwin Weeps," 3. Also see Lee Johnson, "The Bronco-Bustin' Pianist of So. Lyme: Tillie Baldwin Slate," *Hartford Courant*, August 18, 1957, SM11.

72 *Chicago Daily News*, August 15, 1925, box 1, album 3, Chicago scrapbook, Tex Austin Collection; *New York Eve Telegram*, October 30, 1922, box 8, album 16, 1922 Madison Square Garden Rodeo, Tex Austin Collection.

73 "Tex Austin Discusses Rodeos and Their Origin," *New York Sun*, November 9, 1922, box 8, album 16, 1922 Madison Square Garden Rodeo, Tex Austin Collection.

74 "Thrills Aplenty in Cowboy Show," *New York Eve Telegram*, October 29, 1922, box 8, album 16, 1922 Madison Square Garden Rodeo, Tex Austin Collection.

75 Wild West Program, 1917, box 1, folder 18, Harvard Theatre Collection.

76 "101 Ranch Wild West to Appear Here This Month: Tillie Baldwin, Oklahoma Rough Rider, Will Be Feature of Interesting Show," *San Francisco Chronicle*, April 7, 1912, 49.

77 William Lee Howard, "Effeminate Men and Masculine Women," *New York Medical Journal* (May 5, 1900): 686–87.

78 101 Ranch program, undated, box 1, folder 24, Harvard Theatre Collection.

79 According to Laegreid, cowgirls were not totally considered New Women and therefore got much better press than actresses and other public women, mostly

because they were considered to be doing things important to their heritage as pioneers; see *Riding Pretty,* 52–53.

80 Richard von Krafft-Ebing wrote about this theory of inversion in his foundational work *Psycopathia Sexualis* (1886), which presented a set of case studies concerning supposed sexual ailments. Mary Lou LeCompte, in *Cowgirls of the Rodeo,* argues that many cowgirls attempted to mitigate the masculine aspects of their careers through their appearance.

81 "A 98-Pound Heroine Who Trembles Only for Others," *Literary Digest,* August 1, 1925.

82 "Beautiful but Brave These Cowgirls Here from the West."

83 Quoted in Patton and Schedlock, *Gender, Whiteness, and Power,* 35.

84 See, for examples, "Ninety-One Images of Cowgirls, the Rodeo, and the American West," Elizabeth West Postcard Collection, 1887–1955, Cowgirls and Rodeo folder, Schlesinger Library on the History of Women in America, Radcliffe Institute, Cambridge, Massachusetts. Interestingly, rodeos began to explicitly traffic in the language of authenticity in the 1920s as they sought to distinguish themselves from Wild West shows. By the 1920s, audiences were demanding unrehearsed contests between humans and beast rather than staged battles between cowboys and Indians.

85 "Mamie Francis: Girl Who Rides Diving Horse," unidentified clipping, Mamie Francis Hafley file, NCHF.

86 McGinnis, *Rodeo Road,* 91. These experiences were similar to circus performers' feelings about performance; see Josephine DeMott Robinson's *The Circus Lady* (New York: Thomas Y. Cromwell, 1927).

87 LeCompte, *Cowgirls of the Rodeo,* 2.

88 Transcript of interview of Mitzi Riley by Kim Moslander, Tad Lucas file, NCHF.

89 See, for example, Janya Brown, *Babylon Girls: Black Women Performers and the Shaping of the Modern* (Durham: Duke University Press, 2008), and Adria Imada, *Aloha America: Hula Circuits through the US Empire* (Durham: Duke University Press, 2012).

90 "Eleanor Williams, A Rebel in the West," *New Mexico Magazine,* October 1984, Eleanor McClintock Williams file, NCHF. Many other rodeo women went on the road with their husbands; for example, one woman bet Tex Austin that she could accompany her husband on the rodeo train dressed as a man. "She Wins," unidentified clipping, August 3, 1927, Tex Austin Collection; "Blakemore's Bride Home as Cowgirl," unidentified clipping, undated, Tex Austin Collection; and "Society Bride Rides Train as Cowboy on Bet," *Chicago Herald and Examiner,* April 23, 1927, box 2, album 5, Tex Austin Collection.

91 Interview with Juanita Hackett Howell by Kim Moslander, 1994, Juanita Hackett Howell file, NCHF.

92 "Girl Cow Puncher Drives Nails with Gun, Ropes Steer in 30 Seconds," *Evening Post* (Cincinnati), August 29, 1907, Lucille Mulhall file, NCHF.

93 "Oklahoma Girl at the Temple Theater Yearns to See Western Plains," unidentified clipping, Lucille Mulhall file, NCHF.

94 "Dare Devil Girls Who Ride for Ranch 101: Lulu Parr and Tillie Baldwin Who Challenge World in Feats of Riding," *Idaho Statesman*, July 15, 1912, 3.

95 "Miss Mulhall to Amend an Adage," *Sheridan Post*, August 15, 1915.

96 See Steven E. Weil and G. Daniel DeWesse, *Western Shirts: A Classic American Fashion* (Salt Lake: Gibbs Smith, 2004), and Holly George-Warren and Michelle Freedman, *How the West Was Worn* (New York: Harry N. Abrams, 2001), for an in-depth look at the development of western wear.

97 McGinnis, *Rodeo Road*, 23, 182, 186.

98 Joan Burbick, *Rodeo Queens and the American Dream* (New York: Public Affairs, 2002), 14.

99 "Will Rogers: He Pays a Tribute to an Old Friend and Showman," *Hamilton Daily News*, October 10, 1931, 3.

100 "Thousands See Fair Second Day."

101 Rowdy Waddy, "The Corral," *Billboard*, November 27, 1915.

102 Laegreid, *Riding Pretty*, 160.

103 Richard White, "Frederick Jackson Turner and Buffalo Bill," and Patricia Nelson Limerick, "The Adventures of the Frontier in the Twentieth Century," in *The Frontier in American Culture* (Berkeley: University of California Press, 1994).

104 Biography, Reine Shelton file, NCHF.

105 Michael Allen, *Rodeo Cowboys in the North American Imagination* (Reno: University of Nevada Press, 1998), 28.

106 Laegreid, *Riding Pretty*, 14.

107 Margie Greenough, unidentified source, Margie Greenough file, NCHF.

108 McGinnis, *Rodeo Road*, 43.

109 LeCompte, *Cowgirls of the Rodeo*, 13.

110 Teresa Jordan, *Cowgirls: Women of the American West* (New York: Anchor Press, 1982), 198.

111 "Rain and Cold Fail to Keep Eleven Thousand Away from the Second Performance," *Calgary Daily Herald*, September 4, 1912, 6; "Native Hanover Girl a Feature with Wild West Show at York last Saturday," *Hanover Herald*, May 24, 1913, Lulu Bell Parr file, NCHF.

112 "Tillie May Be a Trifle Horsey."

113 Many historians have looked at the changes in cowgirl costume. For example, LeCompte, *Cowgirls of the Rodeo*, 71.

114 "Champion Lady Broncho Buster." Also see "Girl to 'Bulldog' Steer: Tillie Baldwin Training to Enter Contest at Pendleton," *Oregonian*, morning edition,

August 2, 1913, 11, and "Tillie to Try New Trick: Oregon's Champion Cow Girl to Bulldog a Steer at 'Roundup,'" *Idaho Statesman*, August 3, 1913, 9.

115 Whistling Annie, "Wimmen's Writes" (column), *Billboard*, October 2, 1915, 8.

116 *Bridgeport Evening Farmer*, second section, December 15, 1916, 20.

117 "Little New York Hairdresser Outrides Montana Cowpunchers," *Ekalaka Eagle*, September 26, 1916, 9.

118 "Champion Lady Broncho Buster."

119 "Champion Lady Broncho Buster."

120 Laura Ingalls Wilder would soon publish her "true stories" about growing up in a pioneer family. See Caroline Fraser, *Prairie Fires: The American Dreams of Laura Ingalls Wilder* (New York: Metropolitan Books, 2017).

121 Rodeos drew young men, especially, into visiting the US West. At the Chicago Rodeo an annual roping contest was held for young Boy Scouts to win a trip to rodeo organizer Tex Austin's New Mexican ranch for one week. "Boy Winners Off for Rodeo Ranch," *South Bend (Indiana) News-Times*, September 6, 1927, box 2, album 4, Tex Austin Collection.

122 Dude ranches and rodeos were intimately entwined as both venues attempted to sell westernness to eastern tourists. These tourist industries also helped create a universal imagined West, in which the cowboy, instead of the miner or sheepherder or military scout, became the occupation of all westerners. These spaces conditioned real westerners to perform westernness in particular ways. For a discussion of how these processes operated on a local level, see Bonnie Christensen's *Red Lodge and the Mythic West* (Lawrence: University Press of Kansas, 2002). Hal Rothman's *Devil's Bargains: Tourism in the Twentieth-Century American West* argues that many of these tourist industries were increasingly controlled by Eastern corporate interests (Lawrence: University Press of Kansas, 1998). For more historical information on the dude ranching industry in particular, see Lawrence Borne, *Dude Ranching: A Complete History* (Albuquerque: University of New Mexico Press, 1983). For a look at authenticity and country western music see Richard Peterson, *Creating Country Music: Fabricating Authenticity* (Chicago: University of Chicago Press, 1997); Pamela Fox, "Recycled 'Trash': Gender and Authenticity in Country Music Autobiography," *American Quarterly* 50, no. 2 (June 1998): 234–67; Aaron Fox, *Real Country: Music and Language in Working-Class Culture* (Durham: Duke University Press, 2004); Rebecca Scofield, "'Nipped, Tucked, or Sucked': Dolly Parton and the Construction of the Authentic Body," *Journal of Popular Culture* 49, no. 3 (June 2016): 660–77.

123 Loraine Hornaday Fielding, *French Heels to Spurs* (New York: Century, 1930), 32.

124 Fielding, *French Heels to Spurs*, 35.

125 "Champion Lady Broncho Buster."

126   "Champion Lady Broncho Buster."

127   "Champion Lady Broncho Buster."

128   See Laegreid, *Riding Pretty*, 54.

129   Roach, *The Cowgirls of the Rodeo*, 112.

130   LeCompte argues that Gene Autry in particular helped marginalize women in both film and rodeo by featuring women in decorative instead of active roles as neo-Victorian gender norms resurfaced in the 1940s emphasis on the home. Due to Autry's increasing influence in the rodeo business after World War II, women's chances to ride broncs dwindled in mainstream rodeos.

131   Eugene Kinkead, "The Cowboy Business," *New Yorker*, October 26, 1940, box 1, folder 34, Harvard Theatre Collection.

132   Girls Rodeo Association Handbook (1949), 12, Tad Lucas file, NCHF.

133   George Morris Jr., "Tillie Baldwin Reappears," *Hartford Courant*, October 19, 1930, E5.

134   Owen, "Sports among Women," C7.

135   The policewoman story is repeated in Ann Baldelli, "The Consummate Cowgirl," *Day*, June 7, 2001, D1, though this particular story has not been substantiated.

2. RESTORATIVE BRUTALITY: VIOLENCE AND SOCIAL SALVATION AT THE TEXAS PRISON RODEO

1   "18,000 Fans See Opening Rodeo Oct. 5," *Echo*, October 1941, 1.

2   "Eleventh Annual Prison Rodeo Begins Here Sunday, October 5," *Item*, September 25, 1941, 1, 10.

3   "Old West Lives Again in Big Arena," *Echo*, September 1941, 1–2. Also see "The Mad Scramble: A Madman's Dream of Chilling Confusion," *Echo*, rodeo edition, 1957, 1.

4   "Item Editor to Cover 88th Prison Rodeo Performance," *Echo*, rodeo edition, September 1959, 2.

5   "Echoing the Penal Press," *Echo*, rodeo edition, 1951, 2.

6   "30,000 Fans Present at First Show," *Echo*, October 1940, 1. Four sold-out shows in 1940 first hit this number, "100,000 Fans Witness Four Sunday Shows," *Echo*, November 1940, 1.

7   See Ethan Blue, *Doing Time in the Depression: Everyday Life in Texas and California Prisons* (New York: New York University Press, 2012); and Mitchel P. Roth, *Convict Cowboys: The Untold History of the Texas Prison Rodeo* (Denton: University of North Texas Press, 2016).

8   Melissa Schrift, "The Angola Prison Rodeo: Inmate Cowboys and Institutional Tourism," *Ethnology* 43, no. 4 (Autumn 2004): 331. The Oklahoma State Penitentiary Prison Rodeo ran from 1940 until 2010, closing due to low staff

and stadium disrepair. Also see Daniel Bergner, *God of the Rodeo: The Search for Hope, Faith, and a Six-Second Ride in Louisiana's Angola Prison* (New York: Crown, 1998); Jessica Adams, "'The Wildest Show in the South': Tourism and Incarceration at Angola," *Drama Review* 40, no. 2 (Summer 2001): 94–108.

9   Michelle Brown, *The Culture of Punishment: Prison, Society, and Spectacle* (New York: New York University Press, 2009), 4; Mary Rachel Gould, "Discipline and the Performance of Punishment: Welcome to 'The Wildest Show in the South,'" *Liminalities: A Journal of Performance Studies* 7, no. 4 (December 2011): 1. Some informants gestured to rehabilitation as a theme; see pp. 12 and 15. Also see David Wilson and Sean O'Sullivan, *Images of Incarceration: Representations of Prison in Film and Television Drama* (Winchester, UK: Waterside, 2004); Dawn K. Cecil, *Prison Life in Popular Culture: From the Big House to Orange Is the New Black* (Boulder: Lynne Rienner, 2015); Bill Yousman, *Prime Time Prisons on U.S. TV: Representation of Incarceration* (New York: Peter Lang, 2009).

10   For histories of the convict leasing system in Texas, see Donald Walker, *Penology for Profit: A History of the Texas Prison System, 1867–1912* (College Station: Texas A&M University Press, 1988); Martha Myers, *Race, Labor and Punishment in the New South* (Columbus: Ohio State University Press, 1998); Robert Perkinson, *Texas Tough: the Rise of America's Prison Empire* (New York: Picador, 2010).

11   Perkinson, *Texas Tough*, 143.

12   "Courage," *Echo*, March 1934, 1.

13   Richard Slotkin, *Gunfighter Nation: The Myth of the Frontier in Twentieth-Century America* (Norman: University of Oklahoma Press, 1998), 350.

14   O. J. S. Ellingson, "Greetings," rodeo program, 1939, 5, box 1998/038–404, programs and related materials, Texas Prison Rodeo records, Texas Department of Criminal Justice, Archives and Information Services Division, Texas State Library and Archives Commission, Austin, Texas. Hereafter TPR records.

15   As Foucault has argued, the modernization of prisons sought to make inmates "the object of a collective and useful appropriation." Michel Foucault, *Discipline and Punish: The Birth of the Prison* (New York: Vintage, 1979), 109. Also see David Garland, *Punishment and Modern Society: A Study in Social Theory* (Chicago: University of Chicago Press, 1990).

16   C. C. Springfield, "Underworld Rodeo," *Echo*, September 1946, 1, 8.

17   Lee Simmons, *Assignment Huntsville: Memoirs of a Texas Prison Official* (Austin: University of Texas Press, 1957), 91.

18   Simmons, *Assignment Huntsville*, 92.

19   This impulse to keep taxes low and government small was the mainstay of the Democratic Party after Radical Reconstruction ended. Walker, *Penology for Profit*, 172.

20 Perkinson, *Texas Tough*, 84–85.

21 Perkinson, *Texas Tough*, 84–85.

22 Walker, *Penology for Profit*, 112–14.

23 Blue, *Doing Time*, 1. Also see Jeffrey Alder, "Less Crime, More Punishment: Violence, Race, and Criminal Justice in Early Twentieth-Century America," *Journal of American History* 102, no. 1 (June 2015): 34–46.

24 Simmons, *Assignment Huntsville*, 62.

25 Simmons, *Assignment Huntsville*, 66–67.

26 Blue, *Doing Time*, 165.

27 Don Sabo, "Doing Time, Doing Masculinity: Sports and Prison," in *Prison Masculinities*, ed. Don Sabo, Terry Kupers, and Willie London (Philadelphia: Temple University Press, 2001), 62. Similarly, over the past several decades, activists have introduced more therapeutic theater programs into prisons, hoping to teach self-reflection and bodily control. Jonathan Shailor, ed., *Performing New Lives: Prison Theater* (Philadelphia: Jessica Kingsley, 2011), 7. See also Michael Balfour, *The Use of Drama in the Rehabilitation of Violent Male Offenders* (New York: Edwin Mellon Press, 2003).

28 Simmons, *Assignment Huntsville*, 84.

29 "Third Annual Prison Rodeo Opened Saturday, October 7," *Echo*, October 1933.

30 Simmons, *Assignment Huntsville*, viii.

31 Simmons, *Assignment Huntsville*, vi.

32 Paul M. Lucko, "Counteracting Reform: Lee Simmons and the Texas Prison System, 1930–1935," *East Texas Historical Journal* 30, no. 2 (October 1992): 1, 25.

33 Simmons, *Assignment Huntsville*, x.

34 Perkinson, *Texas Tough*, 94.

35 Kristine Fredrikson, *American Rodeo: From Buffalo Bill to Big Business* (College Station: Texas A&M University Press, 1985), 21–40.

36 "New Rodeo Dates," *Echo*, September 1942, 4.

37 "Old West Lives Again in Big Arena," *Echo*, September 1941, 1–2.

38 "Reader's Digest and The Baltimore Sun Carry Rodeo Story," *Echo*, November 1941, 8 (reprint of Loring Schuler's untitled article from *Reader's Digest*, November 1941).

39 See repeated concerns over audiences' experience throughout the *Echo*, September 1937.

40 "Inmates Eagerly Await Opening of Rodeo," *Echo*, September 1940, 2.

41 Perkinson, *Texas Tough*, 172.

42 For a detailed description of the development of this fund see Charlotte A. Teagle, *History of Welfare Activities of the Texas Prison Board* (Huntsville: Texas Prison Board, 1941).

43 Texas Prison Rodeo program, 1950, box 1998/038–404, TPR records.

44 Blue, *Doing Time*, 10.

45 Photo captions, the *Echo*, August 1938, 4. Also see Simmons, *Assignment Huntsville*, 108. The prison newspaper at the time linked the racialized idea of cotton picking and the rodeo. Milton Tom Harris, "Spicy Dark Town Jumpin' Jive," *Echo*, September 1940, 13.

46 "'Wildest Rodeo' Is behind Bars," *Hartford Currant*, November 23, 1978, 41A. Also see "Wildest Rodeo Is behind Bars," *Los Angeles Times*, June 15, 1979. Even as black men were accepted as bona fide competitors and men of color like O'Neal Browning would become the all-time winningest cowboy, the imagery surrounding the black cowboy remained deeply racist.

47 "Convict Riders Share $1,636 in Prize Money at Big Rodeo," *Ebony* 8, no. 4 (February 1, 1953), 44.

48 Rodeo program, 1939, box 1998/038–404, TPR records.

49 Rodeo program, 1955, box 1998/038–404, TPR records.

50 See Khalil Gibran Muhammad, *The Condemnation of Blackness: Race, Crime, and the Making of Modern Urban America* (Cambridge: Harvard University Press, 2010), for a historical analysis of Progressive-era statistics that nurtured an association of blackness and criminality.

51 Blue, *Doing Time*, 38.

52 Peter Caster, *Prisons, Race, and Masculinity in Twentieth-Century Literature and Film* (Columbus: Ohio State University Press, 2008), 3.

53 "Local Writer Recalls Other Famous Rodeos," *Echo*, August 1938.

54 "Courage," *Echo*, March 1934.

55 "New Rodeo Dates," *Echo*, September 1942, 8.

56 "The Other Rodeo," *Echo*, September 1940, 4.

57 "Woman Inmate May Take Part in 1938 Rodeo," *Echo*, August 1938, 1.

58 "Goree's All-Girl String Band," *Echo*, September 1940. Rodeo program, 1939, box 1998/038–404, TPR records. For discussions of the lives of incarcerated women see Talitha LeFlouria, *Chained in Silence: Black Women and Convict Labor in the New South* (Charlottesville: University of North Carolina Press, 2015), and Estelle Freedman, "The Prison Lesbian: Race, Class, and the Construction of the Aggressive Female Homosexual, 1915–1965," *Feminist Studies* 22, no. 2 (Summer 1996): 397–423.

59 See Perkinson, *Texas Tough*, 171.

60 Stuart Merritt, "Production for Use," *Echo*, August 1938, 4.

61 "Roy White to Try for First Place in Rodeo," *Echo*, August 1938, 10.

62 Good even took credit for inspiring the rodeo in his memoir *Twelve Years in a Texas Prison*; see Roth, *Convict Cowboys*, 37.

63 Ellingson, "Greetings."

64 Roth, *Convict Cowboys*, 56–57. See Slotkin's discussion of the "cult of the outlaw," in *Gunfighter Nation*, 293.

65 "Within Prison Walls Texas' Wildest Rodeo," *Sun*, October 5, 1941. For the influence of the "outlaw" on country music and cowboy lore see Michael Dunne, "'I Fall upon the Cacti of Life! I Bleed!': Romantic Narcissism in 'Outlaw' Cowboy Music," *Studies in Popular Culture* 11, no. 2 (1988), 22–39, and Martin Parker, "The Wild West, the Industrial East, and the Outlaw," *Cultural and Organization* 17, no. 4 (September 2011): 347–65.

66 "New Rodeo Dates," *Echo*, September 1942, 8.

67 "Reader's Digest and The Baltimore Sun Carry Rodeo Story," 8.

68 "Within Prison Walls," *Sun*, October 5.

69 "Convict Exposed to Super-Thief," *Echo*, October 30, 1948.

70 "Convicts Ride Em," *Sun*, November 2, 1947. Mitchel Roth states that audiences came "to get the vicarious thrill of being in close proximity with hardened outlaws, who no doubt were often just as thrilled to be contemplating what must go on in the lives of free world spectators once the show was over." Roth, *Convict Cowboys*, 150.

71 Perkinson, *Texas Tough*, 161–62.

72 Meeting minutes, September 6, 1943, Department of Corrections Administrative Correspondence Board of Criminal Justice Minutes and Meeting, Minutes, January 1943–January 1944, box 1998/038-8, Texas Department of Criminal Justice, Archives and Information Services Division, Texas State Library and Archives Commission, Austin, Texas.

73 Rodeo program, 1963, box 1998/038-404, TPR records.

74 Springfield, "Underworld Rodeo." For mainstream rodeo's growing obsession with the "good guy" cowboy see, "Rodeo Is Clean of 'Bad Men,'" *Chicago Herald*, July 31, 1925, box 1, album 3, Chicago scrapbook, Tex Austin Collection, Museum of New Mexico, Fray Angelico Chavez History Library, Santa Fe, New Mexico.

75 "Opening Day Show Sets Attendance Record," *Echo*, October 1940, 1.

76 "My Sunday Shot," *Echo*, September 1941. John "Snake" Parker, for instance, was also marked out as a particularly good black cowboy in the 1940s in "Lynching," *Echo*, September 1946, a column that capitalizes on the racialized violence of the author's name.

77 "Riders Who Draw Brahmas Must Be Ready for Anything," *Echo*, September 1937, 11.

78 Nance particularly investigates how certain landscapes and animals were used by rodeo organizers and riders to craft narratives about authority in the West. In her analysis of the life of Greasy Sal she looks at how the "outlaw bronc" character "was produced at the intersection of wild horse behaviour, local business cultures, and the Western genre and seems to have appealed specifically to rodeo people and audiences living on the cusp of the post-equine era in North America (1910–1930), in which most people no longer employed horses

for labour." Greasy Sal "was a post-equine horse employed primarily for nostalgic entertainment purposes—just (and this is important, I think) as people were transitioning to the gasoline engine." "Outlaw Horses and the True Spirit of Calgary in the Automobile Age," in *Calgary: City of Animals*, ed. Jim Ellis (Calgary: University of Calgary Press, 2017), 12–13. Texas, too, was rapidly industrializing and looking nostalgically at equine performers.

79 *9th Texas Prison Rodeo Souvenir Book*, 1939, 5. Quoted in Roth, *Convict Cowboys*, 29.

80 Roth, *Convict Cowboys*, 134.

81 "Rodeos to Be Held on Thursdays," *Echo*, September 1942, 1, 8.

82 Blue, *Doing Time*, 175–76.

83 Billie Burcalow, "Miscellany," *Echo*, October 1940.

84 "Rodeo Days in October," rodeo program, 1965, box 1998/038–404, TPR records. This explanation of participation was a common one: "Surely he wants to finish in the money. But above all, he wants the applause of the fans, the heart-warming cheers that tell him that he's not just a convict, but a man, a man whose efforts are lauded and appreciated." Rodeo program, 1965, box 1998/038–404, TPR records. See also "Rider Applications Now Being Accepted," *Echo*, rodeo edition, 1959, 2.

85 Simmons, *Assignment Huntsville*, 97.

86 Simmons, *Assignment Huntsville*, 98.

87 Schuler, "Reader's Digest," 8.

88 Travis Brumbeau, "Shoe Shop Findings," *Echo*, September 1940, 13.

89 "Around the Yard," *Echo*, September 1940.

90 "Rodeo Highlights," *Echo*, November 1941.

91 Rodeo program, 1970, box 1998/038–405, TPR records. Also see "Mr. Redshirt," rodeo program, 1973, box 1998/038–405, TPR records.

92 "'62 Rodeo Draws 81,000," *Echo*, November 1962.

93 Mark Zienman, "At the Prison Rodeo, Texas Outlaws Earn Loot the Hard Way," *Wall Street Journal*, October 21, 1985. The rodeo was a release from monotony in "the crowds passing, the swirl of gay and colorful clothes, happy smiles and carefree laughter and in the shouts of children." "Letters of Appreciation," *Echo*, September 1958. Men often mentioned children, as well as women, as a joy to see. For example see "Cowboys at Rodeo All Belong in Prison, and That's Where They Are," *Wall Street Journal*, October 20, 1975.

94 *Echo*, November 1941. Candy Barr, for instance, became a beloved figure of the rodeo. A popular striptease artist and burlesque dancer who was arrested on drug charges, Barr became of member of the Goree Girls band and even came back to perform at the rodeo after her release. Inmates adored the self-consciously sexual Barr. See Candy Barr interview in the *Echo*, August 1966.

See "Texas Prison Rodeo," *Echo*, special edition, undated, clippings about the rodeo, 1931–1986–2, box 1998/038–404, TPR records; and "Grueling Work, Sweat, Blood Makes 1960 Prison Rodeo Most Thrilling," *Echo*, November 1960. Barr also appeared at the same rodeo as Anita Bryant in 1962, stating that she hoped this would be her final rodeo performance as an inmate. "'62 Rodeo Draws 81,000," *Echo*, November 1962.

95   "Rodeo Highlights," *Echo*, October 1941.

96   Ellingson, "Greetings."

97   "45 Annual Texas Prison Rodeo Aim to Advantage Inmates' Rehabilitation," *Echo*, September 1976.

98   "Voc Ed. to Remain Active during Rodeo," *Echo*, rodeo edition, 1959, 3. "Notice," *Echo*, rodeo edition, 1963.

99   "Notice," *Echo*, rodeo edition, 1953, 16. In 1951, the *Echo* announced the transfer of all able-bodied men to the farms to pick cotton, which shut down the shoe shop, tag plant, and textile mill for the next thirty days. "Million Dollar Cotton Crop Shuts Down Walls Industries," *Echo*, rodeo edition, 1951, 1. See also, "21st Rodeo Tops All Former Records" and "Another New Record: Prison's 1952 Cotton Crop worth 2.3 Million," *Echo*, November 1952, 1.

100   Springfield, "Underworld Rodeo," 1.

101   Blue, *Doing Time*, 195–96.

102   "Shoe Shop Will Be Well Represented in Coming Rodeo," *Echo*, September 1946, 2.

103   "Board Unanimously Approves Mr. Ellis' $4,200,000 Prison Modernization Program," *Echo*, February 1948, 1.

104   Rodeo program, 1948, box 1998/038–404, TPR records. Ellis was successful in his attempts to raise money for these reforms in part because of the prosperity of postwar Texas and Governor Jester's willingness to provide financial support. Ellis himself delivered 250 speeches over the course of a year in order to drum up support for the plan. Perkinson, *Texas Tough*, 226–31.

105   In September 1940, the *Echo* reported that the print shop completed five thousand programs and a special edition. "Print Shop Squibs," 3.

106   Perkinson, *Texas Tough*, 229.

107   Detailed in "Board Unanimously." This new form of segregation was thought to protect "rehabilitative" prisoners by designating individual cells for nonrehabilitative prisoners.

108   The influence of 1970s drug laws on mass incarceration has been well documented; for instance see David Garland, *The Culture of Control: Crime and Social Order in Contemporary Society* (Chicago: University of Chicago, 2001), and Michelle Alexander, *The New Jim Crow: Mass Incarceration in the Age of Colorblindness* (New York: New Press, 2010). These policies drew on racially

coded "color-blind" and "law-and-order" campaigns to urge for a reduction in welfare aid; see Mathew Lassiter, *The Silent Majority: Suburban Politics in the Sunbelt South* (Princeton: Princeton University Press, 2006), and Michael Javen Fortner, *The Black Silent Majority: The Rockefeller Drug Laws and the Politics of Punishment* (Cambridge: Harvard University Press, 2015). Who should be entitled to welfare was a significant debate of the twentieth century. Jennifer Klein in *For All These Rights: Business, Labor, and the Shaping of America's Public-Private Welfare State* (Princeton: Princeton University Press, 2003) examines the New Deal foundation for these debates in the mixture of public and private welfare policy. The gendered, racialized, and sexualized aspects of these debates are detailed in Linda Gordon's "Social Insurance and Public Assistance: The Influence of Gender in Welfare Thought in the U.S., 1890–1935," *American Historical Review* 97 (February 1992): 19–55, and Margot Canaday's *The Straight State: Sexuality and Citizenship in Twentieth-Century America* (Princeton: Princeton University Press, 2009).

109   "The 18th Annual Prison Rodeo," *Huntsville Item*, September 29, 1949, clippings about the rodeo, 1931–1986–1, box 1998/038–404, TPR records.

110   "Biggest Prison Show on Earth," ca. 1948, clippings about the rodeo, 1931–1986–2, box 1998/038–404, TPR records.

111   "Convict Riders Share," 44.

112   C. C. Springfield, "The Dang'dest Show on Earth," *American Legion Magazine* (reprinted in the *Echo*, September 1947, 1).

113   "Echoing the Penal Press," *Echo*, rodeo edition, 1951, 2.

114   "Seen by Thousands Who Attended the Annual Prison Rodeo," *Echo*, August 1938, 4; "Convicts Ride Em," FA23. The rodeo was referred to as the fastest and wildest "on earth" by the 1940s. "Rodeo's First Press Day a Huge Success," *Echo*, November 1940, 8.

115   Rodeo program, 1950, clippings about the rodeo, 1931–1986–1, box 1998/038–404, TPR records.

116   "The Biggest Show of Its Kind on Earth," rodeo program, 1956, box 1998/038–404, TPR records.

117   "30th Anniversary," rodeo program, 1961, box 1998/038–404, TPR records.

118   "Mile a Minute Action at 'The Show of Shows,'" *Echo*, September 1941, 10.

119   Springfield, "Dang'dest."

120   Rodeo also produced new opportunities for escape and the spread of the fear of prison violence into the public's backyard. Escapes were not frequent but were at times successful because of the rodeo. In the 1930s, while being transported back to their farm after attending the rodeo in Huntsville, several inmates took the opportunity of being stopped in Houston traffic to jump from the prison vehicle. The guards could not shoot because of the crowded streets, and they

could not pursue the men as they still had prisoners in the van. "5 Convicts Escape in Texas, 2 Caught," *Washington Post*, October 26, 1936. In another break, construction crew members building the rodeo stadium used their equipment to tunnel under the walls and forced several local teenagers to drive them to another town. The most famous escape happened at the rodeo itself when two inmates who had worn street clothes under their uniforms dropped beneath the bleachers and were crawling over the fence when a guard saw them. The guard yelled at the two seemingly ignorant visitors, warning them the prisoners' area was strictly off limits. The guard was later fired. Springfield, "Dang'dest." All of these reported escapes happened in the early years of the rodeo and the need to crack down brought about stricter control of the rodeo grounds as part of larger reform efforts.

121 Roth, *Convict Cowboys*, 263.

122 Fred Massengill, "Old Engineer," *Terrell Daily Tribune* (reprinted in the *Echo*, October 1939, 1).

123 Springfield, "Dang'dest."

124 For a discussion of the culture of domination under Ellis, see Perkinson, *Texas Tough*, 237.

125 For stories on early escapes, see, "5 Convicts Escape."

126 For incarceration statistics on state and federal prison in the mid-twentieth century, see Patrick Langan, "Race of Prisoners Admitted to State and Federal Institutions, 1926–86," (Washington, DC: US Department of Justice, Bureau of Justice Statistics, May 1991).

127 "100 Mile Dash," rodeo program, 1969, box 1998/038–405, TPR records.

128 Slotkin, *Gunfighter Nation*, 379.

129 "Outlaw vs. Outlaw No Mere Figure of Speech," *Echo*, rodeo edition, September 1956, 1.

130 "The Prison Rodeo . . . Its Reasons," *Echo*, second rodeo edition, 1952, 1.

131 "Around the Yard," *Echo*, September 1940, 6, noted the Walls was a hive of activity. "The Unremembered," *Echo*, second rodeo edition, 1953, 6, particularly highlights the work of the backstage stockmen doing real cowboy labor while receiving little or no credit.

132 In 1946, advertising director C. C. Springfield bragged that "despite the speed and recklessness of the show, injuries are few and deaths are practically nil." "Underworld Rodeo," 1. But death was a possibility. "Few Get Bad Hurts in Rodeo Here," *Echo*, August 1954, 2, stated, "Only one death is recorded in the rodeo's 23-year history. In 1932 a Negro contestant got his foot hung in a stirrup and was kicked in the head by a bucking horse." Mitchel Roth, author of *Convict Cowboys*, states that this was the only verifiable death, though prison medical records are difficult to access, 66–67. Another man was reported to

have died in 1977 due to his injuries; see Peter Applebome, "Last Roundup Feared at Texas Prison Rodeo," *New York Times*, March 19, 1987, A18. In 1985, thirty-nine of the one hundred cowboys were treated for some kind of injury. Zienman, "At the Prison Rodeo," 1.

133 Springfield, "The Dang'dest."

134 Lewis Nordyke, "These Convicts Make Fun of Themselves," *Saturday Evening Post*, January 3, 1953, 24.

135 Kevin Kruse, *One Nation under God: How Corporate America Invented Christian America* (New York: Basic Books, 2015).

136 "Kilgore Jaycees Back Ellis Plan," *Echo*, rodeo edition, 1948, 3. Also see "Prison Reform Battle, Victory," *Echo*, March 21, 1949, 1.

137 "Your Rodeo Dollar," *Echo*, second rodeo edition, 1953, 8.

138 "Huntsville Is Proud of the Accomplishments of Mr. O. B. Ellis, General Manager, and the Texas Prison Board" and "The 18th Annual Prison Rodeo," *Huntsville Item*, September 29, 1949, clippings about the rodeo, 1931–1986–1, box 1998/038–404, TPR records.

139 Robert Perkinson notes that the reported numbers of heel-stringing only increased after Simmons's tenure, rising from 174 in the late 1930s to 341 in the mid-1940s. *Texas Tough*, 215.

140 Perkinson, *Texas Tough*, 229.

141 Reprinted version of Ellis's plan, rodeo program, 1948, box 1998/038–404, TPR records.

142 e.m.m., "This Is My Home," *Echo*, rodeo edition, September 1959, 2.

143 Robert Chase, "'Slaves of the State' Revolt: Southern Prison Labor and the Prisoners' Rights Movement in Texas, 1945–1980," in *Life and Labor in the New, New South: Essays in Southern Labor History since 1950*, ed. Robert Zieger (Gainesville: University of Florida Press, 2012), 186. Chase also notes this in part because of the costliness of rehabilitative programs in other states, which the rodeo paid for in Texas.

144 Roth, *Convict Cowboys*, 219–29. Also see "Prison Rodeo Profits Used to Hike Income of Officials," *Houston Post*, December 27, 1959, 11, and "Not Right Way to Raise Prison Salaries," *Houston Post*, November 29, 1959.

145 Elizabeth Hinton, *From the War on Poverty to the War on Crime: The Making of Mass Incarceration in America* (Cambridge: Harvard University Press, 2016); Naomi Murakawa, *The First Civil Right: How Liberals Built Prison America* (New York: Oxford University Press, 2014); and Julilly Kohler-Hausmann, "Guns and Butter: The Welfare State, the Carceral State, and the Politics of Exclusion in the Postwar United States," *Journal of American History* 102, no. 1 (June 2015): 89.

146 Perkinson, *Texas Tough*, 231–35.

147 Lyndon B. Johnson, foreword to *The Texas Rangers: A Century of Frontier Defense*, 2nd ed., by Walter Prescott Webb (Austin: University of Texas Press, 1965), ix–x.

148 Chase, "Revolt," 187.

149 "Thrills, Chills, and Spills," *Echo*, rodeo edition, September–October 1964, 3.

150 Kohler-Hausmann, "Guns and Butter," 89; Robert Chase, "We Are Not Slaves: Rethinking the Rise of Carceral States through the Lens of the Prisoners' Rights Movement," *Journal of American History* 102, no. 1 (June 2015): 74.

151 "We're Going Places," *Huntsville Item*, September 29, 1949, clippings about the rodeo, 1931–1986–1, box 1998/038–404, TPR records.

152 Fred Burke, "The Cowboys," rodeo program, 1978, 19, box 1998/038–405, TPR records. Also see references to individualism in rodeo program, 1979, box 1998/038–405, TPR records; rodeo program, 1981, box 1998/038–405, TPR records; rodeo program, 1983, box 1998/038–405, TPR records.

153 "Texas Prison Rodeo," undated press release, ca. 1975–79, clippings about the rodeo, 1931–1986–2, box 1998/038–404, TPR records.

154 "Rider Applications Now Being Accepted," *Echo*, rodeo edition, 1959, and "Prison Rodeo Rated with Best, 47Stitches for Winner," *New York Times*, October 22, 1973, 51.

155 "Cowboys at Rodeo All Belong in Prison," 1.

156 Benjamin Lach, "Ride Em Cowboy," rodeo program, 1980, box 1998/038–405, TPR records.

157 "Growth of Prison Industry," *Echo*, January 1965, 7.

158 Rodeo program, 1966, box 1998/038–404, TPR records.

159 Rodeo program, 1969, box 1998/038–405, TPR records.

160 Interestingly, the rodeo helped pay for "female impersonators" alongside blackface performers; see the *Echo*, September 1940. Therefore, while the rodeo reasserted proper sexual and gender roles, it also funded the subversion of these roles through other entertainments. For more on southern popular mixings of drag and blackface see Brock Thompson's *The Un-Natural State: Arkansas and the Queer South* (Fayetteville: University of Arkansas Press, 2010).

161 Other concerns were related to labor and violence, including the spike in the practice of self-maiming in order to gain work release and stabbings in the large dormitories. Department of Corrections Administrative Correspondence Board of Criminal Justice Minutes and Meeting, Minutes, March 1944–July 1945, box 1998/038–8, Texas Department of Criminal Justice, Archives and Information Services Division, Texas State Library and Archives Commission, Austin, Texas. For a discussion of sexuality and prisons see Regina Kunzel,

Criminal Intimacy: Prison and the Uneven History of American Sexuality (Chicago: University of Chicago Press, 2008).

162　Chase, "Revolt," 188.

163　"Rodeo Performers," rodeo program, 1939, box 1998/038-404, TPR records.

164　"Leadership Comes Natural for Lala Markovich," *Echo*, September–October 1966, 2; "Hard Money," rodeo program, 1965, box 1998/038-404, TPR records. Schrift also notes how money operates as a key inducement at Angola. "Angola Prison Rodeo," 334.

165　Zieman, "At the Prison Rodeo," 1.

166　*Historical Statistics on Prisoners in State and Federal Institutions, Yearend 1925–86* (Washington, DC: US Department of Justice, Bureau of Justice Statistics, May 1988).

167　See James Lamare, *Texas Politics: Economics, Power, and Policy* (St. Paul: West, 1981). Originally from Texas Department of Corrections, *1975 Annual Statistical Report* (Huntsville: Texas Department of Corrections, 1975).

168　Joseph Weshifesky, "Redshirts," rodeo program, 1980, 16, box 1998/038-405, TPR records.

169　"Redshirts," rodeo program, 1979, 21, box 1998/038-405, TPR records.

170　A Redshirt could become a cowboy, and Mr. Redshirt became its own award in the 1970s. Rodeo program, 1973, 26, box 1998/035-405, TPR records.

171　Rodeo program, 1968, box 1998/038-405, TPR records.

172　"Browning Upsets Abbott, Miller to Take 'Top Hand' Rodeo Title," *Echo*, November 1968.

173　Rodeo program, 1973, 22, box 1998/038-405, TPR records. Women's participation ended in the late 1970s because of the reorganization of the prison system.

174　"Prison Rodeo," 51.

175　Hinton, *From the War on Poverty*, 65.

176　Perkinson, *Texas Tough*, 6.

177　Chase, "We Are Not Slaves," 75. As Perkinson argues, Ellis's reforms in education, though limited in scope, provided incarcerated men the opportunity to create a prison intelligentsia who formed the center of this movement; see *Texas Tough*, 224.

178　Chase, "Revolt," 179, 193.

179　For a full description of *Ruiz* see James Marquart and Ben Crouch, "Judicial Reform and Prison Control: The Impact of *Ruiz v. Estelle* on a Texas Penitentiary," *Law and Society Review* 19, no. 4 (January 1, 1985): 557–86. For a discussion of TDC's failure to implement the changes imprisoned men fought so hard to achieve see Perkinson, *Texas Tough*, 270–87, and Steve Martin, *Texas Prisons: The Walls Came Tumbling Down* (Austin: Texas Monthly Press, 1987).

180 "A Look Back at a Texas Tradition," *Clock Wise*, November 1986, clippings about the rodeo, 1931–1986-2, box 1998/038–404, TPR records.

181 Zienman, "At the Prison Rodeo"; Applebome, "Last Roundup Feared at Texas Prison Rodeo," A18.

182 Gould, "Discipline," 24.

3. HISTORY UNEDITED: BLACK RODEO, PROGRESS, AND THE PERFORMANCE OF HERITAGE

1 *Black Rodeo*, dir. Jeff Kanew (1972; Scorpion Releasing, 2011), DVD. Much of the filming for the rodeo was done in Harlem the day before the rodeo. The rodeo itself was held on Randalls Island. Philip Deloria explains the ways in which indigenous people are shown to be unexpected in modern American culture in *Indians in Unexpected Places* (Lawrence: University Press of Kansas, 2004).

2 Jeff Kanew, *Black Rodeo*, DVD director commentary.

3 "Michigan Cowboy, 23, in 6th Year as Rodeo Rider," *Baltimore Afro-American*, October 28, 1961, 14.

4 On the history of ranching cultures see Richard Slatta, *Cowboys of the Americas* (New Haven: Yale University Press, 1990); Paul Starr, *Let the Cowboy Ride: Cattle Ranching in the American West* (Baltimore: Johns Hopkins University Press, 1998); Simon Evans, Sarah Carter, and Bill Yeo, *Cowboys, Ranchers, and the Cattle Business* (Calgary: University of Calgary Press, 2000). For literature on African American range workers see Sara Massey, ed., *Black Cowboys of Texas* (College Station: Texas A&M University Press, 2000). Also see Philip Durham and Everett Jones's foundational *The Negro Cowboys* (New York: Dodd, Mead, 1965) and William Loren Katz's *The Black West* (New York: Doubleday, 1971).

5 In 1792, Spanish records showed almost three thousand people living in Texas, of whom fifteen percent listed African ancestry. Alwyn Barr, introduction to *Black Cowboys of Texas*, ed. Sara Massey (College Station: Texas A&M University Press, 2000), 1–5.

6 Ranches owned by black or mixed-raced people were well established in some areas of Texas, but these prominent black families also faced sustained attacks on their right to own land. The Ashworths of Jefferson County, for instance, owned extensive grazing lands near the Louisiana border. Like other Mexican nationals after the war, the Ashworths spent a great deal of time, money, and effort attempting to save their property from Anglo squatters and rustlers. Barr, "Introduction," 5.

7 Barr, "Introduction," 6.

8   Barr, "Introduction," 4–5.

9   Women like Johana July, a black Seminole *vaquera*, broke horses alongside their fathers and husbands. While July would have been raised with gender-specific tasks, her ability with animals, especially horses, cattle, and goats, as well as a longer Seminole tradition of female stock raisers, allowed her to enter the male-dominated sphere. After the death of her father, July continued to raise and break horses by riding them out into the Rio Grande and letting them tire themselves while swimming. Cecilia Gutierrez Venable, "'Havin' a Good Time': Women Cowhands and Johana July, a Black Seminole Vaquera," in *Black Cowboys in the American West: On the Range, on the Stage, behind the Badge*, ed. Bruce Glasrud and Michael Searles (Norman: University of Oklahoma Press, 2016), 26–28.

10 Douglas Hales, "Black Cowboy: Daniel Webster '80 John' Wallace," in *Black Cowboys in the American West: On the Range, on the Stage, behind the Badge*, ed. Bruce Glasrud and Michael Searles (Norman: University of Oklahoma Press, 2016), 75–84.

11 Nat Love, *The Life and Adventures of Nat Love* (repr.; London: Forgotten Books, 2017). For analysis of the life and legend of Nat Love, see Blake All-mendinger, "Deadwood Dick: The Black Cowboy as Cultural Timber," *Journal of American Culture* 16, no. 4 (Winter 1993): 79–90; Charity Fox, "Cowboys, Porters, and the Mythic West: Satire and Frontier Masculinity in *The Life and Adventures of Nat Love*," in *Fathers, Preachers, Rebels, Men*, ed. Peter Castor (Columbus: Ohio State University Press, 2011), 184–202; Micheal Searles, "Nat Love, a.k.a. Deadwood Dick: A Wild Ride," in *Black Cowboys in the American West: On the Range, on the Stage, behind the Badge*, ed. Bruce Glasrud and Michael Searles (Norman: University of Oklahoma Press, 2016), 85–98; Richard Slatta, "Deadwood Dick," in *The Mythical West: An Encyclopedia of Legend, Lore, and Popular Culture* (Santa Barbara: ABC-CLIO, 2001), 119–20; Dan Moos, "Recasting the West: Frontier Identity and African American Self-Publication," in *Outside America: Race, Ethnicity, and the Role of the American West in National Belonging* (Hanover: Dartmouth College Press, 2005); Michael Johnson, *Black Masculinity and the Frontier Myth in American Literature* (Norman: University of Oklahoma Press, 2002).

12 Michael Johnson, *Hoo-Doo Cowboys and Bronze Buckaroos: Conceptions of the African American West* (Jackson: University Press of Mississippi, 2014).

13 John A. Lomax, *Cowboy Songs and Other Frontier Ballads* (New York: Sturgis and Walton, 1915), xxi.

14 Robert Cantwell, *When We Were Good: The Folk Revival* (Cambridge: Harvard University Press, 1996), 72. This persistent effacement of black cowboys through biography and collection is discussed in Johnson, *Hoo-Doo Cowboys*, 8.

15　See for instance Emily Lutenski, *West of Harlem: African American Writers and the Borderlands* (Lawrence: University Press of Kansas, 2016), and Dan Moos, *Outside America: Race, Ethnicity, and the Role of the American West in National Belonging* (Hanover: Dartmouth College Press, 2005).

16　Oscar Micheaux, *The Forged Note* (Lincoln: Western Book Supply, 1915). Quoted in Moos, *Outside America,* 65. Micheaux also wrote two articles for the *Chicago Defender* urging young black men to move west.

17　"Black Rodeos," *Black Enterprise,* April 1972, 44.

18　See Peter Iverson, *Riders of the West: Portraits from Indian Rodeo* (Seattle: University of Washington Press, 1999), and *When Indians Became Cowboys: Native Peoples and Cattle Ranching in the American West* (Norman: University of Oklahoma, 1997); Jan Penrose, "When All the Cowboys Are Indians: The Nature of Race in All-Indian Rodeo," *Annals of the Association of American Geographers* 93, no. 3 (September 2003): 687–705; Laura Barraclough, "Contested Cowboys: Ethnic Mexican Charros and the Struggle for Suburban Public Space in 1970s Los Angeles," in *The Chicano Studies Reader: An Anthology of Aztlán, 1970–2015,* ed. Chon A. Noriega, Eric Avila, Karen Mary Davalos, Chela Sandoval, and Rafael Pérez-Torres (Los Angeles: University of California Chicano Studies Research Center, 2016), 714–39.

19　See Bruce A. Glasrund and Michael N. Searles, eds., *Black Cowboys in the American West: On the Range, on the Stage, behind the Badge* (Norman: University of Oklahoma Press, 2016.)

20　The prominence of heritage in the late twentieth century has often been conflated with a valuing of history, but as David Lowenthal famously explained, heritage and history are separate: "Heritage is not inquiry into the past but a celebration of it, not an effort to know what actually happened but a profession of faith in a past tailored to present-day purposes." See *The Heritage Crusade and the Spoils of History* (Cambridge: Cambridge University Press, 1998), x. For how this plays out in the contemporary West, see Daniel Maher, *Mythic Frontiers: Remembering, Forgetting, and Profiting with Cultural Heritage Tourism* (Gainesville: University Press of Florida, 2016).

21　Draft of fund-raising letter, March 2, 1998, MS 190, box 2, folder 8, Oakland Black Cowboy Association records, African American Museum and Library at Oakland, Oakland Public Library, Oakland, California. Hereafter OBCA. Also see "Oakland Celebrates Black Cowboy Parade," *Metro,* October 17, 1982, 1.

22　James Baldwin, "The American Dream and the American Negro," *New York Times,* March 7, 1965.

23　Deak Nabers, "Past Using: James Baldwin and Civil Rights Law in the 1960s," *Yale Journal of Criticism* 18, no. 2 (Fall 2005): 221–42. Also see Alison

Landsberg, *Prosthetic Memory: The Transformation of American Remembrance in the Age of Mass Culture* (New York: Columbia University Press, 2004).

24 While members of these tribes had contact with African-descended people from their first contact with Spanish explorers, it was not until the development of stable Spanish colonies in Florida and the English colonies in the Carolinas in the late seventeenth and early eighteenth centuries that black and Native peoples had day-to-day interaction. Daniel Littlefield, *Africans and Creeks: From the Colonial Period to the Civil War* (Westport, CT: Greenwood, 1979), 9. A person could be adopted or marry out of slavery; their bondage was not hereditarily passed down to their children, and they worked communal agricultural lands without the strict supervision of an overseer. This more loosely structured form of slavery began to be threatened after the revolution. As white settlement increased and agriculture gained preeminence over the deerskin trade, chattel slavery became increasingly important to both the Creeks and the Choctaws. Soon aspects of Anglo-American slavery began to transfer into Native societies. Enslaved African Americans who married free Creeks could no longer become citizens, and children soon began to inherit slavery. African Creeks, Cherokees, and Choctaws often created expansive, intergenerational families comprised of both free and enslaved members. Gary Zeller, *African Creeks: Estelvste and the Creek Nation* (Norman: University of Oklahoma Press, 2007), 10–14. Also see Kathryn Holland Braund, *Deerskins and Duffels: The Creek Indian Trade with Anglo-America, 1685–1815* (Lincoln: University of Nebraska Press, 1993); Margaret Zehmer Searcy, "Choctaws Subsistence, 1540–1830: Hunting, Fishing, Farming and Gathering," in *The Choctaws before Removal*, ed. Carolyn Keller Reeves (Jackson: University Press of Mississippi, 1985), 32; Richard White, *The Roots of Dependency: Subsistence, Environment, and Social Change among the Choctaws, Pawnees, and Navajos* (Lincoln: University of Nebraska Press, 1983); James Taylor Carson, *Searching for the Bright Path: The Mississippi Choctaws from Prehistory to Removal* (Lincoln: University of Nebraska Press, 1999). Also see Circe Sturm, *Blood Politics: Race, Culture and Identity in the Cherokee Nation of Oklahoma* (Berkeley: University of California Press, 2002); Tiya Miles, *Ties That Bind: The Story of an Afro-Cherokee Family in Slavery and Freedom* (Berkeley: University of California Press, 2005); Claudio Saunt, *Black, White, and Indian: Race and the Unmaking of an American Family* (New York: Oxford University Press, 2005); Celia Naylor, *African Cherokees in Indian Territory: From Chattel to Citizens* (Chapel Hill: University of North Carolina Press, 2008); Kevin Mulroy, *The Seminole Freedmen: A History* (Norman: University of Oklahoma Press, 2007); Fay A. Yarbrough, *Race and the Cherokee Nation: Sovereignty in*

the *Nineteenth Century* (Philadelphia: University of Pennsylvania Press, 2008). For classic works on Native and African American relationships see Jack D. Forbes, *Africans and Native Americans: The Language of Race and the Evolution of Red-Black Peoples* (Urbana: University of Illinois Press, 1993); James F. Brooks, ed., *Confounding the Color Line: The (American) Indian-Black Experience in North America* (Lincoln: University of Nebraska Press, 2002); Sharon P. Holland and Tiya Miles, eds., *Crossing Waters, Crossing Worlds: The African Diaspora in Indian Country* (Durham: Duke University Press, 2006); Arica L. Coleman, *That the Blood Stay Pure: African Americans, Native Americans, and the Predicament of Race and Identity in Virginia* (Bloomington: Indiana University Press, 2013); Barbara Krauthamer, *Black Slaves, Indian Masters: Slavery, Emancipation, and Citizenship in the Native American South* (Chapel Hill: University of North Carolina Press, 2013); Sharon P. Holland and Tiya Miles, "Afro-Native Realities," in *The World of Indigenous North America*, ed. Robert Warrior (New York: Routledge, 2015), 524–48.

25 Zeller, *African Creeks*, 25.

26 Zeller, *African Creeks*, 32–35.

27 Zeller, *African Creeks*, 44–46. Also see Amy Ware, *The Cherokee Kid: Will Rogers, Tribal Identity, and the Making of an American Icon* (Lawrence: University Press of Kansas, 2015), for a description of how the Cherokee Nation, and particularly Will Rogers's family, participated in these debates.

28 Importantly, the Choctaws and the Chickasaws did not claim their tribes' Freedmen as citizens; instead they asked the federal government to remove them from the territory. The government failed to do so, leaving many people without citizenship in any country. Daniel Littlefield Jr., *The Chickasaw Freedmen: A People without a Country* (Westport, CT: Greenwood, 1980), 51. The Choctaws adopted their Freedmen in 1883; see Choctaw Nation of Oklahoma, *Freedmen Bill: An Act* (Dennison, TX: Murray, 1883).

29 Zeller, *African Creeks*, 77. See Sarah Deutsch, "Being American in Boley, Oklahoma," in *Beyond Black and White: Race, Ethnicity, and Gender in the U.S. South and Southwest*, ed. Stephanie Cole and Alison Parker (College Station: Texas A&M University Press, 2004), 97–123, for a discussion of the differences between "full blood" Creeks with African ancestry and the Freedmen at the turn of the century.

30 Gary Zeller, "'If I Ain't One, You Won't Find Another One Here': Race, Identity, Citizenship, and Land; the African Creek Experience in the Indian Territory and Oklahoma, 1830–1910" (PhD diss., University of Arkansas, 2003), 2.

31 Zeller, *African Creeks*, 194.

32 Political and social justice were not the only potential opportunities. Kenneth Hamilton, historian of black towns, argues that "economic motives" were central

to the formation of these communities, noting that "their founders were specula-
tors aiming to profit by fostering a migrant population's quest for social equality
and financial security." Kenneth Marvin Hamilton, *Black Towns and Profit:
Promotion and Development in the Trans-Appalachian West, 1877–1915* (Urbana:
University of Illinois Press, 1991), 1, 100. Also see Thomas Knight, "All Black
Towns in Oklahoma: The Development and Survival" (PhD diss., University of
Oklahoma, 1975); Charlotte Hinger, *Nicodemus: Post-Reconstruction Politics and
Racial Justice in Western Kansas* (Norman: University of Oklahoma Press, 2016).

33 Hamilton, *Black Towns*, 101.

34 US Bureau of the Census, *Negro Population in the United States, 1790–1915*
(Washington: Government Printing Office, 1918, repr. New York: Arno Press,
1968), 786.

35 Kendra Field describes how earlier waves of black settlement often required a
separation of people from a larger African American community and an
attempt at assimilation into Native societies. See "'Grandpa Brown Didn't Have
No Land': Race, Gender, and an Intruder of Color in Indian Territory," in
Interconnections: Gender and Race in American History, ed. Carol Faulkner
and Alison Parker (Rochester: University of Rochester Press): 105–30. Also see
Kendra Field, *Growing Up with the Country: Family, Race, and Nation after
the Civil War* (New Haven: Yale University Press, 2018), and David Chang, *The
Color of the Land: Race, Nation, and the Politics of Landownership in Oklahoma, 1832–1929* (Chapel Hill: University of North Carolina Press, 2003),
158–59. David Chang explicitly analyzes the problematic deployment of the
word "Freedmen" to all Creeks of African descent as a way to essentialize all
African Creeks as non-Creek, as well as designate all African Creeks as
descendants of slaves, which was historically untrue. However, many African
Creeks also embraced the term as a way to distinguish themselves from
migrant African Americans, using it to structure their identity as native to
Indian Territory. See "Where Will the Nation Be at Home?: Race, Nationalisms,
and Emigration Movements in the Creek Nation," in *Crossing Waters, Crossing
Worlds: The African Diaspora in Indian Country*, ed. Sharon P. Holland and
Tiya Miles (Durham: Duke University Press, 2006), 81–83.

36 Thomas Haynes exemplified the migration patterns of many African Americans seeking to raise their families in a safe and stable place. Born in Red River
County, Texas, in 1869, Haynes first moved his family in 1899 to Oklahoma
City, a booming land-rush town, where he could find work as a day laborer.
Like most settlers, however, Haynes wished to own land, not simply work it
for others. While the Dawes Commission restricted the sale of tribal allotments
for a period of years, white and black people looked first to rent Native lands,
especially Freedmen lands, which could be sold more quickly, and then to buy.

Taking his family east into Indian Territory in 1901, Haynes built a simple dugout on rented land. He laboriously cleared the land and began to prepare it for farming. He also attempted to draw more black settlement to the area by proposing an all-black community called Oxford; unlike the future Boley, however, this town failed due to legal difficulties with buying and selling Native lands. *Boley Progress,* December 22, 1910.

37   Melissa Nicole Stuckey, "All Men Up: Race, Rights, and Power in the All-Black Town of Boley, Oklahoma, 1903–1939" (PhD diss., Yale University, 2011), 16–17.

38   E. J. Pinkett, "Over in Boley," *Boley Progress,* May 11, 1905.

39   Knight, "All Black Towns," 55, 79.

40   Chleyon Thomas, "Boley: An All-Black Pioneer Town and the Education of Its Children" (EdD diss., University of Akron, 1989), 43–44.

41   As Stuckey explains, in 1907, both Paden and Boley were included in Paden Township, so knowing how neighboring farm families identified is difficult; "All Men Up," 37. Also see US Bureau of the Census, *Bulletin 89: Population of Oklahoma and Indian Territory in 1907* (Washington, DC: Government Printing Office, 1907), 23, 32.

42   Stuckey, "All Men Up," 104.

43   Booker T. Washington, "Boley, a Negro Town in the West," *Outlook,* January 4, 1908, 28.

44   Hamilton, *Black Towns,* 2, 105.

45   Moos, *Outside America,* 11.

46   "Not Color," *Clearview Patriarch,* reproduced in Clearview Rodeo Souvenir Program, 1983, 6, Towns, Clearview Rodeo, Historic Oklahoma Collection, Research Division, Oklahoma Historical Society, Oklahoma City. Hereafter Historic Oklahoma Collection.

47   David Blight, *Race and Reunion: The Civil War in American Memory* (Cambridge: Harvard University Press, 2001), 368. Also see Kathlyn Gay, *African-American Holidays, Festivals, and Celebration* (Detroit: Omnigraphics, 2007), 252.

48   "Big Summer Carnival," *Boley Progress,* May 18, 1905, 1.

49   For more on the carnival see *Boley Progress,* June 22 and 29, 1905.

50   Boley's town-booster carnival would have been one of many opportunities men of color would have had to participate in early forms of rodeo, though these openings began to close over the early decades of the twentieth century. In the 1876 rodeo, Nat Love reportedly won the name "Deadwood Dick" when he competed in a cowboy competition on July 4 in Deadwood, South Dakota. He "roped, threw, tied, bridled, saddled, and mounted my mustang in exactly nine minutes from the crack of the gun. [. . .] Right there the assembled crowd named me Deadwood Dick and proclaimed me champion roper of the western cattle country." Love, *Life and Adventures,* 91–93. In 1906, a "Grand Roping

Contest and Cowboy Carnival" took place near Boley, featuring local Okemah cowboy Luther Williams as well as Bill Pickett, "the Negro Wrangler, who throws a steer with his teeth." While rodeo producers often forced Bill Pickett to dress as a Mexican performer to draw attention away from his race, places like Boley celebrated the appearance of a professional black cowboy. "Grand Roping Contest and Cowboy Carnival," unknown source, 1906, Boley and Clearview scrapbook, Okfusgee County Historical Society, Okemah, Oklahoma. Hereafter OCHS.

51 Field, "Grandpa," 123.

52 Littlefield, *Chickasaw Freedmen*, 205. See Stuckey's "All Men Up" on the importance of Boley in civil rights activism in the 1910s and 1920s as black Oklahomans fought Jim Crow.

53 Boley Spears, interview by Cheylon Thomas, Boley, Oklahoma, December 11, 1987, cited in Thomas, "Boley," 41. Some white journalists decried the crime as well: "The act of the mob is deeply regretted by all good citizens. There is not a shadow of excuse for the crime, and it is hoped that the officers make every effort to bring the guilty parties to justice and uphold the majesty of the law." "Woman and Boy Lynched," unknown source, ca. 1911, Boley and Clearview scrapbook, OCHS.

54 Velma Dolphin-Ashley, "A History of Boley, Oklahoma" (MS thesis, Kansas State Teachers College, 1940), 36. Kendra Field explains how the horrible conditions faced by migrants has led to a public memory of fraudulence on the part of Chief Sam. See Kendra Field and Ebony Coletu, "The Chief Sam Movement, a Century Later: Public Histories, Private Stores, and the African Diaspora," *Transitions* 114 (2014): 108–30, and Kendra Field, "'No Such Thing as Stand Still': Migration and Geopolitics in African American History," *Journal of American History* 102, no. 3 (December 2015): 693–718. Also see K. Mays, "Transnational Progressivism: African Americans, Native Americans, and the Universal Races Congress of 1911," *American Indian Quarterly* 37, no. 4 (2013): 244–61.

55 Dolphin-Ashley, "History of Boley," 39. Also see Luther P. Jackson Jr., "Shaped by a Dream, a Town Called Boley," *Life Magazine*, November 29, 1968, 72–74. Black folks suffered whether they owned the land or not. Those who owned land often could not afford the mortgage or taxes and lost their house to the bank. Others were sharecroppers whose landlords simply took their share out of production during hard times.

56 "A Dream That Faded," *New York Times Magazine*, December 6, 1964, 47; "A New Chance for Black Town," *Business Week*, August 9, 1969, 98–97.

57 Henrietta Hicks, interview with Rebecca Scofield, Boley, Oklahoma, June 2017.

58 "Boley Round-Up Time," *Ebony*, November 1, 1964, 102.

59   1966 Boley Rodeo, Official Souvenir Program, and 1974 Boley Rodeo, Official
      Souvenir Program, Personal Collection of Henrietta Hicks. Hereafter Hicks
      Collection.

60   "Rodeo Expects More Visitors," *Oklahoman*, May 21, 1967, 159; "Large Crowd
      Due for Rodeo," *Oklahoman*, April 29, 1973, A18; "Rodeo Buffs Flood Boley,"
      Oklahoman, May 28, 1978, 23.

61   "Boley Expects Flip to Lead Rodeo Parade," *Oklahoman*, May 13, 1979, 29.

62   "Boley Round-Up Time."

63   The State Training School for Negro Boys was originally built in 1923 as a
      tuberculosis sanitarium for black people. In 1925 it became the State Training
      School for Negro Boys, which incarcerated young "incorrigibles." The facility
      provided one of the main sources of employment throughout the midcentury.
      In 1965 it integrated and changed its name. In 1983, the Oklahoma Department
      of Corrections reopened it as a prison named the John H. Lilley Correctional
      Center, against community wishes. See "Boley Townsfolk Just Want Their
      School," *Oklahoman*, May 29, 1983.

64   "Youth Acheivements," 1974 Boley Rodeo, Official Souvenir Program, Hicks
      Collection.

65   Clearview Rodeo Souvenir Program, 1983, Historic Oklahoma Collection.
      Also see J. P. Owens, *Clearview* (Okemah, OK: J. P. Owens, 1995).

66   Clearview Rodeo Souvenir Program, 1983, inside cover, Historic Oklahoma
      Collection.

67   Richard D. Hardaway, "Oklahoma's African American Rodeo Performers," in
      *Black Cowboys in the American West: On the Range, on the Stage, behind the
      Badge*, ed. Bruce Glasrud and Michael Searles (Norman: University of
      Oklahoma Press, 2016), 118. Also see "Negro Killed in East Main St. Resort,"
      Daily Ardmoreite, March 4, 1915.

68   Alan Govenar, "A. J. Walker: Cowboy and Rodeo Organizer," in *Black
      Cowboys of Texas*, ed. Sara Massey (College Station: Texas A&M University
      Press, 2000), 293.

69   Men of color had often tried to compete in rodeos at Madison Square Garden.
      In 1948, Carlos Verde of Albuquerque and Nickolas Mann of Yuma were
      unable to raise the seventy-five-dollar registration fee until Sherman Hibbitt,
      "mayor of Harlem," stepped in and sponsored them. See "2 Cowboys Take
      Part in Autry Rodeo," *Baltimore Afro-American*, October 16, 1948, A2, and
      "Bucking Brahma Bull no Trouble to Cowboy," *Baltimore Afro-American*,
      August 16, 1941, 23.

70   Govenar, "A. J. Walker," 291.

71   Govenar, "A. J. Walker," 297.

72   "The Rocky Trail of a Rodeo Cowboy," *New York Times*, September 25, 1981.

73 See Demetrius W. Pearson, "Shadow Riders of the Subterranean Circuit: A Descriptive Account of Black Rodeo in the Texas Gulf Coast Region," in *Black Cowboys in the American West: On the Range, on the Stage, behind the Badge,* ed. Bruce Glasrud and Michael Searles (Norman: University of Oklahoma Press, 2016), and Hardaway, "Oklahoma's African American Rodeo Performers," for discussions of the financial hardships of rodeos.

74 College rodeos began in the 1920s, primarily in Texas. In 1949, several state university teams created the National Intercollegiate Rodeo Association. Sylvia Gann Mahoney, *College Rodeo: From Show to Sport* (College Station: Texas A&M University Press, 2004). "Black Rodeos," 39–44.

75 "Association of Black Cowboys Brings a Rodeo to Jersey City," *New York Times,* April 25, 1971, 64.

76 "150 cowboys expected in Bill Pickett Invitational Rodeo," *Baltimore Afro-American,* July 20, 1985, 3.

77 "Boley Round-Up Time."

78 Michel-Rolph Trouillot, *Silencing the Past: Power and the Production of History* (Boston: Beacon Press, 1995), 7. He also notes: "History is always produced in a specific historical context," 22.

79 Baldwin, "American Dream."

80 C. Vann Woodward, *The Strange Career of Jim Crow* (New York: Oxford University Press, 1955), xvi; Lerone Bennett Jr., *Before the Mayflower: A History of the Negro in America, 1619–1962* (Chicago: Johnson, 1962); Howard Rabinowitz, "More Than the Woodward Thesis: Assessing the Strange Career of Jim Crow," *Journal of American History* 75, no. 3 (December 1988): 842–56.

81 See Russell Rickford, *We Are an African People: Independent Education, Black Power, and the Radical Imagination* (New York: Oxford University Press, 2016). Also see Robert Self, *American Babylon: Race and the Struggle for Postwar Oakland* (Princeton: Princeton University Press, 2003).

82 Boley rodeo program, 1982, M2012.188, box 50, folder 5, Clara Luper Collection, Research Division, Oklahoma Historical Society, Oklahoma City. Hereafter Clara Luper Collection.

83 "Take a Road to a Rodeo," Boley Rodeo Souvenir Program, 1987, 50, Historic Oklahoma Collection.

84 "Take a Road to a Rodeo."

85 *Time,* March 28, 1977, 54. For other critical responses to *Roots* see "After Haley's Comet," *Newsweek,* February 14, 1977, 97–98; Maya Angelou, "Haley Shows Us the Truth of Our Conjoined Histories," *New York Times,* January 27, 1977, 27; Gloria Greene, "Roots Uprooted and Rerooted," *Los Angeles Sentinel,* February 3, 1977, A1; Charlayne Hunter-Gault, "*Roots* Getting a Grip on People Everywhere," *New York Times,* January 28, 1977, B1; "*Roots* Takes Hold in

America," *Newsweek*, February 1, 1977; Richard Schickel, "Viewpoint: Middle-
brow Mandingo," *Time*, January 24, 1977. For scholarly analysis of the *Roots*
phenomenon see George Lipsitz, "The Meaning of Memory: Family, Class,
Ethnicity in Early Network Television Programs," in *Private Screenings:
Television and the Female Consumer*, ed. Lynn Spigel and Denise Mann
(Minneapolis: University of Minnesota Press, 1992), 71–110; Michael Steward
Blayney, "*Roots* and the Noble Savage," *North Dakota Quarterly* 51, no. 1
(Winter 1986): 1–17; Amy Harmon, "Blacks Pin Hopes on DNA to Fill Slavery's
Gaps in Family Tree," *New York Times*, July 25, 2005; David Chioni Moore,
"Routes: Alex Haley's *Roots* and the Rhetoric of Genealogy," *Transition* 64
(1994): 4–21; Matthew Delmont, *Making "Roots": A Nation Captivated* (Berke-
ley: University of California Press, 2016).

86 Leslie Fishbein, "*Roots*: Docudrama and the Interpretation of History," in
American History, American Television, ed. John O'Conor (New York:
Frederick Ungar, 1983), 285.

87 Fishbein, "*Roots*," 287.

88 Fishbein, "*Roots*," 281. Also see Kathleen Fearn-Banks, *Historical Dictionary of
African-American Television* (Lanham, MD: Scarecrow, 2006), 371.

89 Jacobson, *Roots Too*, 9.

90 Fishbein, "*Roots*," 301. Also see Matthew Fry Jacobson, *Roots Too: White
Ethnic Revival in Post-Civil Rights America* (Cambridge: Harvard University
Press, 2006).

91 Lauret Savoy, *Trace: History, Race, and the American Landscape* (Berkeley:
Counterpoint Press, 2015), 28.

92 M. J. Rymsza-Pawlowska, *History Comes Alive: Public History and Popular Culture in the 1970s* (Chapel Hill: University of North Carolina Press,
2017), 4.

93 Rymsza-Pawlowska, *History Comes Alive*, 118–38. Also see Tony Horowitz,
Confederates in the Attic: Dispatches from the Unfinished Civil War (New York:
Vintage Press, 1999); Ian McCalman and Paul Pickering, *Historical Reenact-
ment: From Realism to the Affective Turn* (London: Palgrave, 2010); Rebecca
Schneider, *Performing Remains: Art and War in Time of Theatrical Reenact-
ment* (New York: Routledge, 2011).

94 Rymsza-Pawlowska, *History Comes Alive*, 10.

95 Dolphin-Ashley, "History of Boley." Henrietta Hicks also noted that Boley was
"cotton country." Henrietta Hicks, interview with Rebecca Scofield, June 2017,
Boley, Oklahoma.

96 Dolphin-Ashley, "History of Boley," 19, 28.

97 Boley rodeo program, 1982, M2012.188, box 50, folder 5, 18, Clara Luper Collection.

98 1974 Boley Rodeo, Official Souvenir Program, Hicks Collection.

99 "Take a Road," Boley Rodeo Souvenir Program, 1987, 1, Historic Oklahoma Collection.

100 "Bank President, Two Bandits Slain in Attempted Hold-Up, Third Member of Trio Held Here, May Not Live," unknown source, November 32, 1932, OCHS.

101 Leon Smith, *High Noon at the Boley Corral* (Detroit: L. E. Smith, 1980), OCHS. This historic event was further linked with the performative West when an all-black cowboy film *The Crimson Skull*, featuring Bill Pickett, was filmed in Boley soon afterward.

102 Boley rodeo program, 1982, M2012.188, box 50, folder 5, 5, Clara Luper Collection.

103 Afro-American Bicentennial Corporation, *Summary Report of Thirty Sites Determined to Be Significant in Illustration and Commemorating the Role of Black Americans in United States History* (Washington, DC: Afro-American Bicentennial Corporation, 1973), 4. Emily Isberg, "Black Landmarks," *Washington Post*, July 28, 1974; Angela Terrell, "Black Landmarks," *Washington Post*, August 3, 1974; "Six Historic Sites Are Named," *Washington Post*, March 18, 1977. For an examination of how communities and individuals experienced the Bicentennial as an opportunity to embody history, especially through organizations like the Afro-American Bicentennial Corporation, see Rymsza-Pawlowska, *History Comes Alive*.

104 Christopher Capozzola, "It Makes You Want to Believe," *America in the Seventies*, ed. Beth Bailey and David Farber (Lawrence: University Press of Kansas, 2004), 38.

105 William V. Francis Jr., "Boley Community Settled by Blacks in 1903," *Okemah News Leader* (reprinted from *Kansas City Star*, December 22, 1974), Boley and Clearview scrapbook, OCHS.

106 *Clearview Patriarch*, February 20, 1911, 1, reproduced in Clearview Rodeo Souvenir Program, 1983, 3, Historic Oklahoma Collection.

107 Thad Martin, "The Disappearing Black Farmer" (reproduced from *Ebony*, June 1985, 146–50), MS 179, box 23, folder 17, Oakland Vertical File Collection, African American Museum and Library at Oakland, Oakland, California. Hereafter Oakland Vertical File.

108 For some foundational works on black migration to the West, see Nell Painter, *Exodusters: Black Migration to Kansas after Reconstruction* (New York: Alfred A. Knopf, 1977); James Grossman, *Land of Hope: Chicago, Black Southerners, and the Great Migration* (Chicago: University of Chicago Press, 1989); Quintard Taylor, *The Forging of a Black Community: Seattle's Central District from 1870 through the Civil Rights Era* (Seattle: University of Washington Press, 1994).

109 See "Michigan Cowboy, 23, in 6th Year as Rodeo Rider," *Baltimore Afro-American*, October 28, 1961, 14; "Urban Cowboys," *Baltimore Afro-American*,

September 13, 1980, 16; "Yo-Ho Baby!: Charlie Sampson's Mighty Rides at the National Invitational Black Rodeo," *Washington Post*, May 23, 1981, C1.

110 Barraclough, "Contested Cowboys," 721. Also see Laura Barraclough, *Charros: How Mexican Cowboys Are Remapping Race and American Identity* (Berkeley: University of California Press, 2019).

111 Peter Harris, "Rugged Rodeo Rider Resents Racism," *Baltimore Afro-American*, June 4, 1983, 10; "Black Champ Featured in Rare DC Rodeo Show," *Baltimore Afro-American*, September 24, 1983, 10; "Bill Pickett: 1870–1932," *Baltimore Afro-American*, July 20, 1985, 3; "Sampson Doesn't Dwell on Accident: It's History," *Courier* (Prescott, Arizona), July 6, 1984, 9A.

112 Michael Allen, *Rodeo Cowboys in the North American Imagination* (Reno: University of Nevada Press, 1998), 49.

113 Rebecca Scofield, "'Chaps and Scowls': Play, Violence, and the Post-1970s Urban Cowboy," *Journal of American Culture* 40, no. 4 (December 2017): 325–40.

114 For instance, Philadelphia's Fletcher Street Urban Riding Club and New York's Federation of Black Cowboys.

115 Bob Queen, "All-Black 'Jersey' Rodeo Pulls 25,000," *Baltimore Afro-American*, May 8, 1971, 19.

116 Barraclough, "Contested Cowboys," 721.

117 Marilynn Johnson, *The Second Gold Rush: Oakland and the East Bay in World War II* (Berkeley: University of California Press, 1993); Self, *American Babylon*, 218–19.

118 Lionel Wilson, "Black Cowboys Day," October 19, 1977, MS 190, box 1, folder 13, OBCA.

119 "Black Cowboy Rides the Range in Oakland," *San Francisco Examiner*, November 9, 1975, MS 179, box 23, folder 16, Oakland Vertical File.

120 The BCA became the Oakland Black Cowboy Association in 2004. "Executive Members of the Black Cowboy Association," MS 190, box 1, folder 3, OBCA. Booker T. Emery and Charles Wright (chairperson and co-chairperson) were two driving forces of this organization. Wright often visited the mountains for horseback riding. The parade route shifted over the years, often going down Broadway or around Lake Merritt. This route was often up for debate as a letter from the Brookside Horsemen's Association on December 13, 1978, showed. The horsemen's group expressed disappointment that the parade route did not go into West Oakland that year and many of their members missed it, denigrating the path as going through "Skid Row" and "Wino Park."

121 Press releases, March 1979, June 1983, MS 190, box 1, folder 14, OBCA.

122 Self, *American Babylon*, 222.

123 Letter from Booker T. Emery, Chairman, 1980, MS 190, box 2, folder 8, OBCA.

124 "Black Cowboy Rides the Range in Oakland," *San Francisco Examiner,* November 9, 1975, no page, MS 179, box 23, folder 16, Oakland Vertical File.

125 Parade history, MS 190, box 1, folder 3, OBCA.

126 Letter from Lionel J. Wilson, Mayor, April 29, 1978, MS 190, box 2, folder 8, OBCA.

127 Ben Sandmel, *Zydeco!* (Jackson: University of Mississippi Press, 1999), 12–13.

128 Mark DeWitt, *Cajun and Zydeco Dance Music in Northern California: Modern Pleasures in a Postmodern World* (Jackson: University of Mississippi Press, 2008).

129 Northern California Black Horsemen's Association, September 1991, MS 179, box 23, folder 16, Oakland Vertical File.

130 "Association of Black Cowboys Brings a Rodeo to Jersey City," *New York Times,* April 24, 1971, 64.

131 Also see "Rodeo Tour Is Tribute to Black Frontiersmen," *Baltimore Afro-American,* June 21, 1986, 7.

132 "Black Cowboy Association," MS 190, box 1, folder 1, OBCA.

133 T. J. Williams, interview with Tony Sherman, Live Oak, Texas, August 1989, cited in Sherman, "Troy John Williams: The Tennis Shoe Cowboy," in *Black Cowboys of Texas,* ed. Sara Massey (College Station: Texas A&M University Press, 2000), 286.

134 Queen, "All-Black 'Jersey' Rodeo," 19.

135 See Daniel Geary, *Beyond Civil Rights: The Moynihan Report and Its Legacy* (Philadelphia: University of Pennsylvania Press, 2015).

136 "Yo-Ho Baby!," C1.

137 "Executive Members of the Black Cowboy Association," MS 190, box 1, folder 1, OBCA; Steve Estes, *I Am a Man! Race, Manhood, and the Civil Rights Movement* (Chapel Hill: University of North Carolina Press, 2005).

138 Bruce Glasrud, introduction to *Black Cowboys in the American West: On the Range, on the Stage, behind the Badge,* ed. Bruce Glasrud and Michael Searles (Norman: University of Oklahoma Press, 2016), 10. Much of the writing on black women in the West has been from the past two decades. See Tricia Martineau Wagner, *African American Women of the Old West* (Helena, MT: TwoDot, 2007); Dee Garceau-Hagen, ed., *Portraits of Women in the American West* (New York: Routledge, 2005).

139 Gavin Esler, "The Whitewashed Cowboy," *London Times,* December 26, 1994.

140 Roger Butterfield, "Hard Reality of Freedom," *Life Magazine,* November 29, 1968, 63.

141 Queen, "All-Black 'Jersey' Rodeo," 19.

142 Kanew, *Black Rodeo.*

143 Kanew, *Black Rodeo.*

144 "African American—What Does It Mean?" MS 179, box 3, folder 5, Oakland Vertical File. The BCA collected a great deal of educational material on black pioneers to share with their members.

145 Woody Strode, interview, *Black Rodeo,* dir. Jeff Kanew.

146 "Rodeo Changes Face of the West," *Washington Post,* June 3, 1985, B3.

147 Love, *Life and Adventures,* 42. Similarly, he referred to other nonwhite men, like Mexicans, as "greasers."

148 Boley rodeo program, 1982, 18, M2012.188, box 50, folder 5, Clara Luper Collection.

149 There are many Buffalo Soldier Reenactment groups throughout the United States, such as the Bexar County Buffalo Soldiers Association.

150 2014 National Cowboys of Color Rodeo Finals, official program. This journey of Estevanico and his companions established Spanish interest in northern exploration and led to the founding of settlements. See Cyclone Covey, ed., *Cabeza de Vaca's Adventures in the Unknown Interior of America* (Albuquerque: University of New Mexico Press, 1983); Quintard Taylor, *In Search of the Racial Frontier: African Americans in the American West, 1598–1990* (New York: Norton, 1998); and Andrés Reséndez, *A Land So Strange: The Epic Journey of Cabeza de Vaca* (New York: Basic, 2007).

151 See Woody Strode, *Goal Dust* (Indianapolis: Madison Books, 1990), 1–3.

152 Woody Strode, interview, *Black Rodeo,* dir. Jeff Kanew.

153 Washington, "Boley," 30.

154 Washington, "Boley," 31. Sarah Deutsch, in "Being American in Boley, Oklahoma," 108, also comments on the complex racial distinctions at play in Washington's article, noting that black Natives, both Afro Creeks and Freedmen, were often framed as savages in comparison with migrants.

155 "Cleo Hearn Remembers: My Mother," in Don Russell, *Cowboys of Color* (Dallas, TX: Taylor Specialty Books, 2016).

156 Baldwin, "American Dream."

157 Allmendiger, "Deadwood Dick," 87.

158 Toni Morrison, *Paradise* (New York: Alfred Knopf, 1998), 13.

159 Morrison, *Paradise,* 5.

160 Boley's 30th Anniversary Celebration Souvenir Program, 1934, 9, OCHS.

161 Nicole Fleetwood, *Troubling Vision: Performance, Visuality, and Blackness* (Chicago: University of Chicago, 2011), 3.

162 Thomas, "Boley," 26.

4. CAMP AND THE COWBOY: THE SERIOUS FUN OF GAY RODEO

1 Allen Kalchik, "IGRA Finals All Around Cowboy: Greg Olson," *Roundup,* Spring 1994, 17.

2   A note on terminology: when referring to the rodeo community I use "gay rodeoers" and "gay rodeo" as that was how the community defined itself, despite the presence of people of all genders and sexual identities. When referring to broader communities that interacted with the rodeo at the time, I try to use the more expansive terms "queer" and "LGBTQ+" to denote the changing identity labels emerging between the 1980s and the early 2000s. Generational gaps concerning gender and sexual identity, particularly the reclaiming of the word "queer," have been persistent in communities like the rodeo and demonstrate the constant flux of identity labels over time.

3   Mary McGrory, "Reagan Rides High in Saddle at California Ranch," *Boston Globe*, June 2, 1976, 27; letter from President Ronald Reagan to Tennessee Williams, no date, box 31, folder 1, Tennessee Williams Papers, 1920–1983, Rare Book and Manuscript Library, Columbia University, New York.

4   Richard Corliss, "Season of the Night-Soap," *Time*, February 9, 1981, 74–75; James Willwerth, "TV's *Dallas*: Whodunit?" *Time*, August 11, 1980, 60. *Dallas* was so popular, political candidates used characters as campaign fodder. When the main character J.R. was shot in the 1981 season finale, politicians of both parties attempted to claim a piece of the primetime drama. Jimmy Carter told Texan supporters, "I came to Dallas to find out confidentially who shot J.R. If any of you could let me know that, I could finance the whole campaign this fall." More directly, Ronald Reagan's campaign buttons declared, "A Democrat Shot J.R." James N. Gregory argues in "Southernizing the American Working Class: Post-War Episodes of Regional and Class Transformation," *Labor History* 39 (May 1998): 135–54, that western wear was a part of the larger spread of southern culture, but I would not include Carter as an influential southern/western persona. For a labor perspective on the masculinity crisis in the 1970s, see Joshua Freeman, "Hardhats: Construction Workers, Manliness, and the 1970 Pro-War Demonstrations," *Journal of Social History* 26, no. 4 (Summer 1993): 725–44; Eileen Boris, "On Cowboys and Welfare Queens: Independence, Dependence, and Interdependence at Home and Abroad," *Journal of American Studies* 41, no. 3 (December 2007): 599–621.

5   Rebecca Scofield, "'Chaps and Scowls': Play, Violence, and the Post-1970s Urban Cowboy," *Journal of American Culture* 40, no. 4 (December 2017): 325–40.

6   "Western Standards," *Esquire*, September 1989, 180–99.

7   Peter W. Kaplan, "The End of the Soft Line," *Esquire*, April 1980, cover.

8   Kaplan, "The End of the Soft Line," 44, 41.

9   Michael Gross, *Genuine Authentic: The Real Life of Ralph Lauren* (New York: Perennial, 2003).

10 Peter Hennen discusses the fight of other gay subcultures against assumed effeminacy, namely leather and bears. See *Faeries, Bears, and Leathermen: Men*

in Community Queering the Masculine (Chicago: University of Chicago Press, 2008). Also see Martin Levine, *Gay Macho: The Life and Death of the Homosexual Clone* (New York: New York University Press, 1998), and Eric Anderson, *In the Game: Gay Athletes and the Cult of Masculinity* (Albany: State University of New York Press, 2005).

11 "Churchill Officials Move to Block Gay Rodeo," *Reno Gazette Journal,* October 20, 1988, 16C.

12 Marie Antoinette du Barry, interview with Rebecca Scofield, Gay Rodeo Oral History Project, April 1, 2017, Dallas, Texas. Please note that some of these transcripts have been edited and curated for the online exhibit *Voices of Gay Rodeo*, available online through the University of Idaho's Center for Digital Inquiry and Learning.

13 Sara Warner, *Acts of Gaiety: LGBT Performance and the Politics of Pleasure* (Ann Arbor: University of Michigan Press, 2012), 6, 11.

14 Particularly Christopher Le Cony and Zoe Trodd, "Reagan's Rainbow Rodeos: Queer Challenges to the Cowboy Dreams of the 1980s," *Canadian Review of American Studies* 39, no. 2 (2009): 163–83.

15 Patrick Terry, interview with Rebecca Scofield, Gay Rodeo Oral History Project, October 21, 2017, Santa Fe, New Mexico. Many thanks to the dedicated team who worked on assembling the archives—Frank Harrell, Patrick Terry, Roger Bergmann, Gregory Hinton, and Brian Helander, among many others.

16 See Michael Robert Gorman, *The Empress Is a Man: Stories from the Life of José Sarria* (New York: Haworth Press, 1998), for a history of the Imperial Court System. The courts spread throughout the country, with annual elections of a city's empress and emperor.

17 The history of gay rodeo has been laboriously reconstructed in large part through the efforts of Frank Harrell. His website, gayrodeohistory.org, is a phenomenal resource for archival material and historical summaries. Also see Bill Arsenaux, "Ride 'Em Cowboy: Reno's Gay Rodeo," *In Touch for Men*, November 1978, 74–77; John Calendo, "Gay Rodeo: Wild Time in Reno," *In Touch for Men*, January 1981, 34–35; "National Reno Gay Rodeo: An Editors [*sic*] View," *Skin* 5, no. 1 (1983), 10–17; Charles Farber, "National Reno Gay Rodeo and in the Saddle," *Advocate,* September 16, 1982, 21; "Reno Gay Rodeo Draws Big Crowd," *Reno Gazette Journal,* August 5, 1979, 38. Also see Dennis McBride, *Out of the Neon Closet: Queer Community in the Silver State* (North Charleston, SC: CreateSpace, 2016), 196–200.

18 Eight thousand members is a commonly cited number, mostly found in internal correspondence to prospective sponsors; see for instance letter to Miller Breweries from Wayne Jakino, 1993, MSA.26, box 15, International Gay Rodeo Association Institutional Archives, 1982–2009, Autry National Center,

Los Angeles. Hereafter IGRA. Membership committee records, however, show numbers show verified members in good standing to be 2,817 in 1993, 2,891 in 1995, and 2,641 in 1997. IGRA Association and Division Membership Totals, 1997, box 47, IGRA. Similar discrepancies appear in today's reporting of membership numbers. For instance, on February 12, 2015, *Echo Magazine* reported that the IGRA had almost 5,000 members. Official annual conference reports place it closer to 1,600, however. Personal correspondence, IGRA officers, January 8, 2016. The same reporting system shows a 2013 membership of 1,685 and a significant dip in 2014 with 1,345. The 2015 number of 1,600 is therefore encouraging for many in the association.

19 Some of these rodeos were explicitly nontraditional. In 1990, an All People's Rodeo, held by Tri-State International Gay Rodeo, included events like Stud Decorating, Wild Cowboy Riding, and Fastest Blow Job. No subsequent rodeos were held by this association. Once again I would like give credit to cowboy Frank Harrell for his tireless work. Other key dates came from materials in the IGRA archive at the Autry National Center.

20 Bruce Gros, interview with Rebecca Scofield, Gay Rodeo Oral History Project, September 10, 2016, Duncans Mills, California.

21 John King, interview with Rebecca Scofield, Gay Rodeo Oral History Project, July 7, 2017, Denver, Colorado. Nancy Achilles notes the fundamental role gay bars played in the development of gay subcultures throughout the twentieth century. Bars provided both opportunity for and legitimacy to subcultural interactions. This role, however, has been challenged in the past twenty years by the growing presence of the internet. See Nancy Achilles, "The Development of the Homosexual Bar as an Institution," *Sexual Deviance*, ed. John Gagnon and William Simon (New York: Harper and Row, 1967). Also see *Quest*, Seventh Annual Rocky Mountain Regional Rodeo program, 1989, IGRA, box 3. Kathryn Alexander, "Politely Different: Queer Presence in Country Dancing and Music," *Yearbook for Traditional Music* 50 (2018): 187–209.

22 John Toss, "Nightlife: Charlie's Denver," *First Hand Events*, 1989 Gay Rodeo Souvenir Issue, 16. IGRA incorporated this bar-centricity by encouraging large pub crawls after official rodeo events had ended for the night. For instance, the program for the 1983 inaugural Rocky Mountain Regional Gay Rodeo, held in Denver, included a full-page map of the city with each participating gay bar's logo and location displayed. First Annual Rocky Mountain Regional Rodeo program, 1983, IGRA, box 1.

23 1996 Saguaro Regional Rodeo program, 1996, box 30, IGRA.

24 Carline Symons notes in her work *The Game Games: A History* (London, Routledge, 2010) that the Vancouver Games marked a turning point as the event nearly tripled in size, though many of the organizers remained fairly

conservative in their exclusion of some of the more radical contingents of the LGBTQ+ community. Judy Davidson, "The Necessity of Queer Shame for Gay Pride," in *Sport, Sexualities and Queer/Theory*, ed. Jayne Caudwell (London, Routledge, 2006). Also see Patricia Nell Warren's *Lavender Locker Room: 3000 Years of Great Athletes Whose Sexual Orientation Was Different* (London: Wildcat Press, 2006), for information on gay rodeo in sporting culture.

25 Celeste McGovern, "Homo on the Range," *Alberta Report*, July 18, 1994, 29.

26 Email received by IGRA, 1998, box 47, IGRA.

27 This is in contrast to many officials who wrote letters of support to the gay rodeo, thanking the organization for bringing business to the city. These officials still refused to attend, however. Rodney Food, "Commissioner's Fight against Gay Rodeo 'Dead,'" *Nevada State Journal*, June 9, 1981, box 6, church files, IGRA.

28 John King also described a variety of acts of vandalism and attacks on his bars over the years. Many gay rodeoers were reluctant to share their experiences with blatant homophobia, often transitioning to focus on their more positive experiences. King, interview.

29 See *Quest*, Seventh Annual Rocky Mountain Regional Rodeo program, 1989, box 3, IGRA; "County Wants to Stop Gay Rodeo," *Lahontan Valley News*, October 20, 1988, 1–2; "Churchill Officials Move to Block Gay Rodeo," *Reno Gazette Journal*, October 20, 1988, 1C, 16C; "Last Minute Appeal Denied," *Lahontan Valley News*, October 22, 1988, 1; "Tense Aftermath to Banned Gay Rodeo," *Reno Gazette Journal*, October 20, 1988, 1.

30 Copeland and the regional rodeo association filed suit against the arena in 1992. Jennifer Comes, "Gay Rodeo to Make First Foray into Kansas," *Wichita Eagle*, July 19, 1991, box 1, IGRA; "Regional Rodeo Files Suit against Wichita Arena," *OGRA Newsletter*, February 1992, box 12, IGRA.

31 AGRA bid for 1992 IGRA Finals Rodeo, 1992, box 8, IGRA; fact sheet for new media, 1992, box 12, IGRA.

32 Calendo, "Gay Rodeo," 33.

33 "Gay Rodeo," *Jerry Springer Show* (Multimedia Entertainment, 1993). After the airing of this show, the IGRA president graciously wrote an apology to the PRCA commissioner for having promoted a negative image of rodeo by showing a fight on TV with other cowboys. The commissioner responded with similar disappointment in the show's portrayal of the rodeo community. Already sensitive to media issues, the IGRA moved to institute protective measures against mainstream coverage of gay rodeo life. Letter from Roger Bergmann to IGRA board of directors, 1993, box 12, correspondence, IGRA.

34 Calendo, "Gay Rodeo," 91. Many participants eschew both intellectualism and political organization, emphasizing the social aspects. See Craig McClain,

"Gay Rodeo: Carnival, Gender, and Resistance" (MA thesis, University of New Mexico, 2005). Also see Darrell Yates Rist's *Heartlands: A Gay Man's Odyssey across American* (New York: Dutton, 1992), 110, which chronicles his uncomfortable experiences with the patriotism and religious aspects of the gay rodeo, even as he notes that gay rodeoers were dedicated to reclaiming their rural upbringings. One gay rodeoer, Joe Rodriguez, expressed his concern when an otherwise supportive Sacramento gay community labeled United Way's Saddle Pals not deserving of the rodeo's donations because it was not an explicitly gay organization. "Paniolo Joe" Rodriguez, interview with Rebecca Scofield, Gay Rodeo Oral History Project, September 10, 2016, Duncans Mills, California.

35 John Calendo, "Interview with Ron Brewer," *In Touch for Men*, January 1981, 77.

36 Farber, "National Reno Gay Rodeo and in the Saddle," 21.

37 "Women of Northside Assail Rodeo: Brand Sport Event Orgy of Brutality," *Northside Citizen*, July 10, 1925, box 1, album 3, Chicago scrapbook, Tex Austin Collection, Museum of New Mexico, Fray Angelico Chavez History Library, Santa Fe (hereafter Tex Austin Collection); "Against the Rodeo," *Chicago Tribune*, May 12, 1925, box 1, album 3, Tex Austin Collection; "The Rodeo in New York and London," *Chicago Tribune*, May 19, 1925, box 1, album 3, Tex Austin Collection; "Humane Society Will Not Interfere with Roundup Program," *Chicago Illinois News*, May 13, 1925, box 1, album 3, Tex Austin Collection; "Murder, Rape, and the Rodeo," *Chicago Tribune*, July 23, 1925, box 1, album 3, Tex Austin Collection.

38 Eulalia Bourne, *Woman in Levi's* (Tucson: University of Arizona Press, 1967), 176.

39 Liz Galst, "Sacred Cows," *Advocate*, July 27, 1993, 47–51, box 14, IGRA, quoted in Michael Szymanski, "Renaissance Cowboy," *Roundup*, August 1995, 26.

40 Letter from Anna Moretto to IGRA, August 2, 1994, box 22, animal rights correspondence, IGRA.

41 Szymanski, "Renaissance Cowboy," 26.

42 Animal rights discussion at 1994 annual convention, 1994, box 19, IGRA.

43 Letter from Panda Bear, August 30, 1995, box 29, folder 2, correspondence, meeting minutes, IGRA.

44 "Wrangler: Interview with Glen Hostetler," *First Hand Events*, 1989 Gay Rodeo Souvenir Issue, 20.

45 Farber, "National Reno Gay Rodeo and in the Saddle," 21.

46 John Calendo, "Interview with Dave Wilson," *In Touch for Men*, January 1981, 77.

47 Bella Stumbo, "A Rip-Snorting Rodeo with a Special Brand," *Los Angeles Times*, March 30, 1987, box 2, minutes, IGRA.

48 Bob Claypool, *Saturday Night at Gilley's* (New York: Grove Press, 1980), 17.

49 Gordon Jaremko, "Gay Rodeo Attracts Big Crowd," *Calgary Herald,* July 2, 1994, 1.

50 Paula Gautheir, "Steers and Queers" (MFA thesis, University of California, San Diego, 2000).

51 Quoted in Gautheir, "Steers and Queers."

52 At many points, the IGRA encouraged nonrural people to join the rodeo, emphasizing that one did not need a rural background to be a cowboy. See Roger Bergmann, "President's Corner," *Roundup,* Spring 1993, 18–19.

53 See Jim Wilke, "My Lover Is a Cowboy: Homosexuality on the Open Range," *Roundup,* May 1996, 6–8; "The Lost Pardner," *Roundup,* February 1996, 11; Mitch Gould, "Solitary, Singing in the West," *Roundup,* December 1995, 24–29; Jim Wilke, "Frontier Comrades: Homosexuality in the American West," *Frontiers,* May 23, 1996, 18–21. See Peter Boag, *Re-Dressing America's Frontier Past* (Berkeley: University of California Press, 2011) for information on gender-bending and memory in the US West.

54 Dedication to Teddy Roosevelt in Roadrunner Regional Rodeo program, January 13–15, box 3, IGRA.

55 Pride Guide, North Star Regional Rodeo program, 1993, box 14, IGRA.

56 Hennen, *Faeries, Bears, and Leathermen.*

57 As Tom Bianchi writes, Fire Island Pines was a place to be open and free, with parties and cruising areas. However, "for some, the rant went like this: Too many drugs. Too sex obsessed. Too body obsessed. Too fashion obsessed. Too shallow. Too sleazy. Too wild. Too queer." Tom Bianchi, *Fire Island Pines, Polaroids 1975–1983* (Bologna: Damiani, 2013), 16. The body culture of the 1970s and 1980s has developed into current forms of gay male self-presentation, for instance, the emergence of "Insta-studs." These men often have substantial followings. See Mike Albo, "Meet the #Instastuds: Hot Gay Men on Perma-display," *NYMAG.com,* August 5, 2013.

58 For instance, advertisements for leather-levi bars in the 1980s often included a "Welcome Cowboys" call out. An ad for the Triangle Bar in Denver featured pictures of both leathermen and cowboys; *Out Front,* July 1, 1988, box 2, IGRA. An ad for The Buffalo offered a free cover with rodeo tickets; advertisement from IGRA Finals Rodeo, Reno '88, October 19–23, box 2, IGRA.

59 Micha Ramakers, *Dirty Pictures: Tom of Finland, Masculinity, and Homosexuality* (New York: St. Martin's Press, 2000), xi.

60 John R. Burger, *One-Handed Histories: The Eroto-Politics of Gay Male Video Pornography* (New York: Hawthorn Press, 1995), 38. Edward Buscombe asserted that when western pornographic movies ceased to draw in straight audiences, the genre survived in the gay niche market; Edward Buscombe, "Generic Overspill: A Dirty Western," in *More Dirty Looks: Gender, Pornography, and Power,* ed. Pamela Church Gibson (London: British Film Institute, 2004), 30.

61 Mark Thompson, ed., *Leatherfolk: Radical Sex, People, Politics, and Practice* (Boston: Alyson, 1991), xvii.

62 Thompson, *Leatherfolk*, xv.

63 1990 IGRA Rodeo Finals, 1990, box 3, IGRA. Similar ads ("David's: A Man's Party" and "Polish Your Rocks and Prepare for a Party") appeared in the First Annual Rocky Mountain Regional Rodeo program, June 3–5, 1983, box 1, IGRA. Charlie's Bar was promoted as "A Man's Bar" in *First Hand Events*, 1989 Gay Rodeo Souvenir Issue.

64 "Write in the Saddle," *North Star GRA Newsletter*, January 1995, box 28, IGRA. While leathermen and cowboys drew from the same notions of American masculinity and intermingled in a variety of contexts, there was also the need to distinguish between the two subcultures. For instance, in 1995, a man from Norway wrote to the association to ask for more information. He stated, "I am a Norwegian 'open' gay leather-man and cowboy." He goes on to explain that he is "changing between" the two and "everybody knows it." This comment illuminates the tightly bound yet distinct identities between leathermen and cowboys. While both are similarly interested in the performance of hypermasculinity, there are enough differences to warrant comment. Black leather culture and brown leather culture have developed differently over the past several decades. Letter from John Olav Hakegard to IGRA, February 22, 1995, box 29, correspondence, IGRA.

65 Gary Swartz, "American Brotherhood Contest," *Roundup*, December 1995, 8–10.

66 This man wrote to IGRA in 1994 asking for information about gay cowboys in the Michigan, Wisconsin, and Minnesota area. Letter from Pat Kaarite to IGRA, May 3, 1994, box 22, correspondence, IGRA.

67 See Les Wright, ed., *The Bear Book: Readings in the History and Evolution of a Gay Male Subculture* (New York: Harrington Park Press, 1997), 21. Letter from David Richardson to IGRA, November 9, 1994 (Bears Club UK) and letter from Bernard Bucan to IGRA, October 25, 1994 (Bears Club UK), box 29, correspondence, IGRA.

68 Quote from *The Panhandle* cited in Susan Faludi, *Backlash: The Undeclared War against American Women* (New York: Crown, 1991), 196.

69 Will Fellows, *Farm Boys: Lives of Gay Men from the Rural Midwest* (Ann Arbor: University of Wisconsin Press, 1996), 20–21. Also see Michael Riordon, *Out Our Way: Gay and Lesbian Life in the Country* (Toronto: Between the Lines, 1996).

70 Szymanski, "Renaissance Cowboy," 25; Roger Bergmann, interview with Rebecca Scofield, Gay Rodeo Oral History Project, November 19, 2016, Austin, Texas.

71 Bruce Roby, interview with Rebecca Scofield, Gay Rodeo Oral History Project, September 10, 2016, Duncans Mills, California.

72 Ann Kinney, interview with Rebecca Scofield, Gay Rodeo Oral History Project, September 11, 2016, Duncans Mills, California.

73 Jeannine Tuttle, "A Woman's Point of View," *Roundup*, Spring 1993.

74 Bruce Gros, interview. Also see Lexie Farrar, interview with Rebecca Scofield, Gay Rodeo Oral History Project, March 21, 2017, Dallas, Texas.

75 *Bylaws, Standing Rules, and Rodeo Rules*, 1986–1987, Article II: Objects and Purposes, 8, box 2, IGRA Rules, IGRA.

76 "Minutes of the 1987 IGRA Convention," Albuquerque, New Mexico, July 11–12, 1987, box 2, IGRA.

77 As rodeo was already a fluid world, gay rodeo's refusal to collect information—including legal names—made it difficult to gather statistics based on race and gender. Also, while the gender imbalance was the norm on a national level, there are local associations that have approached gender equity.

78 "Flaming Saddles," *Genre*, August–September 1993, 32, box 14, IGRA.

79 Great Plains Regional Rodeo program, Kansas City, September 1994, box 17, IGRA.

80 Windy City's Illinois Regional Gay Rodeo program cover, 1994, box 17, IGRA.

81 Calendo, "Ron Brewer," 77.

82 For instance, Craig Rouse told *Frontiers* magazine that he "rode his first horse at the age of 6, but later admitted that his fondness of cowboys preceded his love of the rodeo." T. X. Enoicaras, "Forget Vampires . . . Interview with a Cowboy," *Frontiers*, May 23, 1996, 25–26.

83 Hennen, *Fairies*, 171. Many theorists, including J. Halberstam, have seen all westerns as inherently homoerotic. See "Not So Lonesome Cowboys: The Queer Western," in the *Brokeback Book: From Story to Cultural Phenomenon* (Lincoln: University of Nebraska Press, 2011). Chris Packard, *Queer Cowboys and Other Erotic Male Friendships in Nineteenth-Century American Literature* (New York: Palgrave, 2005).

84 Waide Aaron Riddle, "A Rodeo Story: Then and Now," *4 Front Magazine*, April 2, 1997. John Carroll also mentions his deep love of westerns in "Rodeo Rookie, or the Virgin Cowpoke" printed in the Bay Area Regional Rodeo program, 1993, box 7, IGRA (originally printed in *Frontiers* magazine, April 9, 1993).

85 Szymanski, "Renaissance Cowboy," 23.

86 Hennen, *Fairies*, 171.

87 Hank Stuever, *Big Sky Gay Rodeo Association Newsletter* 1, no. 2, May 1991, box 6, BSGRA news, IGRA (originally printed in *Albuquerque Tribune*, April 29, 1991).

88 See Jaremko, "Gay Rodeo Attracts Big Crowd," 1; "Reno Gay Rodeo Draws Big Crowd," 38.

Even scholars who have studied gay rodeo use terms that deride femininity. For instance: "The rodeo deconstructs presumptions about cowboy heterosexuality, while offering the opportunity to embrace homosexuality without being pigeonholed as an Oscar Wilde swish"; Le Cony and Trodd, "Reagan's Rainbow Rodeos," 179. Another popular rhetorical tactic by association members was to emphasize that animals don't know participants are gay or, alternatively, the animals aren't gay and therefore "it's just as tough as any other rodeo." See Rick Reilly, "Queer Eye for the Sports Guy," *Sports Illustrated*, November 10, 2003. Of course, this statement leaves intact the assumption that gayness is inherently effeminate and it is only through interaction with uninformed and apparently straight animals that gay men can prove their masculinity.

89 *Albuquerque Tribune*, 1991, box 6, IGRA.

90 *TGRA Newsletter, Saddle Up*, and the *Saddle, the North Star Gay Rodeo Newsletter*, June 1994, box 21, IGRA.

91 Brian Helander, interview with Rebecca Scofield, Gay Rodeo Oral History Project, July 8, 2017, Denver, Colorado.

92 Thomas J. Linneman, "Risk and Masculinity in the Everyday Lives of Gay Men," *Gay Masculinities*, ed. Peter Nardi (Thousand Oaks: Sage, 2000), 85. Also see Michael Shernoff, *Without Condoms: Unprotected Sex, Gay Men, and Barebacking* (New York: Routledge, 2006).

93 Richard Labonte, ed., *Country Boys: Wild Gay Erotica* (Jersey City: Cleis, 2007), 104.

94 Phil Julian, "A Bullrider's View in Less than Six Seconds," *Frontiers*, May 23, 1996, 22.

95 Brooke Hayward, "Home on the Range," *Vanity Fair*, February 1988, 108, 141–44.

96 Bruce Gros, interview. Alex Hunt, scholar of the American West and ex–bull rider, asserts when considering straight rodeo in the context of *Brokeback Mountain* that "in their exaggeration of masculinity beyond the bounds of the traditionally masculine, rodeo cowboys seem to be camp," *Brokeback Book*, 141.

97 Bob Ames, "Rodeo Ramblin'," *Roundup*, Spring 1993, 14–16.

98 Carroll, "Rodeo Rookie." Cowboy and Indian drag was also popular at rodeo fund-raiser events. See "A View from the Mardi Gras Ball," *Dallas-Chapter TGRA Newsletter, Saddle-Up*, March 1992, box 11, IGRA.

99 David Thomson, *In Nevada: The Land, the People, God, and Chance* (New York: Knopf, 1999), 294.

100 Patrick O'Driscoll, "10,000 Hoot, Holler at Gay Rodeo," *Reno Evening Gazette*, ca. 1982, box 6, church files, IGRA; Stumbo, "A Rip-Snorting Rodeo." This marginalization of people considered to be at the fringe of the gay community

was also experienced by the drag queens at the Gay Games; see Carline Symons, *The Game Games: A History* (London: Routledge, 2010), 109.

101 Email from D. Pepper to IGRA, 1997, box 37, IGRA, and email response from R. Washburn to D. Pepper, 1998, box 38, IGRA.

102 "The Rodeo Issue," *Camp*, September 2010. Also see newsletter, TSGRA, February 1992, box 12, IGRA.

103 Bruce Roby, interview. Also see "An Interview with Nurse Strange," *First Hand Events*, 1989 Gay Rodeo Souvenir Issue, 31–33.

104 Stumbo, "Rip-snorting."

105 Warner, *Acts of Gaiety*, 9.

106 Colin Johnson, *Just Queer Folks: Gender and Sexuality in Rural America* (Philadelphia: Temple University Press, 2013), 196. Also see Hugh Campbell, Michael Mayerfeld Bell, and Margaret Finney, eds., *Country Boys: Masculinity and Rural Life* (University Park: Pennsylvania State University Press, 2006); Mary Gray, *Out in the Country: Youth, Media, and Queer Visibility in Rural America* (New York: New York University Press, 2009); Scott Herring, *Another Country: Queer Anti-Urbanism* (New York: New York University Press, 2010); Andrew Gorman-Murray, Barbara Pini, and Lia Bryant, eds., *Sexuality, Rurality, and Geography* (Lanham, MD: Lexington Books, 2013).

107 "Why a Gay Rodeo? Why Not!," *QC*, June–July 1995, 5–8, box 8, IGRA. Reprinted in *Roundup* magazine, August 1995, "Why a Gay Rodeo? Why Not!" box 25, IGRA.

108 Szymanski, "Renaissance Cowboy," 24.

109 "Flaming Saddles," 32.

110 Arsenaux, "Ride 'Em Cowboy," 75.

111 Carroll, "Rodeo Rookie."

112 Tammy Crowder, "Behind the Chutes," *Roundup*, October 1996, 61.

113 See Fabio Cleto, ed., *Camp: Queer Aesthetics and the Performing Subject: A Reader* (Ann Arbor: University of Michigan Press, 1999).

114 "Forget Vampires . . . Interview with a Cowboy," 25. The journalist also jokes that "I still don't know if he meant 'camp' like Camp Fire Girls or 'camp' like Joan Crawford."

115 For instance, Brian Helander states that even though he didn't have a background in rodeos, the gay rodeo looked like "fun" and he just started goat dressing. See "The Rodeo Issue," *Camp*, September 2010.

116 Bruce Roby, interview.

117 Questionnaires, 1990, box 4, IGRA.

118 GSGRA proposed rule book changes for IGRA Convention, 1996, box 35, IGRA.

119 Personal conversation, Santa Fe, New Mexico, 2014.

120 Included in rule books at least as far back as the mid-1990s.

121 At the Reno Gay Rodeo the titles of Ms., Miss., and Mr. were awarded. Ms. went to a lesbian community member, Mr. to a gay male community member, and Miss to a female impersonator. In 1978 there were no lesbian entrants for the Ms. competition, demonstrating the early lack of female participation. See Arsenaux, "Ride 'Em Cowboy," 74. In 1986, the IGRA adapted Reno's local royalty competition into an organization-wide pageant, which would be held at the annual convention. Each local association was allowed to send its representatives to the national competition. In 2005, the MsTer title was added for a female-to-male transgendered person. Interesting that this title was added almost a decade after Drag King shows became popular and that this delay happened in a place that actually valued masculine women; see Jack Halberstam, *Female Masculinity* (Durham: Duke University Press, 1998). The three original scored categories—western wear, horsemanship, and personality—have been expanded to five categories: western wear, horsemanship, interview, public presentation, and entertainment. This format more closely mimics a beauty pageant.

122 Ron Neff, "He, She, & ??," *Roundup,* Spring 1993, 26.

123 "Secret Heart," *First Hand Events,* 1989 Gay Rodeo Souvenir Issue, 58–64. Evidence for continued connections to the Imperial Court exist in letters sent between the organizations; see for instance letter from Jaye Sutherland Empress XI to Mr. Wayne Jakino, June 1984, box 1, Colorado gay rodeo documents, IGRA.

124 Rist, *Heartlands,* 104.

125 Todd Heibel, "An Arena for Belonging?: A Spatial Hingepoint Perspective on Citizenship at the Gay Rodeo" (PhD diss., Pennsylvania State University, 2005): 179–80.

126 Calendo, "Gay Rodeo," 31.

127 Letter from Paul Schaming to IGRA, 1996, box 34, correspondence, IGRA.

128 Craig J. Forsyth and Carol Y. Thompson, "Helpmates of the Rodeo: Fans, Wives, and Groupies," *Journal of Sport and Social Issues* 31, no. 4 (November 2007): 403.

129 Daniel Harris, *The Rise and Fall of Gay Culture* (New York: Hyperion, 1997), quoted in Nardi, *Gay Masculinities,* 5.

130 Susan Sontag, "Notes on 'Camp,'" *Parisian Review* 31, no. 4 (Fall 1964), reprinted in *Camp: Queer Aesthetics and the Performing Subject—A Reader,* ed. Fabio Cleto (Ann Arbor: University of Michigan Press, 1999), 62. Camp is a practice that has a complex and heterogeneous history, with very diverse forms. Larger debates about camp include its relationship to homosexuality, sexism, and high and low culture.

131 D'Lane Compton reads current gay rodeo as a "spoof" of heteronormative rodeo, noting that the more invested the rodeo participants and workers are in a "serious" rodeo, the less invested the audience becomes. Few gay competitors would characterize their performances as a parody, but this interpretation captures gay rodeoers' dedication to play as potentially transgressive even as it often collapses into misogyny—as she notes, there is "a subtle line between spoofing masculinity and mirroring hypermasculinity." See D'Lane Compton, "Queer Eye on the Gay Rodeo," in *Gender in the Twenty-First Century: The Stalled Revolution and the Rodeo to Equality*, ed. Shannon Davis, Sarah Winslow, and David Maume (Oakland: University of California Press, 2017), 234.

132 2005 Southern Spurs Rodeo, video 2, gayrodeohistory.org, by Cowboy Frank Harrell.

133 Convention report from Health and Safety Committee, 1995, box 35, convention schedules, meeting minutes, reports, IGRA.

134 Szymanski, "Renaissance Cowboy," 26.

135 "The Brassy Cowboy," *CGRA Newsletter*, November 1992, box 8, IGRA.

136 *NMGRA Connection Newsletter*, March 1991, box 4, IGRA.

137 Kalchik, "IGRA Finals All Around Cowboy: Greg Olson," 16.

138 "Send in the Clowns," *First Hand Events*, 1989 Gay Rodeo Souvenir Issue, 45.

CONCLUSION: PERFORMANCE AND EMBODIED EPISTEMOLOGIES

1 That morning I had seen firsthand how the racial regimes of this southwestern state still operated, even in spaces that were meant to contest inequality. Sitting in a mostly white crowd, sipping free alcohol that was served to me by a mostly black wait staff, I watched as prominent and wealthy Houstonites gathered together to bid on champion stock. Their money would go to 4H, a youth farming organization, providing hundreds of scholarships to underprivileged, often rural, kids in Texas. I sat shocked as the grand champion steer was auctioned off for a whopping four hundred thousand dollars. The other spectators roared their approval of this gargantuan contribution to the scholarship fund by banging yardsticks against the wooden bleachers, creating a thunderous endorsement for charity through public spectacle.

2 Ed Godfey, "The Real Stars," *Oklahoman*, February 15, 2007 and Michael Park, "No Bull: Bull Riding Fastest Growing Sport," *Fox News*, February 7, 2006.

INDEX

National High School Rodeo Association, 21

National Intercollegiate Rodeo Association, 17, 223n74

National Invitational Black Rodeo, 129

National Park Service, 120

National Reno Gay Rodeo, 137, 142, 144–45, 147, 151, 164

Native Americans, 35–36, 52, 104–5, 132, 194n26, 217n24. *See also* Afro-Indians; Cherokees; Chickasaws; Choctaws; cowboy culture; Creeks; Five Civilized Tribes; Seminoles

Native dispossession, 102, 104, 105–6

neurasthenia, 37

New Women, 51, 198–99n79

New Yorker on cowgirls, 60

New York Medical Journal on masculine women, 46

New York Times: on Boley, Oklahoma, 110; on pioneer women, 47–48; on prison rodeo spectators, 92; on rodeo, 12

Northern California Black Horsemen's Association, 127

Norwegian immigrants, 33

O

Oakland (California), black rodeo activism in, 104, 123–24

Oakland Black Cowboy Association. *See* Black Cowboy Association

Oakland Museum's Cultural and Ethnic Affairs Guild, 124

Oakley, Annie, 40

Oklahoma Prison Rodeo, 202–3n8

Olson, Greg, 137, 150, 171

Oregonian on Tillie Baldwin, 41

outlaw broncs, 20, 48, 68, 75, 80–82, 189n53, 206n78

outlaws, western mythology of, 67–68, 78, 80–81, 82, 88, 93, 206n65

outriders in history and in rodeo, 5, 10–11, 184n20

over-civilization, 30, 34, 38, 59, 192n13

P

Parker, John "Snake," 206n76

Parr, Lulu Bell, 51, 54

Patriarchs of America, 108

PBR. *See* Professional Bull Riders (PBR) association

Pendleton Round-Up, 52, 53, 55

People for the Ethical Treatment of Animals (PETA), 148

performance: of belonging, 25; as epistemological tool, 15; gender as, 170; generating knowledge through, 5–6. *See also* authenticity; belonging and inclusion; black rodeo; convict cowboys; cowgirls; gay rodeo; heritage, performance of; hypermasculinity

performative spaces, 5

Perkinson, Robert, 69, 89, 211n139, 213n177

physical and moral fitness, 36–40

Pickett, Bill, 35, 55, 100, 103, 221n50, 225n101

pioneer women. *See* authentic western women; Baldwin, Tillie (Anna Mathilda Winger); Roosevelt, Theodore

power and humiliation, 70, 93–95, 96, 98, 175, 176–77

Pozzobon, Ty, 22

PRCA. *See* Professional Rodeo Cowboys Association (PRCA)

PRCA rodeo, 113

Pretty Boy Floyd gang, 119

primitivism, 30, 194n30

prisoners' rights movement, 68, 91–92, 96–97, 213n177

Prisoner Welfare Fund. *See* Educational and Recreational (E&R) Fund

prison labor system: as abusive system, 68; criticism of, 97–98; farm labor, 66–67, 68, 83–84, 85, 89, 208n99; formalizing discrimination in, 85; link with rodeo, 66, 77–78, 205n45; post-Civil War practices, 69–70; slave plantation, evocation of, 74; social benefit of, 64, 68; violence of, 91

prison reform, 71–72, 84–91, 97